Beauty's Vineyard

A Theological Aesthetic of Anguish and Anticipation

Kimberly Vrudny

A Michael Glazier Book

LITURGICAL PRESS
Collegeville, Minnesota

www.litpress.org

A Michael Glazier Book published by Liturgical Press

Cover design by Ann Blattner. Photo © Thinkstock.

1   2   3   4   5   6   7   8

Library of Congress Cataloging-in-Publication Data

Names: Vrudny, Kimberly J., 1969– author.
Title: Beauty's vineyard : a theological aesthetic of anguish and anticipation / Kimberly Vrudny.
Description: Collegeville, Minnesota : Liturgical Press, 2016. | "A Michael Glazier book."
Identifiers: LCCN 2015038993 | ISBN 9780814684078 | ISBN 9780814684320 (ebook)
Subjects: LCSH: Communities—Religious aspects—Christianity. | Church work. | Christianity and justice. | Social justice—Religious aspects—Christianity. | Vineyards—Biblical teaching. | Christianity and art.
Classification: LCC BV625 .V78 2016 | DDC 230—dc23
LC record available at http://lccn.loc.gov/2015038993

"In *Beauty's Vineyard*, Kimberly Vrudny has woven together profound insights from her reading of Scripture and her own rich experience that help us to see both the harsh reality of suffering and the imperative of hope in fresh and connected ways. This is a significant contribution to theological aesthetics, especially as it relates to and informs the struggle for justice, peace, and the integrity of creation."

> —John W. de Gruchy
> Emeritus Professor
> University of Cape Town

"Like the stunning contemporary paintings that embody the themes explored, Kimberly Vrudny's book combines many distinct elements into a satisfyingly coherent whole. At once biblically centered and reverently interreligious, robustly Catholic and expansively ecumenical, grounded in a materially anguished creation and radically open to mystery, this unique approach to key themes of systematic theology significantly advances the field of theological aesthetics. This movingly personal and richly sourced work deftly demonstrates the unity of the aesthetic and the ethical. Here Beauty is the efficient marker for the indwelling of Goodness and Truth, calling us ever and lovingly to itself."

> —Cecilia González-Andrieu
> Associate Professor of Theology, Loyola Marymount University
> Author of *Bridge to Wonder: Art as a Gospel of Beauty*

"This book is a major contribution to the work of theological aesthetics. Beautifully written, it locates beauty as the 'vineyard' of the just and loving community and integrates the idea of beauty and the role of art as crucial to the work of theology. Constructive and systematic theologians as well as theologians of art will welcome this splendidly written book."

> —Wilson Yates
> Distinguished Professor Emeritus of Religion, Society and the Arts
> United Theological Seminary of the Twin Cities

"Kimberly Vrudny's *Beauty's Vineyard* provides a much-needed theological aesthetic that is at once lucid, wide-ranging, scripturally probing, and ethically engaged. Informed in part by liberation and feminist theology, this is a passionate and compassionate work of theology that is exceptional in combining a prophetic tone with a core concern for beauty and for artistic expression. Rooted in the North American context, Vrudny's outlook is also international in perspective, profoundly shaped by her experiences and work in South Africa in particular."

> —Frank Burch Brown
> Frederick Doyle Kershner Professor Emeritus of Religion and the Arts
> Christian Theological Seminary

Carmen

for Richard,
my South African friend,
whose gentle questions
guided me in these directions

Contents

Beauty's Anguish
On Tenants

Let me sing for my beloved
   my love-song concerning his vineyard:
My beloved had a vineyard
   on a very fertile hill
He dug it and cleared it of stones,
   and planted it with choice vines;
he built a watchtower in the midst of it,
   and hewed out a wine vat in it;
he expected it to yield grapes,
   but it yielded wild grapes. . . .

For the vineyard of the L*ord* *of hosts*
   is the house of Israel,
and the people of Judah
   are his pleasant planting;
he expected justice,
   but saw bloodshed;
righteousness,
   but heard a cry! . . .
[T]he L*ord* *of hosts is exalted by justice,*
   and the Holy God shows himself holy by righteousness. . . .

Ah, you who call evil good
   and good evil,
who put darkness for light
   and light for darkness,
who put bitter for sweet
   and sweet for bitter!

> *Ah, you who are wise in your own eyes,*
>   *and shrewd in your own sight.*
> *Ah, you who are heroes in drinking wine*
>   *and valiant in mixing drink,*
> *who acquit the guilty for a bribe,*
>   *and deprive the innocent of their rights!*
> *Therefore, as the tongue of fire devours the stubble,*
>   *and as dry grass sinks down in the flame,*
> *so their root will become rotten,*
>   *and their blossom go up like dust;*
> *for they have rejected the instruction of the* Lord *of hosts,*
>   *and have despised the word of the Holy One of Israel.*
>
>   (Isa 5:1-2, 7, 16, 20-24)

The prophet Isaiah drew on vineyard imagery to describe the people of Judah. God's holy nation—a people meant to look unlike other nations by producing the good fruit of justice and the choice wine of righteousness in the vineyard they had been granted—traded the former for bloodshed, according to the prophet, and the latter for a bribe. The prophet lamented his people's fate, interpreting that they were experiencing the consequences of their injustice in the stripping of their land and the nation that had been their inheritance. Their sanctuary, their vineyard, the land that had been promised to their ancestors, was now in flames because of their transgression against the stranger, the poor, the widow, the orphan. Because they called evil good and good evil, because they put darkness for light and light for darkness, because they called bitter sweet and sweet bitter, their vineyard went up in flames. Its vegetation was reduced to ash. Its inhabitants went into diaspora. The author of Isaiah 5 understood war to come to Israel with divine sanction, for the nation had failed to live as it was intended to live—with care and concern for the immigrant, the prostitute, the destitute, and the sick.

When Jesus speaks of the vineyard, he is intentionally drawing on a tradition of thought sacred within his own Jewish culture. The author of the Gospel of Matthew recounts two parables of Jesus set in a vineyard ("The Parable of the Sons" in Matt 21:28-32 and "The Parable of the Tenants" in Matt 21:33-46). Jesus shares these stories, according to Matthew, in the temple, with chief priests and elders in attendance among others who are also following him. After overturning the table of the money changers and cursing a fig tree, religious leaders ask Jesus to disclose the source of his authority. In addressing their inquiry, Jesus asks which of two sons better pleased their father who had instructed his sons to work in the vineyard—the first, who initially refused to work in the vineyard but later changed his mind and went, or the second, who promised initially to go but never did? When those assembled around Jesus answer that the first son did the will of his father, Jesus endorses their reply by pointing out that the ones in their community who are despised, like tax collectors and prostitutes—those like the disobedient first son—are entering the kingdom of God ahead of the religious leaders who had promised to participate in the kingdom of God but are not. According to Matthew's Gospel, they were insufficiently producing fruit for the kingdom in the form of justice and righteousness. Those whom they considered to be sinners, Jesus disclosed to them, were surpassing them in righteousness.

Jesus was situating his comments squarely within his Jewish community's prophetic tradition. He expressed how working in the vineyard had to do with living one's life according to the will of the Father—that is, living in relation to the good and gracious will of God as revealed by the prophets. This entailed commitment to performing works of justice and righteousness, such as securing care for the immigrant, the orphan, the widow, the leper, the poor—the ones marginalized by the social structures operating in Judah during Jesus' day, a situation made only more complex by the reality of Roman occupation. Within such a vineyard, where allegiance to the will of God was normative, was the potential for a great yield—with grapes in plenty growing on a multitude of twisted vines, transformed over time into choice wine. The fruit of this vineyard that Jesus describes, in line with the prophets, is a community of attention to those who are most vulnerable. The fruit—the yield of the vineyard for which God, the landowner, is asking—is a community of *hesed*, of loving-kindness, a community living in right relation to God and to neighbor as outlined in the books of the Law, upheld as sacred by Jesus' own Jewish brothers and sisters. Writing decades after Jesus' ministry, the author of the Gospel of Matthew characterizes Jesus as insinuating that the religious leaders were like the second son, the one who promised his father he would participate in the harvest but who never followed through. Tax collectors and prostitutes, however—representing a group of people despised by the religious elites for their moral laxity—were being transformed in Jesus' sight. Initially unrepentant, they were turning and, like the first son, were among those serving first in the vineyard, enjoying the dawning kingdom of God present among them. By living righteously through their care for one another, and by living justly by resisting harmful socioeconomic systems in place in the first century, they were entering what I am calling Beauty's vineyard.

NB

The early Christian community called Jesus their "Messiah" in part because he was able to imagine the possibilities of a just and righteous community, this vineyard, this kingdom of God, coming into being in the midst of them. Within the Jewish tradition, the messiah, literally an "anointed one," was usually a royal figure, one who could make God's vision for such a potential community visible, as such a vision is easily trampled over in our world: dismissed as hopelessly naïve, easily corrupted from the inside, impossible to sustain. Through him, Jesus' followers also perceived this community. He was making God's will known to them. Indeed, it was incarnate among them.

In order to comprehend what was meant by the use of the word "messiah" within the first-century Jewish community, we might consider the teachings of the rabbis. Rachel Farbiarz, a 2008 writing fellow of the American Jewish World Service, an organization dedicated to alleviating hunger, poverty, and disease among people living in the developing world, helps to enliven the contemporary imagination to the ancient Jewish understanding by drawing from a Talmudic exchange imagined between the wise third-century Rabbi Joshua ben Levi and the prophet Elijah:

> Rabbi Levi beseeched the prophet to divulge when the Messiah would come. Not one to gratuitously expend his prophetic prowess, Elijah directed Rabbi Levi to inquire of the Messiah for himself. "Where is the Messiah to be found?" Rabbi Levi persisted. "At the gates of the City," Elijah replied. "And by what sign shall I recognize him?" Rabbi Levi asked. "He is sitting among the lepers," Elijah explained, "untying and changing their bandages one at a time: He is the one who tends to the lepers sore by sore."
>
> Rabbi Levi went to the city's gates and there found a man who tenderly cleaned and wrapped the lepers' fetid wounds. "When will you redeem us as the Messiah?" Rabbi Levi asked. "Today," the apparent Messiah answered.
>
> Rabbi Levi returned to Elijah informing him that the Messiah had spoken untruthfully—since he had not yet come. "What did he say to you?" Elijah pressed. "He said he would come 'today.'" "You misunderstood," Elijah rejoined. "He did not say that he would come 'today.' He instead quoted for you the verse from Psalms that instructs: The Messiah will come 'today—if only you will listen to God's voice.'"[1]

Farbiarz interprets the "weighty implications of this story."

1. Rachel Farbiarz, "The Jewish Response to HIV/AIDS," in an unpublished piece she wrote for the American Jewish World Service.

The most holy work resides in the tender care for those whose afflic-
tion renders them cast out, at the margins of society, sitting at the city's
gate. And the mark of the most holy man is that he changes the reviled
lepers' bandages one by one, sore by sore. In doing so, he validates
the shared humanity between them. He wordlessly communicates
his esteem for the bandaged individual, who—like the Messiah himself—is simply and miraculously flesh created from dust, formed in
God's image. Unless and until each person thusly heeds "God's voice,"
implies the Messiah's terse response to Rabbi Levi, the Redemption
will surely remain beyond our collective reach.[2]

Farbiarz's reflection helps contemporary Christian readers understand the kind of community about which Jesus spoke by reference
to the vineyard. Because salvation in the ancient Jewish tradition had
primarily to do with the healing of the community in the here and now,
even as there was development of thought in some Jewish circles by
Jesus' day that included belief in a heavenly afterlife, Jesus was critical
of those who claimed to have some association with God without doing
that which God required—the redeeming work of God's beloved community. The ones despised for their lifestyles in the first century, tax
collectors and prostitutes, among others, were producing the fruit of
the vineyard so desired by its owner. They were unlike those Jesus
reprimanded by use of the parable, those who claimed to work in the
vineyard but had never set foot in the rows of vines producing sweet
grapes. They had not set foot in the gate of the city to change bandages
sore by sore, or to feed the hungry, or to care for the ones who had
fallen ill. Indeed, they hid behind religious rules to defend their right
to neglect those in need. It is important to emphasize that Jesus was
not offering a critique of Judaism in preference for Christianity. Jesus
was born a Jew, lived the life of a Jew, and died a Jew. According to the
author of Matthew, however, he challenged religious leaders who were
engaged in a well-intentioned attempt to pass the tradition to the next
generation to abide by the spirit and not simply the letter of the law
(Jer 31:31-32; Rom 2:29).

As the Gospel of Matthew unfolds, another story (also set in a vineyard) follows immediately on the heels of the "Parable of the Two Sons."
In his "Parable of the Tenants," Jesus tells about how a landowner leased
his vineyard to tenants and went away to live in another country. First-
century landowners, especially those who could plant vineyards complete with fences, wine presses, and watchtowers, were wealthy. Clearly,

2. Ibid.

the landowner was privileged, a reality that would not have been lost on Jesus' audience. In fact, so privileged was he that he was able to send slaves to collect the produce when harvest time had come. The tenants beat, killed, and stoned the slaves who did their master's bidding. When the landowner sent more slaves, they were treated in the same way. The landowner thought that if he sent his son, they would respect him—but the tenants killed him as well, hoping nevertheless to receive the son's inheritance. Jesus asked the people assembled before him, "When the owner of the vineyard comes, what will he do to those tenants?" (Matt 21:40). Those in attendance answered that the landowner would kill the tenants and lease the vineyard to others who would hand over the produce as requested at harvest time. Jesus replied, "Therefore I tell you, the kingdom of God will be taken away from you and given to a people that produces the fruits of the kingdom" (Matt 21:43).

Interpretation of this parable requires caution. The author of the Gospel of Matthew, writing about fifty years after the crucifixion of Jesus, is representing the tension within his own Jewish community. Judaism in the first century, which was not a single entity but many different sects (among them Pharisees, Sadducees, Zealots, Covenanters, Essenes, and more), became further divided over the question of whether Jesus was, indeed, the long-awaited Messiah. For the author of Matthew, the Pharisees, chief priests, and elders came to represent the opponents of Jesus for their refusal to see in him the identity of the Messiah. The text is certainly functioning rhetorically here to shame the ones the author of Matthew had come to see as Jesus' opponents. The passage reflects the growing tensions that, by the author's day, were developing within the community between Jews who were followers of the ancient traditions and Jews who were followers of Jesus' interpretations of the same. It is unlikely, however, that the situation was this volatile in Jesus' own day. Rather, the text reflects the author's situation a half century later.

In the decades after Jesus' death, allegiances were being drawn in the Jewish community either to follow an interpretation of the law as proclaimed by Jesus or to follow the more ancient tradition as communicated by the high priests. Both were Jewish options until probably around the turn of the century, when definitions tightened after the destruction of the Temple, and the way of Jesus, the way of the Christ, was understood as clearly distinct from Judaism. Given the decades between the episode recounted in the text and the writing of the text itself, scholars cannot know with certainty the degree of the conflict between the religious leaders and Jesus in his own day, and whether or not in fact Jesus shamed the leaders publicly in the way the author describes. My own experience in varying religious communities informs the opinion that Jesus' posture in solidarity with the marginalized would not have been received enthusiastically by the powerful, those whose professional lives were bound up in protecting the tradition as they had received it and handing it down to the next generation. But whatever authentic historical tensions there were between Jesus and the religious leaders within Jesus' own community, these were most likely much more pointed by the time the author put quill to papyrus. And this historical development is reflected in the text, as the author of Matthew in some places characterizes the Pharisees as opponents of and adversarial to the newly emerging community allegiant to Jesus, even as they are described in other places as inviting him in for conversation, seeming quite genuinely curious about what he is saying.[3]

Given the additional centuries that separate the writing of the Gospel of Matthew from a reading of it in our own day, a second cautionary word is in order. During the Christian Middle Ages, interpreters used these gospel texts to rationalize acts of brutality against Jews. When medieval exegetes read in Matthew's Gospel that the kingdom of God would be taken away from one people and given to another, they understood Jesus to be disclosing through a sacred text that God was ripping the kingdom from those who worshiped in synagogues and was handing it over to people who would worship in churches. By then, because Christians understood the kingdom as predominantly manifest in the life of the church, many Christians threatened Jews with death unless they converted to belief in Christ as their Redeemer and Lord. Medieval commentaries, as well as art decorating medieval cathedrals, show the synagogue blindfolded and the church triumphant over it. In some images, the church holds the synagogue at sword point. For many throughout medieval Europe, the Christian life was the normative standard, the only kind of life worth living, and certainly the only lifestyle they believed could be rewarded in the much-anticipated afterlife. On the basis of passages such as the parable of the tenants, Christians rationalized the idea that God was ripping the covenant from the Jews and delivering it into the hands of the Christians; Jews were not to be inheritors of the kingdom alongside Christians. As a result (at least in

3. Marilyn J. Salmon, *Preaching without Contempt: Overcoming Unintended Anti-Judaism* (Minneapolis, MN: Fortress Press, 2009).

part) of such readings, Christians participated in the persecution of Jewish people—killing them, they reasoned, with God's endorsement.[4]

Suffice it to say that many Christians believed that this text revealed God's displeasure with the alleged unfaithfulness of the entire Jewish people. For Jews, this chapter in Matthew is a text of terror, and rightfully so—as should it be for Christians as well who carry the burden of guilt. No degree of contextualization can undo what has been done in the name of Scripture held sacred by Christians—a reality with which Christians must live, repenting again and again for the atrocities committed in the name of Christianity, and committing generation after generation to the principle: *never again*.

Despite the minefields surrounding interpretation of these passages, given centuries of poor exegesis that have contributed to the current state of anti-Judaism and anti-Semitism in a world still standing condemned in light of the Shoah, there is in the parable of the vineyard a jewel worth extracting. The vineyard about which Jesus teaches is grounded in the prophetic tradition of Isaiah. It remains occupied in some measure by those who sing psalms in synagogues and churches and by singers of songs in temples other than these. But for Jesus, even more than either synagogue or church, the vineyard signifies a place of justice and righteousness, a community of peace and nonviolence, a sanctuary of hope and promise. Jesus conveys through his parable that God is taking it away from those whose wickedness had caused the grapes to wither on the vines and sour and is giving it to those who will see that life in the vineyard is restored. It is not being given to a people on the basis of their ethnicity, nor is it being given to anyone for offering consent to a number of dogmas. It is not being given to a people on the basis of a birthright, nor on the basis of a religious conversion. Rather, all people are invited to enter the vineyard by laboring for the common good in the world so that suffering can be minimized. They are asked to labor for a world where the needs of all are tended; to labor for a world where fewer make choices out of desperation; to labor for a world where more are able to contribute to the endeavors of the community, thereby liberating the liberators as well. These are the grapes that mature on the vine, the fruit of their collective labor. Their works benefit the entire community.

---

4. The history of Christian anti-Semitism is obviously long and complex, and this is an oversimplification for the sake of brevity. For a good starting place, see James Carroll, *Constantine's Sword: The Church and the Jews; A History* (New York: Mariner Books, 2002).

This kind of beloved community, marked by just and right relations, is what the parable discloses as desired by the God revealed in these texts, rooted in a tradition sacred to both Jews and to Christians. Christians believe that, in Christ, the covenant to the Jews was opened in such a way that all of humankind could participate. God's covenantal promises, first granted to the Jews, was broken open in Christ, no longer restricted to a few chosen ones but now extended to all. Membership was no longer on the basis of a bloodline but by faith in what Jesus was teaching—that our collective salvation is received by surrendering our wills to the will of God, a surrender only possible by grace and by following in the footsteps of those who walked this way before: Abraham, — *women* Isaac, Jacob, Moses, David, and now Jesus. Through his simple, peaceful, and joyful existence in service to humankind and its well-being, ultimately laying down his life instead of bringing harm to another of God's beloved creatures, Christ invites us to follow him. For Christians, involvement in the creation of such a society is participation in the mystical Body of Christ. Such a society is Beauty's vineyard, as is testified in John:

> I am the true vine, and my Father is the vine-grower. He removes every branch in me that bears no fruit. Every branch that bears fruit he prunes to make it bear more fruit. You have already been cleansed by the word that I have spoken to you. Abide in me as I abide in you. Just as the branch cannot bear fruit by itself unless it abides in the vine, neither can you unless you abide in me. I am the vine, you are the branches. Those who abide in me and I in them bear much fruit, because apart from me you can do nothing. Whoever does not abide in me is thrown away like a branch and withers; such branches are gathered, thrown into the fire, and burned. If you abide in me, and my words abide in you, ask for whatever you wish, and it will be done for you. My Father is glorified by this, that you bear much fruit and become my disciples. (John 15:1-8)

In a similar vein, the apostle Paul did not understand Jesus' teachings to represent God's rejection of Israel. To the contrary, Israel and its covenant with God was the root that supported additional branches. Gentiles were, through Christ, grafted onto the Jewish vine, the Jewish covenant, the Jewish community. Both Paul and Jesus, however, condemn those branches that are not bearing good fruit. Insofar as faith in God is evident in lives of *hesed*, of loving-kindness, and insofar as unbelief is evident in lives that persist in the perpetuation of injustice, Paul instructs the Gentile believers in Rome:

> But if some of the branches were broken off, and you, a wild olive shoot, were grafted in their place to share the rich root of the olive tree, do not vaunt yourselves over the branches. If you do vaunt yourselves, remember that it is not you that support the root, but the root that supports you. You will say, "Branches were broken off so that I might be grafted in." That is true. They were broken off because of their unbelief, but you stand only through faith. So do not become proud, but stand in awe. For if God did not spare the natural branches, perhaps he will not spare you. Note then the kindness and the severity of God: severity towards those who have fallen, but God's kindness towards you, provided you continue in his kindness; otherwise you also will be cut off. And even those of Israel, if they do not persist in unbelief, will be grafted in, for God has the power to graft them in again. For if you have been cut from what is by nature a wild olive tree and grafted, contrary to nature, into a cultivated olive tree, how much more will these natural branches be grafted back into their own olive tree. (Rom 11:17-24)

Paul's vision is that Jews who had failed to live out their obligation to live justly, and who nevertheless renounce their faithlessness to the covenant by returning to God as demonstrated by their commitment to righteousness and to justice, are grafted back onto the vine more naturally than are Gentiles, who nonetheless are now able to become part of the vine as well.[5] The branches bearing good fruit make the vineyard thrive and flower, producing plump grapes that are pressed into choice wine. This becomes visible when humankind functions as a community living as God intends: embracing one another, assisting one another, listening to one another, enjoying one another's company—not only in our little tribes, but as an entire human race, holistically appreciating the diversity of the human story and learning from the wisdom in one another's stories. Jesus did not specify that only people who shared his ritual practice could enter; indeed, anyone who encountered someone in need with compassion rather than contempt and scorn had already entered. Today, this means that when we look to the teachings of the Buddha, whose own spiritual journey was begun by introduction to the aged, the disabled, and the poor, we see that he too is interested in fostering this kind of being in the world. To the extent that all sacred traditions guide their faithful to this same essence that is Good, Beautiful, and True—and to works of loving-kindness that such just, compassionate, and wise teachings counsel, whether the ideals are expressed in the beauty of the *Bhagavad*

5. See also chapter 4, "Beauty's Veiling: On Sin," where I return to Paul's explication in his letter to the Romans of the redemption of both Jew and Gentile.

Gita and other texts sacred within Hindu traditions, or in the whispers of those spirits Aboriginal peoples hear as they recognize human interconnectedness too with the land—Catholic teaching affirms that all human beings are related, and in our encounter with others sharing a common humanitarian purpose, glimpses of the vineyard come into being.[6] The vineyard represents our meeting place as a people of commitment to creation rather than to destruction, where we acknowledge and celebrate the existence of our distinct rituals, creeds, and codes that distinguish us as people of diverse religious traditions without losing sight of our common humanity, our common dignity—including first and foremost the humanity and dignity of our brothers and sisters who are struggling for survival, and of the earth on which our common existence depends. Certainly not all theological constructions are equally accurate in describing the reality to which they point, and surely all fall short of their ultimate aim, which is, finally, beyond the capacity of finite language to describe. But, regardless, the fruit of the vineyard—these works of loving-kindness that extend care and attention to the vulnerable ones in our midst—produces the peaceable kingdom no matter the faith orientation of the one participating. In this kingdom, all of creation is celebrated as abundant enough to quench our thirst in senses both physical and spiritual.[7]

The wisdom of the parable lies buried beneath the branches of a vineyard often largely neglected and all but abandoned centuries ago. Raking back the dead foliage, however, we can see signs of new life. Reminded that these passages in Matthew intentionally evoke the tradition of the prophet Isaiah who wrote a love song about God's vineyard, the people of Judah—a people in whom God delighted and with whom God entered into covenant by the establishment of a just social order marked by justice for the poor and marginalized—the Jesus of Matthew's Gospel is revealing that this covenant was being extended to all humankind. The blessing promised to the people of Abraham, that the chosen ones would make God known to the nations, was continuing to be fulfilled. The author of Matthew relies on the knowledge of a Jewish audience to make the connection between Isaiah's love song and the parable of the tenants,

---

6. "Those who have not yet accepted the Gospel are related to the people of God in various ways." Second Vatican Council, *Lumen Gentium* (Dogmatic Constitution on the Church), par. 16. English translations from the Second Vatican Council are taken from *Vatican Council II: The Basic Sixteen Documents*, ed. Austin Flannery (Collegeville, MN: Liturgical Press, 2014).

7. Ibid. "Whatever of good or truth is found amongst them is considered by the church to be a preparation for the Gospel and given by him who enlightens all men and women that they may at length have life."

set in the very same vineyard. In Jesus' words, they would understand the tenants to represent the people of Judah, the precious ones most beloved of God who were first invited to live in the vineyard and to live by God's ways within it. In his words, they would understand the slaves to represent those prophets who called the people to repentance when they had failed to live according to the covenants they had entered with God to enact justice for the widow, the orphan, the immigrant, the poor, the hungry, and the sick. In his words they would hear an indictment tied to a failure to live justly—by a failure to feed the hungry, welcome the stranger, clothe the naked, tend the sick, and visit the prisoner. And after still more slave-prophets were killed, as was the landowner's son, in whom is the author's memory of Christ's crucifixion, Jesus informs his listeners in a manner like the prophetic tradition before him that "the kingdom of God will be taken away from you and given to a people that produces the fruits of the kingdom" (Matt 21:43). Jesus' critique is against those who claim to follow God without recognizing that YHWH desires works of justice more than songs of praise. It isn't about ripping the vineyard, as it were, away from one religious group and giving it to another. It is about how those who fail to bring forward its bounty have abandoned the vineyard and how God will welcome in still others to make it flower again. The parable is about welcoming humanity into the vineyard, the kingdom of God—a kingdom once Jewish, always Jewish, and yet now also more than Jewish. In this vineyard, all of humanity is welcome, so long as humanity is compassionately engaged in the care of God's creation. It is *this* that God desires, according to the parable: a community committed to the well-being of the hungry, the weak, the downtrodden—not festivals of worship, a point too that has resonance with the prophetic tradition before Matthew, before Jesus, and even before Isaiah:

> I hate, I despise your festivals,
>   and I take no delight in your solemn assemblies.
> Even though you offer me your burnt offerings and grain offerings,
>   I will not accept them;
> And the offerings of well-being of your fatted animals
>   I will not look upon.
> Take away from me the noise of your songs;
>   I will not listen to the melody of your harps.
> But let justice roll down like waters,
>   and righteousness like an ever-flowing stream. (Amos 5:21-24)

If the Matthean recounting is accurately reflective of a historical episode, Jesus was leveling a critique that could equally be directed against many Christians today who fill churches with songs of praise without attempting to imitate the one who inspired these songs and for whom they must ring hollow. The followers of Jesus have demonstrated throughout history an ability to become oppressors as well, failing to live according to the ways demanded by their God and Lord and enabling the vineyard once again to spoil, turning its grapes sour and mangling its vines, leaving them withered, dried into dust upon the ground. Each generation receives the invitation over again, regardless of religious creed or ethnic identification. Each person is free, ultimately, to contribute to the vineyard's harvest or to speed along its demise. But, according to Matthew, there are consequences. And, of course, we all experience the consequences of a humanity failing to abide by the ways of this vineyard God imagines. We all taste its sour fruit and drink its fermented vinegar in a world brewing fear, hatred, violence, and despair. This is the cause of our collective anguish.

The fence around the vineyard delineates a clear line between those who live within the vineyard and those who exist outside of it. Perhaps this is the meaning of Jesus' words that he comes not to unite but to divide (Matt 10:34). The fence divides the just from the unjust, the righteous from the unrighteous. Too often in Christian churches, the spiritual dimension of this fence has been emphasized to the neglect of the material, such that the fence is seen primarily to exclude those thought not to be righteous (i.e., non-Christians). But given the prophetic passages that the parable references, there are worldly economic and political dimensions to the parable as well. Inside the vineyard, there is an awareness of structural systems like sexism, classism, racism, anti-Semitism, heterosexism, and militarism, to name just a few. These systems harm everyone they touch. Yet inside the vineyard, there is a commitment to bring about just and charitable relief to those harmed by the systems, including a commitment to the transformation of the ones privileged by the systems as they stand as well as a transformation of the systems themselves. Outside of the vineyard are those who do not live in such a way—who profit off the backs of those who labor for mere pennies, if that, and who function within the myth that the systems do not need repair. Such a myth perpetuates the idea that folks need simply to work harder to become part of the consuming classes without recognizing the systems that entrap us all. Yet Jesus offers a counter word to such deception. He extends grace to all and promises that upon entrance to the vineyard, even just a little contribution is appreciated. The community contributing to the good of all humankind creates this vineyard and keeps it thriving—from the widow who contributes a mite (Mark 13:1-2) to the rich man who is expected to give everything he has (Matt 19:21). It is not about the value of what we give but *that* we give. Every contribution is valued equally, for in the contribution itself we find our common redemption. To reference another parable, we reap what we sow (Gal 6:8).

Despite the wide expanse of those who participate in the vineyard, whether they give only a little or a lot, Jesus' grace is not a cheap grace behind which we can hide injustices that dehumanize and humiliate those whose image also bears God's own.[8] Judgment is promised several chapters after this parable in Matthew, on the basis of whether one feeds the hungry, welcomes the stranger, clothes the naked, tends to the sick, or visits the prisoner:

> When the Son of Man comes in his glory, and the angels with him, then he will sit on the throne of his glory. All the nations will be gathered before him, and he will separate people one from another as a shepherd separates the sheep from the goats, and he will put the sheep at his right hand and the goats at the left. Then the king will say to those at his right hand, "Come, you that are blessed by my Father, inherit the kingdom prepared for you from the foundation of the world; for I was hungry and you gave me food, I was thirsty and you gave me something to drink, I was a stranger and you welcomed me, I was naked and you gave me clothing, I was sick and you took care of me, I was in prison and you visited me." Then the righteous will answer him, "Lord, when was it that we saw you hungry and gave you food, or thirsty and gave you something to drink? And when was it that we saw you a stranger and welcomed you, or naked and gave you clothing? And when was it that we saw you sick or in prison and visited you?" And the king will answer them, "Truly I tell you, just as you did it to one of the least of these who are members of my family, you did it to me." Then he will say to those at his left hand, "You that are accursed, depart from me into the eternal fire prepared for the devil and his angels; for I was hungry and you gave me no food, I was thirsty and you gave me nothing to drink, I was a stranger and you did not welcome me, naked and you did not give me clothing, sick and in prison and you did not visit me." Then they also will answer, "Lord, when was it that we saw you hungry or thirsty or a stranger or naked or sick or in prison, and did not take care of you?" Then he will answer them, "Truly I tell you, just as you did not do it to one of the least of these, you did not do it to me." And these will go away into eternal punishment, but the righteous into eternal life. (Matt 25:31-46)

---

8. For a treatment of "cheap grace," see Dietrich Bonhoeffer, *Discipleship*, Dietrich Bonheoffer Works, vol. 4 (Minneapolis, MN: Fortress Press, 2003).

The reality is that just as there is a dimension of the kingdom present in the here and now, perceptible where people are creating this kind of community as, for example, in the Catholic Worker houses and in the St. Vincent de Paul programs in many Catholic parishes, or in many organizations caring for the created world outside of the institutions of our churches, so too is judgment recognizable already.[9] Where this kind of community is not being created, all people are suffering to a greater degree. We are all tormented by the dysfunction of a society whose ill are not cared for properly, whose wealthy are disconnected from the world because they live in gated communities both isolating and despair inducing, whose hungry beg for food on the street. In our society, the desperate readily access drugs, alcohol, and guns, extremists unleash violence, and the masses spiritualize the teachings of ancient philosophers, exclusively postponing liberation until the afterlife, thus underscoring our powerlessness to change anything for the better and thereby assuring that nothing will change. All of this creates a living hell, putting all of us into greater jeopardy, making all of us less safe. It creates the anguish to which the subtitle of this book refers.

All of this is rectified in Beauty's vineyard, the reality to which Jesus' parable points, the reality to which we all, as human beings created in the *imago Dei*, are oriented, and the reality in which our hope lies. Beauty's vineyard, then, ought to become a spiritual anchor for Christians struggling to discern how best to live, given this context of anguish that I have described. And so this book, bearing *Beauty's Vineyard* as its title, will outline such a system as informed by theological aesthetics, a theology anchored in an understanding of beauty, with theological, christological, soteriological, pneumatological, and ecclesiological implications. Taking seriously the understanding of "beauty" as a transcendental aspect of all beings which becomes manifest in the person of Jesus the Christ, and in whose compassion, justice, and wisdom his disciples can participate through the power of grace, each chapter will sketch what Beauty's vineyard might look like by reflecting on a theological theme in conversation with a painting by a contemporary social realist. The paintings, for the most part, are filled with anguish. They will draw us onto religious ground, raising the theological questions that each chapter considers. Chapters follow the outline of a classical theological system, treating in turn such topics as theology (on the Trinity), anthropology (on *imago Dei* and sin), Christology (here emphasizing

---

9. Dorothy Day, *The Long Loneliness: The Autobiography of the Legendary Catholic Social Activist* (New York: HarperOne, 1996).

his humanity not to the exclusion of his divinity, with a focus on his parables), soteriology (on forgiveness and offering a nonviolent theory of atonement), and, after a chapter on suffering, the final word is given to pneumatology and its concomitant hope.

In chapter 1, "Beauty's Allure: On Conversion," and in conversation with a painting by Jerome Witkin, I speak of my own journey of anguish as the glass box of fundamentalism into which I had been born and raised was cracked by learning to read the Bible in a scholarly way and then ultimately shattered by traveling to Israel where I lived, for the first time, among people who did not share the same assumptions I held about the world and our role in it. Learning also from communities where oppression had been evident, first by travel to Palestine, then to South Africa, next to Thailand, and finally to Mexico, I discovered how Beauty's vineyard was coming into being in peaceful, nonviolent, and faithful expressions of resistance to structures of violence and in creative, hopeful, and imaginative communities living out a different understanding of what it means to be authentically human in our increasingly globalized, interconnected, and interdependent world. The ideas for this book took root beside the Atlantic Ocean in South Africa, where my family and I spent a sabbatical during 2009 to 2010, a period of time where I learned better how to be human by attending an Anglican church where we worshiped, in a Presbyterian community center where we tutored pastors and children, and in a Catholic house run by the Scalabrini Brothers where we prepared meals for abandoned refugee children and served meals in a soup kitchen. In all of these places, I entered more deeply into an understanding of how Christ can be found among those living in poverty. Without wanting to romanticize the situations of suffering we encountered among people who are struggling for survival in the midst of abject poverty and devastating illness, I must acknowledge that we did, without question, experience holiness in these places. Each community we encountered is participating in Beauty's vineyard, as I imagine it, each modeling in different ways what it is to be a disciple of Christ. Early drafts of all of these chapters were conceived in Africa.

In chapter 2, "Beauty's Companions: On the Good and the True," and in conversation with a painting by Mark Rothko, I propose a Trinitarian theology that navigates an understanding of reality grounded in an awareness of God's creative presence. After treating prolegomena of how we use language theologically and after examining what is at stake in committing to various theological systems, I sketch a theological aesthetic that informs each remaining chapter. While celebrating endeavors in our wisdom traditions to forward humanity's understanding and embodiment of holiness, it is in this chapter that I retrieve Thomas Aquinas's participation metaphysics. Thomas believed that transcendental categories of being, like the good and the true, are names for God. Beauty sometimes appears in his lists of transcendental categories of being; sometimes it is absent, though I follow Umberto Eco in believing that Thomas did think of beauty as a transcendental. In something of a thought experiment, I imagine Goodness as a name for the Father, the Just Creator; Beauty as a name for the Son, the Compassionate Redeemer; and Truth as a name for the Spirit, the Wise Sustainer. Just as the Father, Son, and Holy Spirit are One by a divine and eternal *perichoresis*, or indwelling, of the Good, Beautiful, and True, so are these persons nevertheless distinct. The distinct but not separate Good, Beautiful, and True Persons are One in Love, and we are invited to participate in their celestial dance, even in the here and now. Love, then, sustains them in their Unity through all eternity, and through which we too become One with them. It is this Love that overflows into the creation of material existence, breaking into time and space, the superabundant expression of all of the transcendentals together. Thus, Being brings being into being out of Being, creating the universe in which we are in the process of becoming that which God intends for us to be. Beauty becomes visible in the person of Christ, hinting at what is truly beautiful: a life so devoted to principles of peace and nonviolence that one's own life might end in its refusal to harm another. In refusing to harm another, however, life and salvation might paradoxically be found, not only for the individual who hopes for an afterlife but also, more fully understood, within the context of a human community that thrives peacefully. Without denying the existence of an afterlife, I suggest that the implications for this world are paramount.

Having arrived at the creation of human beings, I will move into a treatment of theological anthropology, the study of the human person in relation to God. Issues of human dignity and human corruption, or sin, are considered in chapter 3, "Beauty's Trace: On *Imago Dei*." In this chapter, I enter into varying theological "imaginations," a term employed to refer to ways of thinking about a subject. Here, and in conversation with a painting by Samuel Bak, I trace the problematic association between human dignity, *imago Dei*, and human nature, alternatively thought to be damaged (in the Catholic imagination) or destroyed (in the Lutheran and Calvinist imaginations) by original sin. In the first part of this chapter, I treat the issue of human dignity and propose that Christians believe that all human beings are beloved creations of God and thereby possess an inviolable dignity that is not increased by the degree to which one is

sanctified, whether through baptism alone (as in the Lutheran imagination) or by cooperation with God in performance of good works (as
in the Catholic imagination). Distinguishing the sanctity of one's soul
from one's dignity protects those who have struggled and fallen down
through life, ensuring that all, saints and sinners alike, are recognized
to be beloved children of God, worthy of care by the very nature of
their existence, by their very being, created as they were by a Creator
who willed them into existence. Dignity therefore is grounded in one's
imago Dei, which is the image God has in mind regarding each one of
us. As "God's projects," Catholics believe we incrementally live into the
image that God has in mind for us with greater and greater integrity.
Through a process of sanctification, veils of participation in individual,
relational, and structural sin are lifted, enabling us to participate in the
perfect image that is granted to us as a gift and birthright. This image
itself was never compromised by sin nor made holier by sanctification.
It is, indeed, inviolable. Nevertheless, incrementally and by a sanctifying
process, we increasingly embody the goodness, beauty, and truth that
God has in mind for each one of us as we become who we are meant to
be, and as we find deeper and deeper integrity in our being by living
into God's imagination of who we really are and, in a real way, always
have been.

Sin measures the distance between who we are and who we are
meant to be. So in chapter 4, "Beauty's Veiling: On Sin," and in conversation with a painting by Kehinde Wiley, I outline how humankind's
relationship with the Good, Beautiful, and True is damaged by individual, relational, and structural sinfulness which, collectively, most
adequately accounts for the personal behaviors, broken relationships,
and oppressive structures that we experience in the modern world. The
chapter includes discussion of systems of jeopardy that apply to most
of the social issues plaguing the world in its contemporary context,
creating much of the anguish we experience as creatures who share
this planet for a time.

Next, I turn to the healing of the world in a chapter on the person
and mission of Jesus Christ. In chapter 5, "Beauty's Story: On Parables,"
and in conversation with a painting by Sefedin Stafa, I reflect theologically on the power of telling stories within the wider context of Jesus'
own fondness for teaching through the sharing of parables. By treating
his stories about a good Samaritan, a great feast, and a persistent widow,
and by eliciting their subversive meaning in Jesus' own social context,
the chapter points to the core of Jesus' mission as one of creating a holy
community. This community stands in stark contrast to the ways of this

world. Jesus was not primarily concerned about our attainment of an afterlife, though he was mindful of that as well. Rather, Jesus was focused on the creation of a community dedicated to greater intentionality and justice in the here and now—and this was tied to a consummation of the kingdom "on earth, as it is in heaven" (Matt 6:10).

Jesus' stories had political consequences, however. Religious authorities in his own community, as well as political authorities occupying his nation under the auspices of Rome, took notice of him and ultimately conspired to kill him. In chapter 6, "Beauty's Incarnation: On Forgiveness," and in conversation with a painting by Kukuli Velarde, I examine the salvific meaning of Jesus' incarnation. I propose a restorative model of atonement that counters the violence implicit in classical theories of atonement. In contrast to these, I construct a model that properly situates the cross as the instrument of torture it was and, as such, an implement used by Rome that represents everything that is in opposition to the faithful, peaceful, and hopeful way Jesus lived his life, a way that is ennobled in his community of followers by the coming of the Holy Spirit. By emphasizing reconciliation between humans and God, and by thinking about forgiveness as the first step toward a restored relationship after a violation has occurred, the chapter will reimagine atonement in a way that does not implicate God the Father in the use of redemptive violence.

In chapter 7, "Beauty's Lament: On Suffering," and in conversation with a painting by Geoffrey Laurence, I will pause to think through implications of understanding God as Good, Beautiful, and True on classical dilemmas presented by the question of theodicy. How can the monotheistic religions defend an all-Knowing, Good, and Powerful God, given the reality of human experiences of evil and suffering? This book, in large measure, is about the anguish produced by atrocious acts of evil committed by human beings against human beings—not only those committed directly but also those committed by complicity in systems that do great harm. Since an all-Good God would want to create only an all-good creation, and since an all-Powerful God should be able to do so, how can we worship God, given the depths of suffering and evil we experience on earth? If God did not will an all-good creation, God's perfection of Goodness is collapsed, and God must be characterized as evil to some degree. If God could not create an all-good creation, God's perfection of Power is collapsed, and God must be characterized as impotent to some degree. If God did not know it would go badly, God's omniscience is collapsed, and God must be characterized as incompetent to some degree. What alternatives are there?

By differentiating God's foreknowledge from terms such as predestination and predetermination, by retrieving an Augustinian reading of evil as the profound lacking of goodness, and by rethinking the meaning of omnipotence and the proper exercise of power, I propose a way for Christians to navigate through questions of theodicy. My proposal leaves intact a monotheistic worldview that acknowledges, on the one hand, truly brutal experiences we have in a world where a profound lack of goodness creates suffering and anguish. It also affirms the existence of a perfectly Good, Beautiful, and True God, on the other hand, who wields power strategically even if subversively and, yes, perfectly, opening the way to a joyful anticipation of a new world coming into being, opening the way for Beauty's vineyard, having taken root, to flourish even into its ultimate and beautiful consummation.

Recognizing that we live not only in an age of anguish but also in an age of anticipation, where we are expectant and hopeful not only for a heavenly afterlife but also for a new way of being coming into being in the here and now—in a community of peace and loving-kindness I have been calling Beauty's vineyard—in the last chapter of the book, I ponder the work of the Holy Spirit among us. In "Beauty's Imagination: On Hope," and in conversation with a drawing by Ricardo Cinalli, I pick up a theme from the previous chapters about Beauty—understood as Jesus present among us, as the one who compassionately "suffers with" us. When he was among his first followers, he promised to send an Advocate, One who would be the Spirit of Truth in the community—the One who would be with us, to help us navigate our way to this paradise of peace and loving-kindness present in the here and now, culminating finally in a holistic vision in the presence of God, a union of heaven and earth. I speak of the hope inherent in the task of creating this community of peace and loving-kindness—even when there are no reasons to believe it can come into being, even when all evidence points to the contrary, even when there is no optimism whatsoever that it can be achieved. Hope lies in the imagination that there can be a different way, and in the vision that, within such an imagination itself, the new community emerges.

The book concludes with a short epilogue, a reflection called "Beauty's Anticipation: On Workers," about another of Jesus' parables, also set in a vineyard. It is in this chapter, along with the chapter on hope, that the "anticipation" of the subtitle of *Beauty's Vineyard* finds articulation. The workers in the vineyard are those who contribute to the community of *shalom* and *hesed*, of peace and loving-kindness, whether by giving every ounce of energy they have to the community or by laboring in it only lightly. These reflections are borne of an understanding of *ubuntu*—that our humanity is bound up in one another's, such that what affects one affects all, and what harms one harms all. What contributes to one's well-being contributes to the well-being of all. Again, we reap what we sow: if we focus on building a healthy community, we will all benefit; if we greedily exploit one another's labor, we will all live in fear. Within the concept of *ubuntu* lies the promise of a new world coming into being, breathed into existence by a God who wants us to live abundantly, enjoying lives committed to integrity and to simplicity—to the way of justice and righteousness, and by a God who embraces us when the long, hard day is done.

So I begin this book with the parable of the tenants, fittingly, it seems, because it introduces the ideas disclosed throughout the book. *Beauty's Vineyard* is written with the awareness of a conflict between varying theological imaginations at work in relation to the kingdom of God, as well as differing theological languages at work utilizing analogies and metaphors that speak to these varying realities. But explicit is one biblically and philosophically rooted imagination of the being of God as Love, a Trinity who is the essence of Goodness, Beauty, and Truth, persons distinct but not separate within the Godhead. Within this Being a material world is gestating, as it were, in God's womb, developing through evolutionary processes its material goodness, beauty, and truth expressive of the One from whom the creation comes and to whom the creation is oriented. Within this Being, Love is actively producing, degree by degree, faithfulness and peacefulness, kindness and gentleness, hopefulness and joyfulness. Within the world, Love is producing, in other words, a blessed community of God's beloved ones, all of humankind, who tend to Beauty's vineyard in the many and varying ways, large and small, they are uniquely qualified as they go about living their lives. One day, Beauty's vineyard will be fully developed, finding its union in the mind of God, where all tears will be wiped from our eyes, and in which our long journey of anguish is ended—our anticipation ultimately fulfilled. At long last, and in community, we will see Love. We will see God, face-to-face.

Throughout the years, many people have become my teachers. What I have gleaned from them is written in these pages, with a request for the reader's patience as I continue to learn and an appeal for generosity of spirit as readers encounter ideas new to them. Sue Myers should be named first and foremost among those who read these pages carefully and provided feedback at critical stages, as should my colleagues Gerald Schlabach, Philip Rolnick, and Paul Gavrilyuk. I am grateful for their biblical insights, sensitive eyes, and mature spiritual orientation, even while I accept responsibility for any errors that remain. Further afield, Frank Burch Brown, Rod Pattenden, Peter Kjeseth, John de Gruchy, and Bob Albers also read the manuscript and shared their thoughts. I am mindful, too, of my Basilica family, especially Leo and Paul, who in many ways official and unofficial sponsored our family, including our children, as we found our way to Catholicism. Thank you for living out the Catholic faith in joyful ways that drew us more deeply into the Body of Christ. The Center for Faculty Development at the University of St. Thomas provided me with release time from teaching to write the first draft of the book. I am grateful, too, for grants that made publication of this book possible, including support from the College of Arts and Sciences, the Theology Department, and the LuAnn Dummer Center for Women at the University of St. Thomas. I am always grateful to my husband, Joe, and my sons, Abe and Andy, for their love and support and, of course, for the gift of time to devote to research and writing. I am blessed by their encouragement. Finally, I want to name Fr. Richard Cogill, a South African priest and college friend, who has demonstrated so well the way of being human that is described in this book. My friend, I am sorry for those things that I still do not understand. I know you have many spiritual counselors; I hope very much they are for you what you have been for me. I am dedicating this book to you.

Chapter 1

Beauty's Allure
On Conversion

The shards of glass and the artistry with which he had captured them flying through the air captured my eye when I first stood in an art gallery exhibiting Jerome Witkin's five-painting series, *A Jesus for Our Time*. Jimmy, the preacher in the series who, in the preceding panel, was preaching confidently in Beirut, is now, in this third panel titled "The Explosion of the Car Bomb," sheltering his face from the fragments of glass propelled by the force of a blast, its heat melting the cross before which he cowers. Looking from the previous panel, "Jimmy's Mission to Beirut (Late Afternoon)," and back again to the explosion before me, it took me some time to notice the artist's double entendre. The shards of glass may very well be the broken bits of windshield and windows from the exploding car. But more likely, they are shards from the glass box in which Jimmy had been encased as he preached, naïvely believing that his message of God's wrathful judgment and conversion to faith in Jesus Christ, the Lord and Savior, would bring peace to the Middle East. Having only months previously returned from a semester of study in Haifa, Israel, from which students were evacuated because of Saddam Hussein's invasion of Kuwait and the determination of the United States to oust him, I too experienced the shattering of a glass box of sorts in the Middle East, just miles from Beirut. And so for reasons I could scarcely have named at the time, I resonated with the image on a profound level. This book, in some ways, is the story of my journey to

The Explosion of the Car Bomb, A Jesus for Our Time (1986–1987) by Jerome Witkin. Oil on canvas; panel 3 of 5; 88 x 79 inches. Courtesy of Jack Rutberg Fine Arts, Los Angeles.

piece together again a faith system after that life-changing semester in Israel, where I first encountered, in the sense of war, at least, the anguish of the world.[1] It took me a long time, and a great deal of study, before I had erected enough of a faith system to sing genuinely, once again, songs of praise to God.

When the Psalmist sings, trusting in the presence of a God who will, ultimately, bring an end to war and to human suffering, he writes using language that evokes memories of deliverance from Egypt and of the revelation of God's name from the burning bush (Exod 3:14). "Be still, and know that I am God" (Ps 46:10). The Psalmist sings, assuring hearers of God's existence—a consolation found not in frantic searching but in a quiet mindfulness. Likewise, there is in Hebrew Scripture an account of Elijah's experience of God:

> And behold, the LORD passed by, and a great and strong wind rent the mountains, and broke in pieces the rocks before the LORD, but the LORD was not in the wind; and after the wind an earthquake, but the LORD was not in the earthquake; and after the earthquake a fire, but the LORD was not in the fire; and after the fire a still small voice. (1 Kgs 19:11-12, RSV)

Just as in Exodus, in which the name of God was revealed to Moses as Yahweh, the one Who Is, the great and wonderful "I Am," the Psalmist returns to the theme of existence, promising that, when we are silent, when we are intentional about quieting our innermost selves, we too will know the presence of God. We will find assurance that God *is*, and that God whispers to us still. These verses suggest that the God of glory and majesty situated in heavenly grandeur is also a God of intimacy, perceptible in simplicity, present in stillness, perceivable in silence. The belief that God expresses something of God's Being to humanity in a barely audible, still, small voice is an insight shared by wisdom traditions throughout the world. If it is truly the voice of God we hear in our contemplative posture, a way that is so necessary to replenish the wells that dry up quickly in our noisy and busy world, the biblical witness assures us that we can anticipate that the Word will prod God's people

---

1. Among the first articles I published as I was embarking on a career in academia was an essay about this artist and this series in particular. See Kimberly Vrudny, "Indictment of Human Cruelty: Jerome Witkin's Image of *A Jesus for Our Time*," in *ARTS: The Arts in Religious and Theological Studies* 6, no. 3 (1994): 14–19. The best book-length treatment of the artist remains Sherry Chayat, *Life Lessons: The Art of Jerome Witkin* (Syracuse, NY: Syracuse University Press, 1994).

into engagement with the world—God's beloved creation—and particularly with God's beloved ones, those who are neglected and vulnerable.

An experience opened up one meaning of these passages to me in 2002. I had become pregnant for the second time and, after carrying my first child to term and giving birth naturally, I hoped and expected that all would go smoothly this round as well. I went through the first trimester with moments of nausea and overall exhaustion, and the second with its attendant joys in feeling the baby kick along with the requisite impulse to prepare the nest for our baby's impending arrival. We were looking forward to presenting our firstborn son, Abraham, with a baby brother or sister during the summer.

One night after a prenatal care appointment early in the third trimester, however, I had a terrible dream. In my nightmare, the nurse inserted a needle into my arm to take a blood sample. When she withdrew the needle, a tornado of blood rushed from the needle's point of entry and swirled fast and furiously around me. I could hear babies screaming over gusts of wind, babies whose images pressed into the wall of the tornado from either side, leaving behind deformed imprints in the dense, red, rubbery wall of the tornado spinning wildly around me. The imprints were visible from where I lay, still on the table in the clinic, cowering under the storm circling around me. I shook myself awake, promising that I would schedule an appointment and insist on an ultrasound which, for cost-saving purposes, were not being given regularly to patients in my clinic. When I followed through, the doctor appeased me and ordered an ultrasound, rationalizing the expense on the medical and insurance forms as necessary for reasons of "maternal anxiety."

During the ultrasound, I could tell something was wrong as soon as the images appeared on the screen. Within moments, the technician excused herself from the room, returning some minutes later with an order for a level-three ultrasound at the perinatal center at the hospital. "Why?" my husband and I asked, alarmed in part because she would not step back over the threshold into our room. "Is there something wrong?" She disclosed that there was fluid around the baby's heart, and apologetically explained that we would have to wait until the next day to learn more, as she was not qualified to interpret what she had seen on the screen. The next morning, after a thirty-minute ultrasound that was broadcast to a national panel of experts to diagnose the condition of the baby, we waited in the office for an opportunity to meet with the doctor. When he finally arrived, he revealed that the baby was in advanced stages of heart failure. Fluid encircled her heart and was beginning to surround her brain as well. He told us that the baby's condition was most definitely fatal. There was risk to my life as well, for if I attempted to carry her to term, my body would likely begin to mirror what was going on in hers, and so I too could go into heart failure. Second opinions confirmed the doctor's prognosis, and they advised us to induce labor as soon as possible. Because I was entering the third trimester, there was a chance she could survive outside of my womb, though not for long in her condition. But the action would certainly protect my life. Not wanting my husband to have to raise our firstborn son without me, we scheduled the induction.

Our daughter was stillborn eighteen hours after the induction began. I know precisely the moment she died; I felt her last shudder during labor. We named our baby Dora, a name that means "gift." We would have to wait six months for autopsy results to learn that she had Adams-Oliver Syndrome, an inherited but rare congenital disorder. Back in the hospital, however, when I closed my eyes, I saw a net being woven together, I believed, by prayers being spoken by our friends and loved ones—a net to catch us as we were falling. It was in those hours deep in the night, rocking in a chair with my tiny, warm, but dead baby bundled in blankets, that I heard the voice of God in the silence of our room and in the stillness of her half-pound mass in my arms—a baby both beautiful and precious, even if deformed and no longer breathing. In the silence, I heard a gentle voice grieving alongside me, singing a lullaby as I transferred and entrusted her care to the motherly ones who would hold her for me now in the next world, until she could be placed in my arms again, restored, I continue to hope, at the end of time.

Through it all, I most dreaded the questions of our son, Abraham. He would ask what happened, of course, which I was prepared to answer. But I knew he would wonder too *why* this happened. I didn't know what I would tell him. Our pastor visited, as did hospital chaplains. Grief counselors stopped by the room as well, dropping pamphlets about how to cope with this kind of tragedy. But there were no suggestions about how to communicate something of the depth of this loss to an inquisitive three-year-old child, now sibling to a dead baby. When I was discharged from the hospital, I asked my husband what I should say to Abe—and what he had said already. He too could offer no suggestion. When we returned home, he went into the house to greet his parents, who were watching Abraham for us. Before going into the house, I peeked around back and found him playing in his sandbox. I joined him, hugging him and holding him very, very closely for a bit. Before too long, as we rummaged through the sand, dragging dump trucks to imaginary building sites and back again, he asked the question I feared most. Words not mine found voice: "Baby Dora was so fragile. . . . Only God was tender enough to hold her."

As a theologian, long fascinated by questions about how God's Goodness, Beauty, and Truth could be reconciled with a world where goodness, beauty, and truth are perceptible to some degree, and even profoundly so, but aware too of a world in which evil and suffering are real, I recognized that the paradoxical reality of these terms were manifest in our Baby Dora—the tiny gift who graced our lives so briefly, both beautiful and deformed, and in whom we experienced something so good yet so unjust, something precious even if absolutely still. In Dora, the gentleness of God revealed itself to me as well—an image that was not among those shared with me when I was growing up, baptized, and confirmed in the more fundamentalist-leaning denomination of the Lutheran Church Missouri Synod (LCMS). Being raised within this denomination, I gathered that God was a stern judge, one who saw my every misdeed, and whose righteous wrath was taken out on his Son, Jesus Christ, who was crucified, bearing in his body the beating that I was told I so very much deserved, so despicable was humankind to the core. He died for my sin so that I could have everlasting life. Having received such a gift, the greatest thanksgiving I could offer, I was taught, was to share this story with others so that more could believe in Jesus Christ, in order that they too could be spared eternal damnation. When they confessed Jesus Christ as Lord and Savior, the cross would be effective for their salvation as well, I was told. Discriminating minds will recognize that there is little here of a truly grace-filled, Lutheran theology—but this is the message that I took away, nonetheless, from my first eighteen years in the LCMS church in the small town where I was raised in central Minnesota.

The next eighteen years and more were spent studying and then teaching at colleges, universities, and seminaries decidedly *not* the same in theological orientation or denomination—and with professors who opened new worlds to me, and to whom I will be forever grateful. They introduced me to conceptions of God I would embrace over time—a loving God, good, beautiful, and true; just, compassionate, and wise; creatively active and intentionally present in the world. They offered me a more complex approach to theology that ultimately transformed the infancy of my childhood faith into a more mature and nuanced system of belief, into a way of living courageously into the hope that there is more, and that in this something more is the existence of a transcendent, personified Love made immanent through the incarnation and activity of the Holy Spirit among us. They helped me to see that what we believe informs profoundly how we live, often in ways that go unrecognized—and so it matters what we believe. Theological imagination influences how we interact with the world, with ramifications both profound and persistent.

While the fundamentalism of my upbringing was shattered in essentially two strokes, the faith that emerged in its place took years to take root and to flourish. These discoveries, constituting a conversion, of sorts, to a new way of being in the world, took place gradually, over many years of careful study. They were marked at times by sporadic breakthroughs in understanding, sometimes dramatic during encounters with people very much unlike me. Sometimes, the breakthroughs were quite unremarkable, detectable only in a speechlessness that overcame me when reading silently in my study a line from a theologian or philosopher whose insight touched me in a deep and transforming way. It was not a conversion of unbelief to faith, or a conversion from one denomination to another, although at varying moments it entailed these as well—but rather a conversion to a deeper commitment to God and to God's creation that meant a deeper acceptance and embrace of humanity in all its wonder, all its diversity, and all its brokenness.

The first blow to the image of God I acquired as a child came during my first-semester Bible class at Gustavus Adolphus College in St. Peter, Minnesota, a college affiliated with the more progressive branch of Lutheranism, the Evangelical Lutheran Church in America (ELCA). At Gustavus, I was introduced to historical-critical methods of reading the Bible, which are attentive to the vantage point of the human authors who wrestled with religious questions and ultimate meanings in their experience of the unfolding history of the ancient Near East. Acknowledging that the Scriptures were inspired but not dictated, this treatment of the Bible allowed for "both/and"—that there are divine truths to be gleaned from the wisdom of our ancestors in the faith without requiring that we understand the texts as scientific journals or historical chronicles about the origins of the world and the unfolding of the ages in a time span of ten thousand years or less. This method included analysis of the varying perspectives of the gospel writers and entailed an acceptance that they had differing agendas and audiences in mind (and sometimes a different set of facts and assumptions from which they were working) as they shared the stories of Jesus' ministry, death, and resurrection from these unique vantage points. This was a radical departure from how we had understood the Bible in my denomination.

Indeed, as I dug deeper, I learned that the Lutheran Church-Missouri Synod had soundly rejected this method of reading the Bible when I was still a toddler. In 1970, the newly elected and conservative president of the Lutheran Church-Missouri Synod, Jacob Preus, established a fact-finding committee to interview the St. Louis Seminary's faculty. The committee prepared a report regarding faculty allegiance to the inerrancy of Scripture and commitment to orthodox Lutheran doctrine as they defined it. Upon completion, this report was sent to John Tietjen, the president of Concordia Seminary, St. Louis, as well as to its Board of Control.[2] Although the board cleared the faculty of all charges of false doctrine, the synod's convention in 1973 condemned the faculty and elected more conservative members to the Board of Control—members who later suspended Tietjen as president of Concordia Seminary. In 1974, this action led to protests by the seminary's students and faculty. The students organized a moratorium on classes, and forty-five of the fifty professors then employed declared that the charges against their president were *de facto* charges against them. The faculty interpreted this to mean that they too were suspended. The Board of Control responded that the faculty would be in breach of their contracts if they did not return to their classrooms by February 18, 1974, and that their teaching appointments would be terminated. They did not return. On February 19, 259 students voted to study with the terminated faculty at the newly formed Concordia Seminary in Exile (Seminex), in facilities provided by Eden Seminary and St. Louis University, and with accreditation temporarily provided under the Lutheran School of Theology at Chicago. Under the independent church body formed by these dissidents in 1976, the Association of Evangelical Lutheran Churches (AELC), Seminex operated until 1987, with many of its leaders acting as catalysts for merging the American Lutheran Church (ALC) and

---

2. To learn more about this episode in the Missouri Synod's history from the most historical distance, see Paul A. Zimmerman, *A Seminary in Crisis: The Inside Story of the Preus Fact Finding Committee* (St. Louis, MO: Concordia Publishing House, 2007). For accounts appearing in the immediate aftermath, see James E. Adams, *Preus of Missouri and the Great Lutheran Civil War* (New York: Harper and Row, 1977); Frederick W. Danker, *No Room in the Brotherhood: The Preus-Otten Purge of Missouri* (St. Louis, MO: Clayton Publishing House, 1977); and Kurt E. Marquart, *Anatomy of an Explosion: A Theological Analysis of the Missouri Synod Conflict* (Fort Wayne, IN: Concordia Theological Seminary Press, 1977). Further down the road, John Tietjen published his memoirs in which he treats this episode in large measure. See John Tietjen, *Memoirs in Exile: Confessional Hope and Institutional Conflict* (Minneapolis, MN: Augsburg Fortress Press, 1990). The fallout for women is recounted in Mary Todd, *Authority Vested: A Story of Identity and Change in the Lutheran Church-Missouri Synod* (Grand Rapids, MI: Eerdmans, 2000).

the Lutheran Church in America (LCA) into the Evangelical Lutheran Church in America (ELCA). This new denomination within American Lutheranism was formed in 1988 and to this day is the largest Lutheran church body in the United States. Those who retained control of Concordia Seminary in St. Louis and who maintained their support of the synod through this fractured moment in its history, however, influenced the fundamentalist direction that the Lutheran Church-Missouri Synod would take, as well as the theological imaginations of the young men who were entering the ministry and who have steered the direction of the church now in the four decades since this episode in its history.

Since I was a preschooler at the time, I only subsequently learned of the drama that had unfolded in St. Louis, preventing me and mine from learning that the Bible is, rather than a document communicated by God directly into the ears of prophets, evangelists, and epistle writers, a composite of writings prepared by many people who, over many centuries, wrestled to discern God's activity in and message to the world. Learning about the historical-critical method came, for me, as a breath of fresh air as I, like many of my classmates, was struggling to understand the claims of Christianity alongside things we were learning in our science classes. Although my denomination feared that reading the Bible in this way would destroy belief in God, it actually saved my faith from collapsing under the weight of the competing and compelling evidence supporting evolution and the emergence of life from an as-yet inexplicable explosion in space billions of years ago. Reading the Bible in this way opened my mind to the possibility of faith and reason existing harmoniously, and it allowed me entry into Christianity in an age of scientific discovery. By semester's end, I no longer shared the faith of my parents, grandparents, or great-grandparents—all of whom were heavily invested in this branch of the Lutheran Church. And there was no going back. It has created a rift that my extended family of both birth and marriage scarcely understands—and about which we have spoken precious little.

The second blow to my fundamentalism came when I studied abroad at the University of Haifa during the fall semester of my junior year. Because we did not have a lot of money when I was a child (neither of my parents attended college; though now retired, my father was a television repairman and my mother was a stay-at-home mom until I was in the fourth grade when she agreed to assist in classrooms at the elementary school nearest our house), and because I believed I would never be able to go overseas again, when my art history professor and mentor suggested strongly that I study internationally, I selected Israel.

I wanted to see the places I had read about in the New Testament, and because the program at Haifa offered courses in both art history and religion, subjects that had become my major fields of study at Gustavus, it seemed like a natural choice. So in September 1990, I was off to Haifa via New York City and Tel Aviv.

Only a handful of Christians were in attendance at the University of Haifa. Most students, including those who had come from Europe to study in the same program into which I had enrolled that semester, were Jewish by descent, even if they were not practitioners of the religion. Unlike me, they were attending the university at a fraught moment in history, as they considered making "aliya," or "stepping up" to Israeli citizenship. In Israel, I experienced life for the first time as a religious minority and felt the sting of my status as an outsider. My non-Jewish identity was revealed accidentally, and quite publicly so, on the first day of our arrival, when we were asked to take a Hebrew placement exam within hours of deboarding the long, overnight flight from New York. When I held the quarter-inch stack of papers in my hands, unable to decipher a word of the Hebrew, appearing to me as nothing more than illegible scratches on the page, I simply walked up to the proctor and asked to be placed in the elementary class. An elderly woman, she tapped my hand and whispered sweetly, "Just do as much as you are able to, dear." When I responded that I had done as much as I was able, given that I didn't know a single letter of the Hebrew alphabet, I communicated unknowingly to everyone in the room that I was not Jewish, since most Jews of some commitment go to Hebrew school as children and learn, at the very least, the basics of the Hebrew language.

Studying in Haifa was an isolating experience. The Jewish Americans in the program, I came to understand over time, were attempting to escape the Christian dominance of their own country in order to experience life in a Jewish one. Classmates confronted me about the symbol of the cross, the brutality of the crusades, and the anti-Semitism in the New Testament. They were legitimate questions, but they were questions I had never considered, and to which I was ill prepared to respond. Later in the semester, the derogatory word "goy" was painted, graffiti style, over a poster announcing a tour of sites sacred to Christians. It was the goy tour—the tour for goys of sites sacred to the goyim. I was a goy who didn't know Hebrew—someone considered unclean, I learned; someone despised.

I internalized too the tensions experienced by contemporary Israelis. Fearful of attacks at the hands of Palestinians, Israelis lived constantly under a double threat, also wary of invasions from foreign armies surrounding the small country struggling to exist after the horrors of the Shoah, the destruction, the Holocaust—a catastrophe wrought in some measure by interpretations of teachings sacred to my tradition. At the same time, I witnessed firsthand the oppression of the Palestinians as we visited refugee camps. With the help of our Palestinian classmates and dormitory neighbors, we began to understand their struggle for freedom. We took part in mock UN sessions, attempting one week to play the role of Israelis, and the next the role of Palestinians, finally trying to broker our own peace deal. Ours too failed. On top of all of this, the political situation was tense. Saddam Hussein had invaded Kuwait earlier that year, and President Bush promised to expel him from Kuwait. The American military was readying itself for war in the Persian Gulf throughout the summer of our departure, and ultimately setting a deadline of January 15, 1991, for Iraq's withdrawal. A refusal on Iraq's part to acquiesce to demands of the United States would result in war. We were taught how to inject ourselves with antichemical agents and what to do in case of war. Our semester-long program at Haifa was scheduled through the end of January, but most of the students fled as the deadline approached. The university eventually closed temporarily when the United States launched its missiles and when Iraq retaliated by sending scud missiles into Israel, America's staunchest ally in the region. These missiles were aimed at targets in Jerusalem, Tel Aviv, and my own Haifa and detonated just days after I had evacuated.

In many ways, the religious delusions of my childhood exploded with those bombs during those weeks of war in the Middle East—and my academic journey to try to find meaning amid the anguish of human life was begun. I began to search for a faith that was meaningful in a world where children are turned into soldiers, many learning hatred based on differences in skin color, nationality, or religious affiliation from birth; where religion becomes another means by which to segregate ourselves, many becoming violent in adherence to their own ideologies; where men, women, and children are trafficked as slaves, many in situations of sexual servitude; where diseases like diabetes, cancer, and AIDS eat away at bodies of beloved ones, many without access to life-prolonging or life-saving medicines; where poverty and hunger deny people of their inherent dignity, many of whom could be fed given the world's abundance. These conditions were no longer merely abstractions in my mind. I had seen those affected by these situations face-to-face. And I could not turn my back on the complexities of what I had witnessed, nor could I wrap my mind around the condition of a world that produced and tolerated these realities.

In terms of my own academic pursuits, I turned ultimately to Christian doctrine upon acquiring still more experience at seminary in reading the Bible critically, struggling to understand the traditional view of God as Beauty alongside bloody atonement theories and histories of crusades against Muslims and pogroms against Jews. Because ultimately I landed a position at a Catholic university after being trained at Protestant seminaries, I was forced more than most, I think, to examine Lutheran and Catholic doctrines side by side. Over time, and in conversation with many a patient colleague, I began to enter more and more deeply into the Catholic imagination and fell in love with its intellectual tradition, its sense of sacramentality, and its social teaching. I officially broke ties with the Missouri Synod in 2010, a move I had desired for twenty years but did not make in order to maintain peace in my family. An opening to do so came after experiencing the JustFaith curriculum with my husband in 2008–2009, and then a sabbatical journey with our family to South Africa during academic year 2009–2010.

Finally, in 2011–2012, my husband and I participated in the Rite of Christian Initiation for Adults (RCIA) through the Basilica of St. Mary, a Catholic parish in Minneapolis near where we live, where we were received into the Catholic Church and became members of this co-Cathedral during the Easter Vigil of 2012, along with our children who were also undergoing sacramental training that year. Obviously, the Catholic Church is no panacea. I entered with eyes wide open but with joy in coming home after a long, long period in the desert. This book outlines how I have come to think about the human person and sin, evil and suffering, Christ and salvation, and community and hope, after twenty years in an exile of sorts—a period in the wilderness, written by a theologian serving the church without having a church to serve, desiring now to contribute to Catholic scholarship in the post–Vatican II era. This book attempts to explain my conversion to a way of thinking profoundly different from the manner the denomination in which I was raised taught about what it means to be a Christian. Informed both by the study of theology and the arts, especially the visual arts, and by meaningful travel to places where traumatic experiences have shaped people to think critically about power and its abuse in a world of great disparity, *Beauty's Vineyard* is my theological aesthetic of anguish and anticipation.

The ideas that take shape in this book are ideas with which I have wrestled since that glass box was shattered in college and then again with Dora's stillbirth. Immediately after her death, I was grateful for my work at the university, but I was restless as well. I looked for an opportunity to do something meaningful in the community with Abraham—a voluntary commitment that we could do together, without putting Abraham in a toddler room somewhere while I performed a task for a nonprofit organization. I found a placement site online and learned about Open Arms of Minnesota, an organization that prepares meals for and delivers meals to people living with HIV/AIDS in the Twin Cities and thought it would be a perfect fit for us. Abraham could deliver meals with me, and we could get out of the house to do this work together a few times each month.

I fell in love with the organization the minute I walked through its doors. Open Arms, it seemed to me, represented something of an alternative universe, where people were committed to preparing tasty and healthy food so that no one who was sick in the community need also go hungry. Everyone seemed joyful despite the heaviness of the issues to which they were responding. Abraham and I became a part of the place. And I soon incorporated the organization into my work as well, collaborating with administrators at the University of St. Thomas to develop a service-learning partnership with Open Arms, beginning in 2004. Students could learn their discipline-specific coursework by conducting projects for Open Arms of Minnesota and, by their work, learn too about a public health dilemma unfolding in our own backyard. By 2006, I was traveling with Open Arms to South Africa in order to design an international service-learning course, "AIDS, Apartheid, and the Arts of Resistance," in affiliation with a community center with which Open Arms was partnering in the townships outside of Cape Town.

By engaging in this kind of work locally and globally, I was increasingly attentive to the reality that vulnerability to an HIV infection is too often predictable, not only based on the behaviors of individual people to which so much of the global health community was focused, but also on a person's relationship to various systems of jeopardy, among them sexual orientation, race, class, and gender. Wanting to disseminate what I had learned more publicly and beyond the academics more typically my audience, I developed a photography project to conduct on sabbatical and moved with my family to Cape Town during academic year 2009–2010 in order to create *30 Years / 30 Lives*, a photographic documentary project about HIV/AIDS intended to mark the thirtieth anniversary of the virus's known presence in the human community (1981–2011).

The project took me to cities in Thailand and Mexico as well, where I invited people impacted by HIV/AIDS—either directly through an infection or indirectly through the care or loss of a loved one or engagement in humanitarian response—to share their portraits and perspectives with those who would see the exhibit or its website. In addition, my family and I volunteered at the J. L. Zwane Church and Community Center in Guguletu, tutoring children in the Rainbow After-School Program, as well as at the Scalabrini Center in Cape Town, cooking meals for abandoned refugee children at the Lawrence House. To accompany the exhibit and to place the work in a religious framework, I published theological blogs on the project's website, short reflections which are now thoroughly reworked in the book the reader is now holding.

While in South Africa, I again read Alan Paton's novel *Cry, the Beloved Country* and discovered deep resonance with the character named Arthur Jarvis, with whom readers become familiar only through memories of his father who reads Arthur's letters after his death at the hands of a robber. The letters reveal Arthur's active political resistance to racism and oppression. In one of them, Arthur writes of his desire to follow a compass that will never play false to him—a compass I have found too in a Christian appropriation of the African philosophy of *ubuntu*.

> I shall devote myself, my time, my energy, my talents, to the service of [*ubuntu*]. I shall no longer ask myself if this or that is expedient, but only if it is right. I shall do this, not because I am noble or unselfish, but because life slips away, and because I need for the rest of my journey a star that will not play false to me, a compass that will not lie. I shall do this . . . because I cannot find it in me to do anything else. I am lost when I balance this against that, I am lost when I ask if this is safe, I am lost when I ask if men, white men or black men, Englishmen or Afrikaners, Gentiles or Jews, will approve. Therefore I shall try to do what is right, and to speak what is true. I do this not because I am courageous and honest, but because it is the only way to end the conflict of my deepest soul. I do it because I am no longer able to aspire to the highest with one part of myself, and to deny it with another. I do not wish to live like that, I would rather die than live like that. I understand better those who have died for their convictions, and have not thought it was wonderful or brave or noble to die. They died rather than live, that was all. Yet it would not be honest to pretend that it is solely an inverted selfishness that moves me. I am moved by something that is not my own, that moves me to do what is right, at whatever cost it may be.[3]

Through my work in response to HIV/AIDS both in the United States and in Africa, I have been able to connect my current path with the longer journey I have traveled since my college days. The experience

---

3. Alan Paton, *Cry, the Beloved Country* (New York: Charles Scribner's Sons, 1948), 170–71.

of witnessing many tragic situations throughout the world—by seeing Palestinian children holding rocks and sling shots, intimidated by Israeli defense forces manipulating machine guns, just as I was intimidated by soldiers who mounted the buildings surrounding Manger Square outside of the Church of the Nativity on Christmas Eve in order to watch us all night, with guns poised, ready to shoot; by sitting with bedridden men wasting away from opportunistic infections associated with AIDS in shacks built due to apartheid segregation and its aftermath in South Africa; by visiting hospitals mobilizing to provide comprehensive medical and legal care to women raped by men, some of whom were carrying a lethal virus; by sitting with and listening to survivors of human trafficking revisit the trauma they had experienced in the hope that a documentary photography project could make an impact; by interviewing leaders of the Zapatista rebellion against the exploitation of Mayan peoples in Mexico; by visiting with community health workers trying to respond to the crisis of a community in Mexico cut off from governmental assistance; by studying the practice of child soldiering in the context of Sierra Leone; by examining the practice of torture in the context of Argentina; by exploring the dynamics of fundamentalism and acts of terrorism in the context of Lebanon and the rise of al Qaeda, al Shabab, and ISIL; by observing the power of people putting feet to pavement in order to demand justice—all of these experiences have shaped my thinking and inform the theology of anguish and anticipation sketched in the pages of *Beauty's Vineyard*.

Invariably, my ideas will change over the years as I am introduced to still more authors and as I experience more of what life has in store. But, for now, this collection of chapters sketches what the broken pieces of faith began to look like once they were assembled again, especially since that eighteenth day of April in 2002, when I was touched gently by grace, by a "still small voice," by the voice of God singing a lullaby, tugging my heartstrings ever so gently, drawing me to a different way of being in the world, converting me to a way of peace and loving-kindness, to a philosophy of nonviolent resistance to the ways of the world. Beauty continues to invite us in, drawing us all to participate in the creation of such a society, a sisterhood, a brotherhood, a kingdom, a kin-dom,[4] that will sustain us all—Christian, Jew, Muslim, Buddhist, Hindu, indigenous, and secular humanists alike—in a community of *shalom*. For such a community is, I believe, Beauty's vineyard.

4. Ada Maria Isasi-Diaz, "Solidary: Love of Neighbor in the 1980s," in *Lift Every Voice: Constructing Christian Theologies from the Underside*, ed. Susan Brooks Thistlethwaite and Mary Potter Engel (San Francisco: Harper, 1990), 31–450, here 303–5.

Rothko Chapel. Interior View with Northwest-North triptych—Northeast paintings. Photo by Hickey-Robertson. Rothko Chapel, Houston, TX.

Chapter 2

Beauty's Companions
On the Good and the True

*Did I conceive all this people? Did I give birth to them, that you
should say to me, "Carry them in your bosom, as a nurse carries
a sucking child," to the land that you promised on oath to their
ancestors?* (Num 11:12)

*You were unmindful of the Rock that bore you;
you forgot the God who gave you birth.* (Deut 32:18)

*Where were you when I laid the foundation of the earth?
    Tell me, if you have understanding.
Who determined its measurements—surely you know!
    Or who stretched the line upon it?
On what were its bases sunk,
    or who laid its cornerstone
when the morning stars sang together
    and all the heavenly beings shouted for joy?
Or who shut in the sea with doors
    when it burst out from the womb?—
when I made the clouds its garment,
    and thick darkness its swaddling band,
and prescribed bounds for it,
    and set bars and doors,
and said, "Thus far shall you come, and no farther,
    and here shall your proud waves be stopped"?* (Job 38:4-11)

*Listen to me, O house of Jacob,
all the remnant of the house of Israel,*

who have been borne by me from your birth,
carried from the womb;
even to your old age . . . ,
even when you turn gray I will carry you.
I have made, and I will bear;
I will carry and will save. (Isa 46:3-4)

For thus says the Lord:
I will extend prosperity to her like a river,
and the wealth of the nations like an overflowing stream;
and you shall nurse and be carried on her arm,
and dandled on her knees.
As a mother comforts her child,
so I will comfort you;
you shall be comforted in Jerusalem. (Isa 66:12-13)

Yet it was I who taught Ephraim to walk,
I took them up in my arms;
but they did not know that I healed them.
I led them with cords of human kindness,
with bands of love.
I was to them like those
who lift infants to their cheeks.
I bent down to them and fed them. (Hos 11:3-4)

The God who made the world and everything in it, he who is
Lord of heaven and earth, does not live in shrines made by human
hands, nor is he served by human hands, as though he needed
anything, since he himself gives to all mortals life and breath
and all things. From one ancestor he made all nations to inhabit
the whole earth, and he allotted the times of their existence and
the boundaries of the places where they would live, so that they
would search for God and perhaps grope for him and find him—
though indeed he is not far from each one of us. For "In him we
live and move and have our being"; as even some of your own
poets have said, "For we too are his offspring."[1] (Acts 17:24-28)

---

1. Since Acts depicts Paul preaching before an altar constructed to "an unknown God," he is quoting Greek poets to reach his audience. The first line is from Epimenides *Cretica*; the second is from Aratus's poem "Phainomena."

The poets and prophets behind the biblical texts drew extensively from a host of images in order to convey their sense of the divine. In the verses assembled here, God is depicted as divine Mother, the One who gives birth and who carries the people of God first in the divine womb and then on the divine bosom. God nurses them, nourishes them, and plays with them. God comforts them when they are discomforted and consoles them when they seem inconsolable. By drawing on such metaphors, the ancient poets effectively tapped into human experience and, by the language they chose, presented the bond between God and humankind as like the love between a mother and her baby. The poets drew on the universality of that idealized experience to conjure in the reader's mind an image of the relationship between God and God's beloved creation. God lifts the creation like an infant to God's cheek, nuzzling the baby, embracing it, cherishing its sweet innocence even knowing, as does every parent, that there are troubled days ahead. But such a God, trusting that it is better to exist than not to exist, wills creation into being nonetheless and freely brings it into being. Together, divine mother and earthly child rest secure in the knowledge that nothing can separate creation from the love of God (Rom 8:38-39).[2]

Like the biblical poets, we continue to fashion our words in an attempt to approach a reality that always finally transcends that which we are trying to describe. Although they always fall short, our words bring to cognition something of God's nature that can be grasped, adored, and worshiped. The authors of the verses collected here were using language metaphorically to convey something of the beautiful essence of the God to whom their metaphors point. They help the faithful enter into prayer and to imagine the One receiving their petitions and praise.

Choosing what words to use when writing about God is a serious undertaking, for how we speak about God indicates the essence of who

---

2. According to those assembled at the Council of Toledo (635 CE), "We must believe that the Son came from the womb of the Father [*de utero patris*] and was begotten or born [*genitus vel natus*] from the Father's own being." For a discussion, see Elisabeth Moltmann-Wendel and Jürgen Moltmann, *Humanity in God* (New York: Pilgrim Press, 1983), 89. See also John Paul II and his "Letter to Families" (par. 7), in which he writes, "When, in union with the Apostle, we bow our knees before the Father from whom all fatherhood and motherhood is named (cf. Eph 3:14-15), we come to realize that parenthood is the event whereby the family, already constituted by the conjugal covenant of marriage, is brought about 'in the full and specific sense.' Motherhood necessarily implies fatherhood, and in turn, fatherhood necessarily implies motherhood. This is the result of the duality bestowed by the Creator upon human beings 'from the beginning.'" http://w2.vatican.va/content/john-paul-ii/en/letters/1994/documents/hf_jp-ii_let_02021994_families.html.

we believe God *is*—an essence into which we believe we are being transformed. In Christianity, through the process of sanctification, alternatively called deification and divinization, we believe we are being transformed into the One we imagine, the One we cherish as sacred. In Christianity, we confess that we are the imperfect but still developing Body of Christ. So what we ascribe to God and God's Being is of ultimate importance—for these ascriptions construct nothing less than the community we aspire to become and are becoming. If we perceive God as violent, misogynistic, or xenophobic, for example—which are only a few among the characteristics we have divinized and thereby worshiped—we will become violent, misogynistic, and xenophobic. By perceiving God to be a Divine Warrior, the Israelites justified war and Christians used these texts to justify crusades and pogroms; by perceiving God to be male, Jews and Christians, both male and female, elevated men and subordinated women; and by perceiving God to be opposed to intermarriage, our traditions have been laced with ethnocentrism and eventually racism. These are only a few examples of the kinds of images we have glorified, to our great shame. But operating in this book is the understanding that, if we perceive God as Good, Beautiful, and True, the One who calls us to resist oppression, to stand in solidarity with those who suffer, and to reconcile broken relationships, then this is the community we will become—culminating in a restored Eden, a union of heaven and earth where, increasingly in time and culminating in the fullness of time, the beloved will see Love's face, even face-to-face.

The serious and even grave nature of our selection and use of words for God was conveyed to me especially successfully once, long ago, when I studied Jewish philosophy in Israel. My professor firmly instructed us that one must never utter the name of God, revealed long ago from a bush burning yet not consumed by the flame enveloping it. So holy was God's nature that to say God's name aloud desecrated both the name and the one who dared utter it. When a classmate, in a moment of impropriety, emitted the hallowed name, the session ended abruptly. Our professor excused himself from the room. It was most awkward, as we were studying in our professor's home in Haifa; we did not know whether he would come back. Moreover, we were not sure if it would be a further insult to leave the premises without acknowledging the hospitality that had been extended to us. We waited for an excruciatingly long time before gathering our things, finally deciding in silence to take leave of our professor's home. Mercifully, he welcomed us back the next week. We never spoke of the incident, but the lesson was learned.

John de Gruchy, a noted South African theologian, writes of a similar experience in his book, *Confessions of a Christian Humanist*—only the one who spoke was he.

One day I made a terrible mistake. While reading from the Torah I unwittingly uttered the sacred name for God revealed to Moses beside the burning bush (Exodus 3.14). There are many names for God in the Hebrew Bible, Adonai and Elohim among them, but there is one name that is above all others, a name of such immensity and mystery that it should never be uttered. In the original Hebrew text there are no vowels, so the sacred name simply reads: YHWH, usually translated "I Am who I Am," though there is uncertainty about its pronunciation. Other Hebrew names for God bring God within our reach; they describe God in terms we can grasp by analogy with our own experience. But YHWH refers to the God beyond our imagination, literally so. To utter the word is unpardonable for it suggests an arrogant familiarity with God, an ability to "image God," and thus a breaking of the First Commandment. In order to convey the sacredness of this Name, many of my later Jewish students wrote "G-d" in their essays.

Having uttered the sacred Name in my Hebrew teacher's study, there was nothing I could do to reverse the situation. He was deeply disturbed by my indiscretion, not least because he had *heard* the Name however incorrectly pronounced. He closed the Bible, rose from his desk, left the room to wash his hands and face, and, returning sometime later, ushered me firmly out of the house. Few words were spoken; but those that were made it clear that my Hebrew lessons, with him at least, had now come to an end. He did not dare take the risk of hearing me make the same dreadful mistake. . . . The experience remains vivid. We Christians are often too casual in the way in which we talk about God.[3]

As these memories attest, words have power. When we speak of God, we must not do so lackadaisically or nonchalantly but carefully and intentionally, ever mindful of the sacredness of the task we dare to undertake.

Perhaps Mark Rothko knew best. Those who visit the Rothko Chapel say that this God of utter mystery, who is beyond all words and all images, but who Christians believe is nevertheless present to us through the incarnation, is experienced profoundly in those panels of paint described as deeply tranquil and meditative. Through his paintings, Rothko offers the prayerful and meditative a potential experience with the sublime. He gives the viewer an experience of visual silence that draws us paradoxically into sacred mystery. Indeed, in the presence of God, perhaps nothing more ought to be said. Perhaps nothing more

3. John de Gruchy, *Confessions of a Christian Humanist* (Minneapolis, MN: Fortress Press, 2006), 122.

can be said. Perhaps the most appropriate response is precisely this: reverent, peaceful silence.

Cautiously, then, this chapter proceeds with an exploration of this God who is, to use Anselm's words, the One about whom "nothing greater can be conceived"[4]—the one who communicated with us, disclosed God's Being to us, and revealed divine Beauty for us. In this chapter, we attempt to approach something of the unapproachable, to express something of the inexpressible, to say something of the One in whom our curiosity, language, and imagination find their highest aspiration in the Christian religion: the Trinitarian God revealed through the incarnation of Christ. Our attention will be directed, first, to how we must find a means to navigate between the absolutisms and relativisms of contemporary culture in order to say something of God with integrity, lest we lose all capacity to critique religious movements that have embraced violence. Next, we will embrace analogy along with metaphor as a key tool in this attempt to speak of God. Finally, we will explore an analogy of Beauty, along with Beauty's companions: the Good and the True, to suggest that belief in the Trinity ought to prompt political engagement in the faithful. The good in them, with its source in God, desires to restore human society to its original intention and thereby to overcome problems plaguing it.[5] We will enter into a thought experiment to consider Goodness as a name for the Father, Beauty as a name for the Son, and Truth as a name for the Spirit. The three eternally indwell one another and reveal God to be accessible through participation in divine life, as demonstrated in lives devoted to the pursuit of justice, compassion, and wisdom and as evidenced in lives devoted to the creation of a community of faithfulness and peacefulness, kindness and gentleness, and hopefulness and joyfulness.

Earthly encounters with the Trinity inform Christian perception of God's interaction with the world. As perfectly Good, Beautiful, and True, the Trinity, this chapter asserts, is fundamentally attractive, alluring in nature. The Trinity captivates the faithful, graciously building up in

---

4. Eugene R. Fairweather, ed. and trans., "Anselm of Canterbury: *An Address (Proslogion)*," in *A Scholastic Miscellany: Anselm to Ockham* (Philadelphia, PA: The Westminster Press, 1956), chap. 15. "And so, O Lord, thou art not simply that than which a greater cannot be thought; rather, thou art something greater than can be thought." See also the translation by Sidney Norton Deane.

5. Hans Urs von Balthasar constructs another analogy of beauty in his seven-volume work of theological aesthetics, *The Glory of the Lord* (San Francisco: Ignatius Press, 1982). John K. Riches describes von Balthasar's theology by reference to the analogy of beauty specifically: John K. Riches, *The Analogy of Beauty: The Theology of Hans Urs von Balthasar* (Edinburgh: Bloomsbury T & T Clark, 1986).

them an anticipation for fullness of life already but not yet fully realized in the vineyard into whose origins and *telos* we have been inquiring. Underlying all three sections of this chapter is the belief and the hope that God does, indeed, continue to communicate with us in the same manner in which God has always made God's own Being known to us—through earthly manifestations of the good, beautiful, and true. God is among us always, but often in ways we fail to recognize, so limited is our comprehension. "For now we see in a mirror, dimly, but then we will see face to face. Now I know only in part; then I will know fully, even as I have been fully known" (1 Cor 13:12).

Beauty's Disclosure: On Curiosity

Perhaps it is an overstatement to suggest that our survival as a people may be rooted in theological curiosity, especially in a day when theology is taught less and less. But there is not much hope for a society when it goes without an ability to examine the implications of varying truth claims, and when its own truth claims go without challenge. Likewise, there is not much hope when people simply believe what they have been taught without inquiring into why those particular things are believed instead of alternatives. But this is precisely the kind of claim made by Prince Myshkin in Dostoevsky's novel, *The Idiot*.[6] Dismissed as a fool, as are most down through the ages who think like him, Prince Myshkin saw what too many cannot see and understood what many cannot understand. He perceived that Beauty could save the world. And he was bold to proclaim that the survival of the world was somehow bound up in Beauty. His was a theological claim. Therefore, in order to understand what he meant, one must develop theological curiosity. Maybe our survival does depend on it.

Of course, there are many competing imaginations about God. At the most fundamental level, we dispute the issue of God's very existence. Those who are theists argue over the nature of the God or gods they perceive. There are polytheistic conceptions of the divine suggesting there are many spiritual beings that have power and influence over the world, as opposed to monotheistic perceptions that there is One Supreme Being exercising some kind of providence over the universe. Within monotheism, there are Unitarian and Trinitarian conceptions that debate whether there is or is not distinction within a unified Godhead. Judaism and Islam are Unitarian in orientation—but they differ in terms of which holy books they revere, with Jews holding Hebrew Scripture and

---

6. Fyodor Dostoevsky, *The Idiot*, trans. Eva Martin (Boston: E. P. Dutton, 1934), 238.

its prophets as authoritative in matters of faith, whereas Muslims revere the Qur'an as the incarnation of the Word of God expressed through the prophet Muhammad. Christianity is dominantly Trinitarian in orientation, though there are thousands of different expressions of Christian thought: some Catholic, some Orthodox, some Anglican, some Protestant, some Evangelical, and still there are more. Among the mainline Protestants, there are Lutherans, Presbyterians and Methodists—and among the Evangelicals there are Baptists, not to mention the Pentecostals, with many more denominations that could be named as well, such that at present, with every Christian free church a denomination unto itself, there are more than thirty thousand Christian sects and counting.

Behind all of these views are questions of a universal nature. Is an intelligent Being (whether Unitarian or Trinitarian) or collection of Beings the cause of the universe, or is existence not the result of any kind of intelligent design whatsoever? If a transcendent Being or Beings is the cause of creation, was human existence an intention of this Being? If humanity was an intentional creation, for what purpose were human beings created? Some theoretical physicists tell us that chronological time and three-dimensional space began when two potential particles, which had been in perfect balance between positive charges and negative charges, gained disequilibrium and exploded.[7] The entire universe was created from this dramatic unbalancing. From that spectacular beginning, a cycle of creation and uncreation was begun, setting all the laws into place that were necessary, it turns out, for life to unfold on planet earth. Do these potential particles have a divine source? These are the kinds of ultimate questions that can bring us onto religious ground and into the realm of theology proper.

If we make the jump to suggest that these potential particles had a divine source, the theologian might enter the conversation to assist those who marvel at these questions to avoid beliefs that are less intellectually satisfying or more philosophically dangerous than others, for we have entered the realm of systems of faith and their construction. This brings us into the realm of systematic theology, the field that interprets the theological tradition in light of the religious questions that dawn anew in every historical era. Systematic theology is a science in a more general sense. It is a branch of knowledge, an area of study—but it is not a science in that term's more technical sense. Systematic theology does not operate by empirical experimentation that can be replicated time and again. As such, these matters do not belong in science classrooms but in theology

7. See, for example, Stephen Hawking and Leonard Mlodinow, *The Grand Design* (New York: Bantam, 2010).

classrooms, with trained theologians shaping these discussions. The theologian will likely begin by asking whether it is better to believe that existence springs from Existence or from nonexistence. Since everything in the empirical world suggests that materiality itself has a beginning or, in other words, that all material things generate from a preexisting something, it becomes necessary either to posit that something material produces everything that exists, stretching materiality itself into infinity (a position that contemporary physics itself seems to refute), or to posit that there exists something infinite—that there is something without beginning and without end transcending material existence from which material existence springs. It is entirely theoretically possible that those particles may be (potentially) infinitely existing but, since they are material, and since our experience of the material world suggests that all materiality is finite, with a discrete beginning and a discrete end, Christian philosophers and theologians, including Thomas Aquinas, have tended to posit an infinitely existing immaterial Being who brings material existence into being from within the capacities and will of that Divine Being.[8] This is a theological assertion, though, and not a scientific one. It is a matter of faith—and belongs then in the realm of churches, synagogues, and temples—not in public school classrooms.

Since no one knows with certainty the answers to these questions of an ultimate nature, whatever judgment one makes in response to them is, by definition, a leap of faith. Faith and doubt coexist on a pole between positive certainty (e.g., "I am certain God exists") and negative certainty ("I am certain God does not exist"). To be sure, there are fundamentalists on either side of this pole who proclaim certainty, rather than faith, in regard to God's existence or nonexistence, shaping our pole into something of a loop that connects the absolutists among us—linking in fascinating, even humorous, ways figures like James Baker and Richard Dawkins. Short of the certainty enjoyed at either end of the pole, however, there are degrees of faith, with some persuaded as they are by various proofs from philosophical argument or scientific experiment on the one hand, revelatory encounters with the transcendent on the other, and every combination in between. Any lack of certainty, however—regardless of how much or how little—introduces a degree of doubt. Doubt is neither the opposite of faith nor its enemy. They are life partners, moving their limbs to the same dance. Inseparable, faith and doubt live together. To have one is, by nature, to possess a degree of the latter.[9]

---

8. Thomas Aquinas, *Summa Theologiae* (hereafter ST), I, q. 2, a. 3.

9. For a deeper exposition on this argument, see Paul Tillich, *Dynamics of Faith* (New York: Harper and Brothers, 1958).

All of this is to say that to believe there is a Being or collection of beings who is or who are responsible for the existence of the particles and/or for their collision is a leap of faith. Likewise, to believe there is no Being or collection of beings who is or who are responsible for the existence of the particles and/or for their collision is likewise a leap of faith. So let us not confuse atheism with faithlessness and theism with faithfulness. To be human is to be faithful. But to what or to whom, precisely, is one faithful? This is the question that invites the comment of theologians, who have grappled for countless ages examining the implications of systems of faith and the elements of these systems, devoting their lives to thinking about the validity of certain claims over others. Insofar as the possibility remains that there is a Being or Beings behind creation of the physical universe, and for as long as there are people confessing faith in a Being or Beings who transcend the boundaries of the universe, theologians have great value, for there are many claims about the nature of that Being or Beings and about what such a Being requires. Some of the claims are awe inspiring. Some of the claims are deadly. Theologians can help us distinguish between them. As a theologian myself, I have become less interested in the question "Do you believe in God," than in the question, "What kind of a God do you believe in?" The answer to the latter is much more telling than the answer to the first.[10] And if there is in actuality a Reality behind these claims, if we ascribe to the principle of noncontradiction, which I think we must, then some of these claims must be more accurate than others. If there is a God, God cannot be both Trinitarian or Unitarian simultaneously—unless God morphs into whatever it is we imagine God to be, in which case, both Trinitarian and Unitarian conceptions are proved to be false, because the reality of a morphing God disproves the characteristic of immutability assumed in most Trinitarian and Unitarian models.

That a response to ultimate questions requires a leap of faith does not diminish their importance. My understanding is that scientists cannot prove that gravity exists. Therefore, to believe in gravity requires a leap of faith. Observation has demonstrated with some degree of reliability that, on earth, heavy objects will be pulled to the ground. Now, there may be gravity denialists who claim that gravity does not exist—and certainly only a few might wish to deny the denialist the freedom of speech to promote his or her point of view. If the theories of the scientist and the denialist are each tested, however, by asking each proponent

10. I am grateful to my South African Anglican priestly friend, Richard Cogill, for this insight.

to jump from an aircraft flying twenty thousand feet above the ground without any gear whatsoever, one position will clearly be supported by the experiment time and again. There is a certain degree of reliability to the theory of gravitational pull in relation to the earth.[11] Likewise in theology: there is in reality an authoritative answer to the question of whether there is or is not a Being or a plurality of Beings as first cause of the universe. Humility dictates that the theologian acknowledge that the atheist may very well be right. If there is a divine first cause, however, then Catholic doctrine assumes that exploration of material reality will reveal aspects of that nature. Moreover, if a Being is the cause behind all that exists, then scientists, philosophers, and theologians alike will be interested in learning all we can, from within our varying disciplines, about this initial cause—even if, at this stage, that answer is unknowable.[12] It remains nevertheless possible that the object of our inquiry is one and the same, and thus scientific, philosophical, and theological assertions should complement rather than contradict one another.

In the times in which we live, truth claims in relation to religious questions make many among us nervous. Culturally, we seem to have shifted, in our desire after world wars and nuclear bombs, and wisely so, to a mood of religious tolerance. We have accepted, to a large degree, the posture that your truth is your truth, and my truth is mine. But this movement of our culture to an absolute relativism can be alarming. While it is good to tolerate lots of positions, for a state of constant warfare is not desirable, it is important, too, both to strive to do more than tolerate many approaches to these questions of an ultimate nature and to condemn religious approaches that have embraced violence. Might a Christian

---

11. I am obviously caricaturizing the view of gravity denialists. See Dennis Overbye, "A Scientist Takes On Gravity," in the *New York Times* (July 12, 2010), for an alternative angle in thinking about gravity's "existence," http://www.nytimes.com/2010/07/13/science/13gravity.html?pagewanted=all&_r=0.

12. The existence of a thing and the knowability of a thing are two separate issues. HIV existed before humans knew it existed. For a time, the reality was unknown and unknowable to human beings. We need not dismiss belief in a reality, even if that reality is unknowable. Nevertheless, we might need to defend our epistemologies. That is to say, we ought to be prepared to defend how we know what we believe to be true and to make a persuasive case for our point of view, even if the reality or unreality behind our claims remains unknowable. This is, after all, the work that theoretical physicists and theologians alike are undertaking. Atheists need to support their case, just as theists need to defend theirs. Theologians must take into account scientifically observable and documented data, as well as Scripture, philosophical/theological argument, reason, and experience, with an openness to correction and to a way of thinking widely informed by the other disciplines.

celebrate Yom Kippur with Jewish friends and Ramadan with Muslim friends, and so on, without compromising one's own belief in the Trinity or hope for redemption in Christ? I want not only to tolerate but also to celebrate the beliefs of my Jewish and Muslim friends. I want to learn from their wisdom traditions, just as I want to share something of mine.

More troubling to me is that people in the West seem increasingly unwilling and, indeed, unable, to weigh the relative merits or demerits of a theological argument or truth claim. This indifference does not serve society well when some people in various religious traditions have taught their people to kill in the name of their God. On what grounds can such violence be condemned? And lest one presume I am referring only to the likes of Osama bin Laden, I am quick to point out that Timothy McVeigh, who blew up the federal building in Oklahoma City, for a time was absorbed in the study of a fundamentalist form of Christianity (as are members of the Ku Klux Klan), and Yigal Amir, who assassinated Yitzhak Rabin, was an Israeli Zionist. How do we live in a multicultural world, judiciously and rationally assessing religious beliefs while lovingly and persuasively disarming dangerous imaginations that can prompt violence? How do we promote peaceful and harmonious alternatives without escalating interreligious conflicts among us? These, of course, are difficult questions, among the most pressing of our time.

Drawing lines is not easy. And, to be sure, we have often drawn them too sharply and too narrowly, conveying an absolutism that has exacerbated rather than calmed volatile relations. But the current trend to draw no lines whatsoever (your truth is your truth and my truth is mine) is not the answer. For clearly there are lines that must be drawn. Not every system of belief should be tolerated. Should we accept a position that says that God prefers Christians to Jews? Though we might be tempted to scoff at such a teaching, let us not forget that the Nazi system was dismantled only about seventy years ago, and many of its premises are not challenged but, indeed, are horrifyingly still defended in many of our churches.[13] Should we tolerate a position that suggests that God loves folks who are pale more than God loves folks of more vibrant

---

13. I first became aware of the concept of a "seamless" reading of the Bible after the Holocaust when reading Danna Nolan Fewell and Gary A. Phillips, "Bak's Impossible Memorials: Giving Face to the Children," in *Representing the Irreparable: The Shoah, the Bible, and the Art of Samuel Bak* (Boston: Pucker Art Publications, 2008), 92–110. Quoting Emil Fackenheim, they write, "An abyss has been opened up between the Book, then and there, and this 'generation' here and now." Therefore, we can no longer go on reading the Bible as though the Holocaust never happened. Our reading requires a seam. See also Emil Facken-

shades? Again, we might reject such a thing as utterly implausible. But let us not forget that the apartheid system was rooted in such a belief and was only dismantled about twenty years ago. Indeed, many of its premises are not challenged in our churches today, which in America as in Africa remain largely segregated. Should we tolerate a position that says that God prefers heterosexuals to homosexuals? This teaching is alive and well among us—a line that some are happy to draw. Should we tolerate a position that says that God only calls men but not women to ordained ministry? On what premises is this teaching based—and can such assumptions stand? These systems of faith must be interrogated too.

Much is at stake in these and many other theological discussions that are currently underway, with more to come. But are we educating the faithful in such a way that they are equipped to enter into these conversations? Your truth is not absolute truth, nor is mine. But together, we must plow through the evidence that is available to us, both revealed and hidden, and to have the difficult conversations that are required in order to approach more closely the divine truths that are calling out to us as people of many faiths to create a more beautiful world. It may very well be that God's view is a gracious one, and that God accepts within a particular "zone of acceptability" a number of notions that we articulate in our attempts to find ultimate meaning from our vantage point of relative ignorance. I pray that this is the case. And it may very well be that God loves us despite the errors in judgment we have made along the way. But when our faith leads us to violence, for example, a line has been crossed. God might save us still—but we are not living in a way that promotes life. We need to be courageous in thoughtfully examining teachings we hold precious, encouraging others to do the same, and entering into interreligious dialogue with one another to learn from wisdom traditions beyond our own—even if it means we will need to leave some things behind. We need to imagine new ways of being—maybe even discovering along the way that this wisdom has been embedded in our traditions all along. Otherwise, there is little hope for us. We will continue to ostracize, isolate, and brutalize one another. Beauty's vineyard will never flourish among us.

In our lives of faith, we must continually navigate between too narrow an absolutism and too wide a relativism in order to chart a middle path, or even a new course, where we speak our truth while remaining open to being corrected by the wisdom of the global community, even

---

heim, *The Jewish Bible After the Holocaust: A Re-Reading* (Bloomington, IN: Indiana University Press, 1991), 17.

as we are empowered to correct those who may have veered into absolutism, on the one hand, or into a relativism that has no means even to offer critique of violent movements brewing among us, on the other. We must continually interact with one another across boundaries that traditionally isolate us from one another, so that we learn to hear each other, so that we learn to learn from each other.

Such a search for meaning ignites curiosity, introducing questions we can spend a lifetime pursuing—always searching for a still more excellent way. If St. Anselm was right—if God is that than which nothing greater can be conceived—what are the philosophical justifications to propose, for example, that there is a singular Being behind creation rather than a plurality of Beings? Why might a monotheist consider monotheism a higher perfection than polytheism, and why a polytheist the opposite? If we postulate that the source behind all of creation is a singular Being, what can be said of this Being? Are immutability, impassibility, and infinity indicators of ultimate perfection—or is it more perfect to change, to suffer, and to experience finitude? If there are implications behind each of the ways that we might think of this Being, which beliefs do no harm? Should we believe this singular Being is Unitarian (without internal distinction) or Trinitarian (with internal distinction)? Is Being immanent to the creation, or does Being remain forever distant from creation? What of Being's expression? Is God's nature accessible to us through revelation, prophetic literature, and poetry? Should we maintain that the source of all Being is perfectly Good, Beautiful, and True? If we suggest that the source of all Being is *im*perfectly good, beautiful, and true, are we ready to suggest that we worship a being who is evil, unjust, and violent, even to a degree? What are the implications for human life and human thriving if we admit any of these things into our belief system? How should we imagine this ultimately mysterious Being with whom we enter or are entered into relationship? What do we risk by such articulations?

If any of these questions ignite our curiosity, then our theological task has begun. We begin to evaluate differing theological imaginations, trying to understand what it is that various communities hold sacred and why. In other words, it is with curiosity that our journey of faith is prompted, by grace, to greater maturity, when it is properly nurtured with care and attention and not stifled, on the one hand, or forced, on the other. Indeed, we must foster curiosity. For curiosity will lead us, I hope, to Beauty—to that which has the unifying power to reconcile competing imaginations, to lure us into the vineyard for which we have been seeking, to empower in us the courage to create the peacefulness after which we have been yearning, to enlighten us with the wisdom we will require to live justly, to love kindly, and to walk humbly with our God (Mic 6:8). Perhaps the poor idiot, Prince Myshkin, was right. Perhaps Beauty can save the world, even yet.[14]

Beauty's Communication: On Language

Once our theological curiosity leads us to become invested in a particular theological tradition, it is important to learn how that tradition has come to speak of what is holy. In Judaism, the holy name revealed by a voice from a bush thousands of years ago points mysteriously, most fittingly, to the reality of the Being revealed in the name. "YHWH," technically a verb in Hebrew, not a proper noun (though it takes that function grammatically as well), is most often translated into English with verbs of being, such as, "I Am Who I Am." Whatever the precise meaning, the word points to God's Being—a promise of God's Existence, of God's mystifying presence, in the midst of God's children who are not abandoned but accompanied by their Creator. God is the One who brought them into being, who invited them to share in Existence by creating them in the *imago Dei* (Gen 1:27), and who continually creates, bringing being into being out of Being through Being's ongoing work of creation, an ongoing creation in which created being participates. The nature of God's Being is implicit in the disclosure of the name, as it conveys simply yet profoundly God's existence, God's Being—a Being whose nature will be disclosed in the events that are about to unfold in Moses' own day: through the freeing of the slaves from their situation of bondage, through their miraculous deliverance through the Red Sea, and through the disclosure of the Divine Law.

This tradition of attempting to describe the nature of YHWH, the essence of God, through the unfolding of history, is picked up in the first century of the Common Era by the author of the Gospel of Mark. Jesus asks, "Who do you say I am?" (Mark 8:29). The theological tradition has offered many words in reply to this most perplexing of questions, an activity in which every succeeding generation has been invited, too, to engage. In relation to the Being of God, among the plausible responses to this question are concepts apophatic and cataphatic in nature. Apophatic concepts are those that attempt to describe God by negation. By speaking in terms of who God is not, we are nonetheless able to approach something of an understanding of who God is. Protecting the ineffability of God, apophatic language describes God with such words as uncreated, immutable, impassible, infinite, invisible, immortal,

---

14. Beauty's salvation of the world is treated in chapter 6, on incarnation.

incomprehensible, and uncircumscribable. In contrast to words such as these, cataphatic language attempts to express something of the divine nature through positive terminology, or by statement of who God is, insofar as we can say, such as omnipotent, omnibenevolent, omniscient, and omnipresent. Words that attempt to capture the perfections of God are likewise cataphatic. Among these are a relatively small set of words known as the transcendental properties of being, a category of characteristics believed by medieval scholastics as applying to every being, such as *Ens* (Being), *Unum* (One), *Bonum* (the Good), and *Verum* (the True).[15] The transcendentals add nothing to Being, they inhere in Being coextensively, and they are discerned to some extent in every being.[16] While they differ from one another conceptually or logically, they are nonetheless convertible into one another.[17] They are essentially the same.

The use of cataphatic language raises a dilemma, however, about the manner in which such words can be used of God—a problem that was not lost on the scholastics. If these words are applied univocally in reference to God, that is to say, in a manner in which there is a 1:1 correspondence between the meaning of the word and God, and so applied to God in precisely the same manner in which such words are applied in human experience, there is a limitation imposed on God, violating the premise that God is unable to be circumscribed and does, as such, transcend all boundaries, including conceptual and linguistic ones. A 1:1 correspondence introduces the risk of idolatry. Such use of language puts us in jeopardy by setting us up to worship our ideas, failing to recognize that the reality behind the words always transcends that to which our words and ideas point.

If the words, however, are applied in an opposite way, that is, equivocally, or in a manner in which there is no correspondence between the meaning of the word and God, the suggestion is that there is absolutely no relationship whatsoever between words applied to God in the divine order and words applied in human experience in the created order. Hence, words would lose all meaning and would be thought to offer no sense of God's nature in any way. In such a frame, it would make no difference whether we referred to God as Good or Evil, for neither of those words nor their underlying meanings would have any correspondence whatsoever to the Being of God. In such a circumstance, words

---

15. For a helpful discussion of transcendental properties of being, see Umberto Eco, *The Aesthetics of Thomas Aquinas* (Cambridge, MA: Harvard University Press, 1988), esp. 20–22.

16. Ibid.

17. Ibid.

would lose all meaning and would be of no use to us as we attempt to speak of divine matters. It would be impossible to create communities of shared meaning, and all piety would disintegrate into personalized and individualized experiences of God that cannot be communicated in community. Thus, to employ language for God in either a univocal or equivocal sense is problematic. This was a conundrum recognized early on in the church and brilliantly treated by Thomas Aquinas in the Middle Ages.

When Thomas Aquinas wrestled with this question of how to use language in reference to the Holy One, he pointed to analogy as a mean between univocal and equivocal application of language in reference to God:

> Some things are said of God and creatures analogically, and not in a purely equivocal nor in a purely univocal sense. For we can name God only from creatures. Thus whatever is said of God and creatures, is said according to the relation of a creature to God as its principle and cause, wherein all perfections of things preexist excellently. Now this mode of community of idea is a mean between pure equivocation and simple univocation. For in analogies the idea is not, as it is in univocals, one and the same, yet it is not totally diverse as in equivocals; but a term which is thus used in a multiple sense signifies various proportions to some one thing.[18]

Thomas adopts analogical language, asserting that our words point to something of the essence of God while always falling short of fully approaching the reality to which they point. Human words can point to the Being of God, while never fully encompassing the fullness of the meaning that still transcends them. Thus, according to Thomas, we can use names for God, such as the Good, the Beautiful,[19] and the True, as long as we recognize that the meaning we ascribe to those words, while

---

18. Aquinas, ST, I, q. 13, a. 5.

19. It is not clear whether Thomas Aquinas considered beauty to be a transcendental property of being. Wisdom and beauty appear in Thomas's lists of divine names early in his career, but in his later works, *pulchrum* is conspicuously absent from such lists. For a discussion, see Eco, *Aesthetics*, 20–48. I generally trust Eco's conclusion: "He did believe that beauty was a transcendental, a constant property of being" (46). And again, "Aquinas returned in his *Summa Theologiae* to a list of just three transcendentals, and rarely mentioned beauty. . . . His conception of beauty was now implicit in his theoretical system as a whole. He had no further need to insist upon the transcendental character of beauty. . . . As a good Aristotelian, he refrained from excessive discussion of beauty, a subject much abused by every variety of Neoplatonist, swooning at universes dissolving in visions of light" (47–48).

approaching to some degree the divine reality to which they point, still falls short of the magnificence of the God mystically unifying them all.

> These names signify the divine substance, and are predicated substantially of God, although they fall short of a full representation of Him. Which is proved thus. For these names express God, so far as our intellects know Him. Now since our intellect knows God from creatures, it knows Him as far as creatures represent Him. Now it is shown above [ST 1.4.2] that God prepossesses in Himself all the perfections of creatures, being Himself simply and universally perfect. Hence every creature represents Him, and is like Him so far as it possesses some perfection; yet it represents Him not as something of the same species or genus, but as the excelling principle of whose form the effects fall short, although they derive some kind of likeness thereto, even as the forms of inferior bodies represent the power of the sun. This was explained above [ST 1.4.3] in treating of the divine perfection. Therefore the aforesaid names signify the divine substance, but in an imperfect manner, even as creatures represent it imperfectly. So when we say, "God is good," the meaning is not, "God is the cause of goodness," or "God is not evil"; but the meaning is, *"Whatever good we attribute to creatures, preexists in God,"* and *in a more excellent and higher way.* Hence it does not follow that God is good, because He causes goodness; but rather, on the contrary, He causes goodness in things because He is good; according to what Augustine says [De Doctrina Christiana 1.32], "Because He is good, we are."[20]

Because we are finite creatures, our concepts—no matter how lofty—remain finite as well. Present in the use of these terms must be the recognition that these words limit God by their mere utterance, as God in actuality transcends our definitions of what these terms mean as well as our experiences of them. If these words were thought to describe God's nature perfectly, we would have fashioned an idol out of our own imperfect conceptions. But if they do not point to God's nature at all, we would have no capacity whatsoever to speak of God or to conceptualize God, making relationship and the theological enterprise utterly impossible and rendering our worship and prayer meaningless. Analogy opens the way to recognize that our words can participate in the reality of God without fully encapsulating who God is. When we say God is Perfect Love, for example, both of these words, "perfect" and "love," describe in some imperfect way the reality of God's Being. The Reality of a God of Love transcends my imperfect notions both of perfection and of love. Nevertheless, analogy enables me to use those

---

20. Aquinas, ST, I, q. 13, a. 2; emphasis mine.

words to approach, even if imperfectly, a description of the reality to which my words are attempting to point. Terms in the transcendental category participate in the reality of God's Being, while protecting me from an idolatry that presupposes identity between my all too human conceptions and God's divine essence on the one hand and the nonsensical view that our words and concepts can have no relationship to the God who has revealed something of God's essence to us through such means as creation, Scripture, and incarnation.

This question of the manner in which we speak of God is alive again, and acutely so, in theological circles. Theologian Sallie McFague has introduced again the question of language for God in her books, *The Body of God: Ecological Theology*, and *Models of God: Theology for an Ecological, Nuclear Age.*[21] In her toolbox, because she understands sin to have so destroyed the relationship between God and creation, language for God functions primarily metaphorically. In these books, she invites readers to think of the world as the body of God in order to foster an awareness, for example, that when we use and dispose of chemicals in our rivers and streams, we are introducing toxins, as it were, into God's own bloodstream. I read her books when I was a graduate student and, while I appreciated what she was attempting to do, her books left me dissatisfied. Although I did not realize it at the time, I was frustrated by the limits of metaphorical language. In the end, although metaphorical language is poetic and has the capacity to expand the concepts by which God is known to us, metaphors also have limitations. They provide only a sense of the reality to which they point. They are not necessarily intimately related to or able to reveal the reality to which they point. To sing "A Mighty Fortress Is Our God" conveys powerfully a sense of God's protective nature. In singing the hymn, I may participate in Martin Luther's sense of wonder at God's willingness to be in relationship with us and to protect us. Metaphors have an important place in Christian theology and spirituality: they provide us with a means by which to speak of Ultimate Reality, to use Paul Tillich's term.[22] But metaphor is not the *only* tool in the linguistic toolbox, and when it was presented to me as such, I was restless. Later, I would learn that functioning, too, in Roman Catholic theology, is analogical language.

To use language analogically is distinct from using language metaphorically, and it is a use that is open to the Catholic theological imagina-

---

21. See Sallie McFague, *The Body of God: An Ecological Theology* (Minneapolis, MN: Augsburg Fortress, 1993), and *Models of God: Theology for an Ecological, Nuclear Age* (Minneapolis, MN: Fortress Press, 1987).

22. Tillich, *Dynamics of Faith*.

tion because of the affirmation that sin does not destroy the relationship between the created order and the divine order. Though Catholicism agrees that the relationship between the Creator and the creature is damaged by sin, analogy remains possible because of the ongoing bond between the Creator and the created, a link damaged by sin but not destroyed by it. The natural world participates in the Being of God and continues to reveal something of the essence of Being. In other words, the being of nature reveals something of the Being of God by analogy, imperfectly to be sure and always in a way that is more dissimilar than similar to the reality beyond it. But analogy has a metaphysical base. Although its roots go back deep into ancient philosophy, Thomas Aquinas developed an understanding of analogy in his *Summa Theologiae* and, especially, he worked out something called the *analogia entis*, or the analogy of being. This concept is an assumption operating in all Catholic faith and doctrine and, as such, it deserves some attention here.

In theological discourse, an analogy stresses the relational quality between two things on the basis of the divine Creatorship. While analogies are used to say something about the divine essence, their first application is creaturely, insofar as they are applied by finite beings possessing finite concepts that they are attempting to apply to an infinite reality. As such, analogies always assume a greater dissimilarity between the term and its reference, even in the midst of a great similarity. If we speak of God's goodness, for example, "goodness" functions analogically. As a human being, my conception of "goodness" remains dissimilar from God's goodness because of my creaturely limitations. I cannot conceive of perfect goodness. My conceptions of goodness always fall short of divine and perfectly holy goodness. Nonetheless, saying "God is good" is different from a metaphorical use of a term in reference to God. My creaturely use of the term "goodness" participates in the reality to which it points. If God is truly good and perfectly good, then God's goodness is infinite. Goodness has its identity in the divine being, and thus the term transcends and points beyond its creaturely limitations.[23] In analogy, because words' referents participate in the reality to which they point, there are only a limited number that can truly be said to function in this way.

> When comparing humans with God, metaphor always implies a denial of the literal, proper, intrinsic meaning of the term applied to God, but properly analogical terms, which are context transcendent, never do. For example, there is traditionally no context in which Christians would deny that God is good. Analogical terms must be flexible

23. Aquinas, ST I, q. 13, a. 2-3, 6.

enough to be applied to humans in a finite context and to God in an infinite one, and they must do so without equivocation in either application. Although numerous metaphors can creatively describe the divine/human relation, only a short list of terms can qualify as properly analogical predicates for God and humans, such as "being," "unity," "goodness," "truth," and "beauty."[24]

The "analogy of being," for example, presupposes that there is a correspondence, correlation, or relation between God and the created order on the basis of the divine creatorship. There is a correspondence between natural being and supernatural Being grounded in the understanding that all being has God as its source. Nature continues to bear the divine fingerprint, so to speak, no matter how damaged it is by sin. Thus, for those who ascribe to the *analogia entis*, God can be known from observations drawn from the natural world. This is typically contrasted to the *analogia fidei*, which maintains that God can only be known by means of God's own self-revelation as, for example, through incarnation or through the revelation of sacred texts. So there is much at stake in this discussion. Can God be known by observing nature, including human nature (since we are said to be made in the *imago Dei*), or can God be known only by God's self-revelation which, for Karl Barth, the *analogia fidei*'s chief modern proponent, is determined by receipt of special grace and the gift of faith? In my book, which develops an analogy of Beauty (*analogia pulchri*) that differs from Balthasar's insofar as it assumes that Beauty prompts the faithful to social and political engagement, it is clear that this author is invested in the existence of an *analogia entis*.

My intention is not to recommend that we use exclusively either analogical language or metaphorical language for God. I opened the chapter with beautiful imagery of God as Mother, which is a metaphorical use of language, as is God as Father. There are fitting rationales for using metaphors when the occasion calls for it. I want us, however, to be mindful of our language and to use language intentionally. I want us to use metaphorical language and analogical language purposefully and to recognize what is at stake in either employment. When Thomas called God "Good," he understood this analogically. Our understanding of goodness does not merely point to the reality of the goodness of God. Our experience of goodness actually participates in the Goodness of God. There is a direct relationship between our experience of goodness

---

24. Philip Rolnick, "Analogy," in *Cambridge Dictionary of Christian Theology*, Ian A. McFarland, David A. S. Fergusson, Karen Kilby, and Iain R. Torrance, eds. (Cambridge: Cambridge University Press, 2011), 10–12.

and the Goodness of God. Since God's Being is, by definition, Good, God brought a good creation into existence. Thomas understood the language of goodness to participate in the very reality to which it pointed. In this way and by intention, the word "good" functioned analogically for him, and so it should for us. If Thomas is right, if goodness participates in the Being of God, then every encounter with what is truly good is an encounter with God, and we may have a way to think of God's constant involvement in the world and an entry to an understanding of omnipresence that would be closed to us if we ceased to understand the analogical sense of these terms in the transcendental category.

The way we speak of God sketches the contours of our theological worldview, simultaneously shaping the dimensions of our life and its own artistry. Faithful people inherit and embody anew in each generation the theological traditions of their ancestors, claiming the tradition as their own. How individuals imagine God is significant enough to most religious people that we share our beliefs with our children, desiring for them to experience and to understand God as we have. Our beliefs become manifest in our lives and in the lives of our children. So, for example, if we believe that eternal things matter most, and that salvation has primarily to do with an experience of the next world accessible in some way by conversion to faith in Christ, our emphasis as people of faith will become proselytization, so that more and more people can look forward to the same. If we believe that there is nothing more to the universe than the empirically verifiable, and that life is a competition where only the fittest survive, we will look out for ourselves and perhaps our "tribe," but at the expense of those more remote from us. This too is a construction shaped by a set of beliefs.[25] If we believe that salvation has not only to do with an afterlife but also with this world, and if we believe that working to realize the community about which Jesus spoke has something to do with resistance to political oppression through the power of nonviolent struggle, then our emphasis will necessarily shift to still a third way of being in the world. There are certainly more ways to construe things than these three. All of this is to say that what we believe and how we dare to speak of it informs how we live, and so we must speak of God carefully, aware of the weighty implications carried by our words.

25. To be clear, I readily recognize many atheists are committed to a secular humanism that is devoted to ensuring that all people have access to the essentials for survival and human thriving: food, shelter, clothing, education, health care, gainful employment, and so on. Secular humanists have put care for humanity rather than care for only oneself at the center of their lives. It is not they to whom I am referring in this paragraph.

Beauty's Revelation: On Participation

Made theologically curious, informed by the biblical metaphors in-troducing this chapter of God as Mother as distinct from analogies that participate in the realities to which they point, and prompted (I hope) by grace to sketch a theological vision that aspires to "do no harm," my own theological proposal is influenced by metaphysical concepts nestled deep within the Christian tradition and applied to political realities in the here and now. My theological construction is grounded in theo-logical aesthetics and takes seriously the idea that Beauty is anchored, by analogy, in the essence of God. Operating here is the conviction that divine Beauty, which becomes visible to us in Christ, calls us to deep and compassionate engagement in the world. Like the scholastics in the Middle Ages who understood the Good, the Beautiful, and the True to transcend creation as its ultimate cause, finding their source in the Being of God, I understand this Being to be the ultimate cause of existence as far as we are able to name it. Being is Mother just as Being is Father—the progenitor from whom all that exists comes into being. Drawing on a line of thought stretching back to Socrates, Being is the Reality against which all truth claims stand to be corrected or modified, proving the false nature of a relativism that has driven us to tolerate the intolerable. Being is conflatable with Beauty and with Love, and Love invites us to engage in the world we inherit as gift to restore goodness and truth when we perceive evil and deception. Love has religious dimensions—and Love has political implications.

According to Plato in his *Symposium* and its speeches on love, Socrates deferred to the instruction of Diotima when he gave his speech on love. Diotima taught Socrates about a *daimon*, a spirit of desire (*eros*), which drives a person to Absolute Beauty and which becomes attrac-tive to those who have been seduced by lesser experiences of the same and who have ascended intellectually to recognize the absolute nature of that which underlies all that is truly beautiful. His "ladder of love" passage is poetic, meriting reproduction in full:

> "He who has been instructed thus far in the things of love, and who has learned to see the beautiful in due order and succession, when he comes toward the end will suddenly perceive a nature of wondrous beauty (and this, Socrates, is the final cause of all our former toils)—a nature which in the first place is everlasting, not growing and decay-ing, or waxing and waning; secondly, not fair in one point of view and foul in another, or at one time or in one relation or at one place fair, at another time or in another relation or at another place foul, as if fair to some and foul to others, or in the likeness of a face or hands or any

other part of the bodily frame, or in any form of speech or knowledge, or existing in any other being, as for example, in an animal, or in heaven or in earth, or in any other place; but beauty absolute, separate, simple, and everlasting, which without diminution and without increase, or any change, is imparted to the ever-growing and perishing beauties of all other things. He who from these ascending under the influence of true love, begins to perceive that beauty, is not far from the end. And the true order of going, or being led by another, to the things of love, is to begin from the beauties of earth and mount upwards for the sake of that other beauty, using these as steps only, and from one going on to two, and from two to all fair forms, and from fair forms to fair practices, and from fair practices to fair notions, until from fair notions he arrives at the notion of absolute beauty, and at last knows what the essence of beauty is. This, my dear Socrates," said the stranger of Mantineia, "is that life above all others which [humankind] should live, in the contemplation of beauty absolute; a beauty which if you once beheld, you would see not to be after the measure of gold, and garments, and fair boys and youths, whose presence now entrances you; and you and many a one would be content to live seeing them only and conversing with them without meat or drink, if that were possible—you only want to look at them and to be with them. But what if [humankind] had eyes to see the true beauty—the divine beauty, I mean, pure and dear and unalloyed, not clogged with the pollutions of mortality and all the colors and vanities of human life—thither looking, and holding converse with the true beauty simple and divine? Remember how in that communion only, beholding beauty with the eye of the mind, he will be enabled to bring forth, not images of beauty, but realities (for he has hold not of an image but of a reality), and bringing forth and nourishing true virtue to become the friend of God and be immortal, if mortal [humankind] may. Would that be an ignoble life?"[26]

Inspired by this speech said to have been uttered by Socrates, and like Augustine before Thomas, and like Thomas before theologians in the contemporary day, I have imagined the Good, the Beautiful, and the True to be different angles from which to approach Divine Being, each One indwelling the Other in divine simplicity, while remaining nevertheless distinct in human perception, ultimately overflowing in Love. Rather than imagining Being to be "out there," however, the highest Existence in some kind of Platonic ladder that climbs ever higher until one arrives at Beauty Absolute—rather than thinking about a God who

---

26. Plato, *Symposium and Phaedrus*, ed. Stanley Appelbaum and Candace Ward, trans. Benjamin Jowett (New York: Dover, 1993), 211A–212B. I have changed "man" to "humankind."

is entirely other, who sort of "bends down" to share the divine nature with earthly life, I'm inviting readers to join me in a thought experiment. I am inviting us to consider earthly experiences of goodness, beauty, and truth to be participatory reflections of the ultimate cause of all that exists. In this way, they are to a degree immanent: the good, the beautiful, and the true are embedded deeply within all that exists, as Uncreated Existence opens up chronological time and three-dimensional space within Being and brings material existence into being out of Being. Traces of the good, beautiful, and true bear witness to the divine in the exquisite elegance of creation's very structure.[27] Speaking metaphorically, I see the material world to be within the womb of God; speaking analogically, I see the existence of the material world to be within Existence itself—within the very Being of God's Goodness, Beauty, and Truth. These earthly manifestations express within themselves varying degrees of the Goodness, Beauty, and Truth of their divine origin.

By their very existence, humans participate in the Being of God and, therefore, in the holiness of divine life. Creation itself exists within Divine Being, interconnected as it is both with the source of its Being and with the community of life brought into being by Being. Goodness, Beauty, and Truth are present in the structure of Being itself, providing evidence of the source from which it all comes and to which it all points. God's Goodness, Beauty, and Truth are evident in nature. As evolutionary processes unfold, they produce canyons and caverns, just as they witness consciousness and compassion emerge in humankind. Deeply embedded within the structure of material existence, the One who is absolutely Good, Beautiful, and True becomes perceptible in the here and now to minds attentive to these realities. Materiality points to a Goodness, Beauty, and Truth that once again transcends material existence. Just as the mind of the mother transcends the awareness of the baby growing in her womb, so does the mind of God remain ultimately mysterious to the creation evolving within the Being of God's divine life. The Good, the Beautiful, and the True are names for God, for Being, for Love—the source of all being, who continually brings being

27. For a helpful discussion of the relation of the Trinity to immanental reality, see Ilia Delio, "Theology, Metaphysics, and the Centrality of Christ," in *Theological Studies* 68, vol. 2 (June 1, 2007): 254–73. Rahner's famous axiom, "The 'economic' Trinity is the 'immanent' Trinity and the 'immanent' Trinity is the 'economic' Trinity," appears in Karl Rahner, *The Trinity*, rev. ed., trans. Joseph Donceel (New York: Crossroad, 1997; orig. ed. 1970), 22. See also Catherine Mowry LaCugna, "Re-Conceiving the Trinity as the Mystery of Salvation," in *Scottish Journal of Theology* 38 (1985): 10–11.

The Trinity
of the Good, Beautiful, and True

MOTHER / FATHER / **GOODNESS**
expressed in **JUSTICE**
produces communities of
FAITHFULNESS • PEACEFULNESS.

JUSTICE requires the grace of **EMPOWERMENT**
to elicit (non-violent) **RESISTANCE**
to varying forms of oppression.

A relative absence of GOODNESS
results in relative degrees of
INJUSTICE & VIOLENCE.
That which has absolutely no Goodness or Justice in it is
ABSOLUTE EVIL or Absence of Being:
Nothingness.

TRINITY
—a divine perichoresis of the—
GOOD, BEAUTIFUL, AND TRUE
is
EXISTENCE • ABSOLUTE BEING • LOVE

SON / **BEAUTY**
expressed in **COMPASSION**
produces communities of
LOVING-KINDNESS • GENTLENESS.

SPIRIT / **TRUTH**
expressed in **WISDOM**
produces communities of
HOPEFULNESS • JOYFULNESS.

COMPASSION requires the grace of
ENCOURAGEMENT
to elicit **ACCOMPANIMENT**
with those who suffer.

WISDOM requires the grace of
ENLIGHTENMENT
to elicit **RECONCILIATION**
of broken relationships.

A relative absence of BEAUTY
results in relative degrees of
INDIFFERENCE & NEGLIGENCE.
That which has absolutely no Beauty
or Compassion in it is
ABSOLUTE DEFORMITY
or Absence of Being:
Nothingness.

A relative absence of TRUTH
results in relative degrees of
IGNORANCE & COMPLACENCE.
That which has absolutely no Truth
or Wisdom in it is
ABSOLUTE DECEPTION
or Absence of Being:
Nothingness.

into being out of Being through something of a microcosmic expression, breaking into time and space, birthing all that is in a complex web of life that lacks the fullness of God's perfection but which continues to testify to Existence's Being: to the Being of the Ultimate "I Am," in whom all beings live and breathe and have their being, and to which all being is continually drawn.

Extending this thought experiment further, if the Ultimate Being is Trinitarian, it is appropriate to think of the Good, Beautiful, and True as names for this Trinitarian God—with the Good, the Creator who makes all things good, expressed in justice and studied in part by ethics; with the Beautiful, the Redeemer who becomes visible, expressed in compassion (from the Latin roots *com-*, meaning "with," and *pati*, meaning "to suffer"), and studied in part by aesthetics; and with the True, the Spirit of Truth, expressed in wisdom, and studied in part by logic. Each one mutually informs the others by completing their union. If the Good, Beautiful, and True are to be identified with the persons of the Trinity—coequal, distinct but not separate, intrinsically relational, and interpenetrating or, better, "indwelling" one another in an eternal *perichoresis* or *circumincessio*—we might say that Goodness is appropriated to the Father without denying the Goodness of the Son and Spirit, interpenetrated as they are by the Good, for the Creator made all things good. We might say that Beauty is appropriated to the Son without denying the Beauty of the Father and the Spirit, interpenetrated as they are by the Beautiful, for Beauty became visible and dwelt among us. And we might say that Truth is appropriated to the Spirit without denying the Truth of the Father and the Son, interpenetrated as they are by the True, for the Spirit of Truth came to be our advocate.

In appropriating the properties of being in this way, we are relying on the Trinitarian teachings stretching back to Gregory Nazianzen, who believed that the perfection of the Father lacks nothing, though the Father is not the Son, and so on:

> We assert that there is nothing lacking—for God has no deficiency. But the difference of manifestation, if I may so express myself, or rather of their mutual relations one to another, has caused the difference of their Names. For indeed it is not some deficiency in the Son which prevents His being Father (for Sonship is not a deficiency), and yet He is not Father. . . . For the Father is not Son, and yet this is not due to either deficiency or subjection of Essence; but the very fact of being Unbegotten, or Begotten, or Proceeding has given the name of Father to the First, of the Son to the Second, and of the Third, Him of Whom we are

speaking, of the Holy Ghost that the distinction of the Three Persons may be preserved in the one nature and dignity of the Godhead.[28]

Likewise, Thomas Aquinas affirmed the appropriateness of appropriation. In answer to the question, "Whether the essential names should be appropriated to the persons?" Thomas answers,

> For the manifestation of our faith it is fitting that the essential attributes should be appropriated to the persons. For although the trinity of persons cannot be proved by demonstration, as was above expounded, nevertheless it is fitting that it be declared by things which are more known to us. Now the essential attributes of God are more clear to us from the standpoint of reason than the personal properties; because we can derive certain knowledge of the essential attributes from creatures which are sources of knowledge to us, such as we cannot obtain regarding the personal properties, as was above explained. As, therefore, we make use of the likeness of the trace or image found in creatures for the manifestation of the divine persons, so also in the same manner do we make use of the essential attributes. And such a manifestation of the divine persons by the use of the essential attributes is called "appropriation."[29]

While I am not appropriating the properties precisely in the same way that Thomas did, I can find Thomistic support for the manner in which I am appropriating these names. For example, Thomas speaks of God as Good, and I am reading this as the Father: "God is the very essence of goodness, so everything must be attributed to God in its highest degree of goodness."[30] Thomas does appropriate beauty to the Son: "Species or beauty has a likeness to the property of the Son."[31] And, finally, in asking "Whether wisdom should be reckoned among the gifts of the Holy Spirit," Thomas answers, "Now man obtains this judgment through the Holy Ghost, according to 1 Cor 2:15: 'The spiritual man judgeth all things,' because as stated in the same chapter (1 Cor 2:10), 'the spirit searcheth all things, yea the deep things of God.' Wherefore it is evident that wisdom is a gift of the Holy Ghost."[32]

---

28. Gregory Nazianzen, *The Fifth Theological Oration: On the Holy Spirit*, http://www.ccel.org/ccel/schaff/npnf207.iii.xvii.html, 9.

29. Aquinas, ST, I., q. 39, a. 7-8.

30. Aquinas, ST, I, q. 103, a. 6.

31. Aquinas, ST, I, q. 39, a. 8.

32. Aquinas, ST, II–II, q. 45, a. 1.

Given this imagination, we might then tweak Jacques Maritain's phrase just slightly to say that "the splendor of all the transcendentals together" is Love, rather than Beauty.[33] This Love is the superabundant expression and overflowing, creative energy present in Being's revelation in creation. Love is the willful expression of God's creative potential that "bubbles up" within Being and explodes, as it were, bringing being into being out of Being. Creation shares intrinsically the divine Love of its Source.

Among the earliest to suggest that the transcendentals might constitute, in a sense, what can be known about the very Being of God (acknowledging that they, by their nature, transcend our experience of them; thus, they are "transcendent"), Augustine contributed significantly to the Christian tradition and its sense that earthly experiences of goodness, beauty, and truth have a relationship with these perfections of Being, albeit to varying and lesser degrees. From there, it was not far for Augustine to make his acclaimed argument about the nature of evil as nothingness, an absolute lacking of being.

> It follows, then, that either destruction harms nothing, which is impossible, or that all things which suffer harm are being deprived of some good; this conclusion is beyond cavil. If, however, they lose all their good, they will not exist at all, for if they were to continue in existence without being any longer subject to destruction, they would be better, because permanently indestructible; and what could be more outrageous than to declare them better for having lost everything that was good in them? Hence, if they are deprived of all good, they will be simply nonexistent; and so it follows that as long as they do exist, they are good.
>
> Everything that exists is good, then; and so evil, the source of which I was seeking, cannot be a substance, because if it were, it would be good. Either it would be an indestructible substance, and that would mean it was very good indeed, or it would be a substance liable to destruction but then it would not be destructible unless it were good.
>
> I saw, then, for it was made clear to me, that you have made all good things, and that there are absolutely no substances that you have not made. I saw too that you have not made all things equal. They all exist because they are severally good but collectively very good, for our God has made all things *exceedingly good*.
>
> For you evil has no being at all, and this is true not of yourself only but of everything you have created, since apart from you there is nothing that could burst in and disrupt the order you have imposed on it.[34]

33. Jacques Maritain, in Eco, *Aesthetics*.
34. Augustine, *Confessions*, 8.17-19, 124-26.

Recognizing the problem of talking about evil as having its own substance (because then from what does it derive—a God of Absolute Evil?), Augustine understood there to be something of a continuum between Absolute Goodness (comprising the very Being of God insofar as our language can express such an essence) and absolute nothingness—the lack of all Being. Thus, he understood the human experience of evil to be located somewhere along that continuum between Existence and nonexistence, between Being and nonbeing, between Absolute Somethingthingness and absolute nothingness. An experience of that which we call evil is not an experience of something *per se*, he thought, but rather an experience of privation, of a corruption of Being—an experience of a lacking of Goodness to a varying degree. Goodness entirely corrupted, or that which is absolutely evil, has absolutely no Goodness in it. Thus, absolute evil has no being, no essence, no substance. Absolute evil is nothingness. As such, Augustine understood absolute evil not to exist. Humans experience what they call evil, even radical evil but, properly understood, according to Augustine, this is not an experience of something. Rather, evil is an experience of corrupted Goodness, or a lacking of Goodness to a high degree.

As a still further extension to this thought experiment, if Goodness is appropriated to the Father since the Father created all things good ("And God saw that it was good," [Gen 1:4, 10, 12, 18, 21, 25, and 31]), and if justice is the expression of divine Goodness made manifest in the creation, since justice describes that which a community properly understands to be good and right, then injustice is the experience of a lacking or a corruption of divine Goodness to a degree, and therefore a lacking of the vision of the Father, of Goodness, to a degree, in creation. The Good and the Just are interchangeable names for the Father, as these cohere with Being Absolute. The more creation expresses the goodness and justice of God, the more creation produces *shalom*, or the faithfulness and peacefulness of a community in relation to God. The enactment or bringing into being of such a vineyard, to use the biblical imagery that we have been using to describe this reality, requires the grace of divine empowerment capable of producing nonviolent resistance to oppression in a world lacking God's perfect justice from the start and becoming more distant from it upon the introduction of sin into the world. This sinful distance from the fullness of Being, from the Good, has resulted in degrees of injustice and violence that we inherit in each successive generation. That which has no Goodness and, therefore, no Justice in it is absolutely evil. It lacks Being altogether: it is nothingness. Absolute evil cannot exist in creation—though that which lacks a high degree of goodness and justice can be enormously powerful, as the anguish to which the subtitle of *Beauty's Vineyard* points—approaching but not able to overtake the power of the Goodness of the God who brought all that exists into being.

Augustine's argument about evil is standard teaching, but in it are implications for the other transcendental aspects of Being as well. For example, Augustine's concept can be extended likewise to Beauty. Just as Augustine understood there to be something of a continuum between Absolute Goodness and absolute nothingness, so there is something of a continuum between Absolute Beauty, cohering with the very Being of God, and absolute nothingness. Thus, the human experience of deformity or ugliness is located somewhere along that continuum between Beauty and absolute nothingness, between Existence and nonexistence, between Being and nonbeing. Like evil, ugliness is not an experience of something *per se* but rather an experience of privation, of a corruption of Being—an experience of a lacking of Beauty to varying degrees. Beauty entirely corrupted, or that which is absolutely deformed, has absolutely no Beauty in it. Thus, absolute deformity has no being, no essence, no substance. Absolute deformity is nothingness. As such, absolute deformity does not exist. Humans experience what they call deformed or ugly, but, properly understood, these are not experiences of something. Rather, to experience something that is ugly is an experience of corrupted Beauty, or even a lacking of Beauty to a high degree.

Extending this thought experiment a degree further, if Beauty is appropriated to the Son since the Son is the dimension of the Godhead that becomes visible and "suffers with" (*patitur cum*) the creation ("And the Word became flesh and lived among us, and we have seen his glory, the glory as of a father's only son, full of grace and truth" [John 1:14]), and if compassion (*compati*) is the expression of divine Beauty made manifest in the creation, since by compassion Beauty is made visible in human lives, then indifference and negligence are experiences of a lacking or corruption of divine beauty and a veiling of the vision of the Son, of Beauty, to a degree, in creation. The Beautiful and the Compassionate are interchangeable names for the Son, as these cohere with Being Absolute. The more creation expresses the beauty and compassion of God, the more the creation produces the loving-kindness and gentleness of a community in relation to God, and the more compassion enters into empathy with a union of all being that transcends suffering by the creation's collective rejection of evil, deformity, and deception. The enactment or bringing into being of such a vineyard requires the grace of encouragement, such that humans are in solidarity with one another, particularly in situations of oppression and suffering. This relative absence of Beauty in a sinful world has resulted in degrees, however, of indifference and negligence. That which has no Beauty and, therefore, no Compassion in it, is absolutely deformed. It lacks Being altogether: it is nothingness. Absolute deformity cannot exist in creation—though that which lacks a high degree of beauty and compassion can be enormously powerful—approaching but not able to overtake the power of the Beauty of the God who brought all that exists into being.

The same might be said of the True. There is something of a continuum between Absolute Truth, cohering with the very Being of God, and absolute nothingness. Thus, human experience of deception is located somewhere along that continuum between Truth and absolute nothingness. Deception is not an experience of something *per se* but, rather, an experience of privation, of a corruption of Being—an experience of a lacking of Truth to a varying degree. Truth entirely corrupted, or that which is absolutely deceptive, has no Truth in it. Thus, absolute deception has no being, no essence, no substance. Absolute deception is nothingness, an absolute lacking of being. As such, absolute deception does not exist. Humans experience what they call deceptive but, properly understood, this is not an experience of something. Rather, deception is an experience of corrupted Truth, or a lacking of Truth to a high degree.

Finally, extending this thought experiment a final time, if Wisdom is appropriated to the Holy Spirit—since Jesus promised to send an advocate after him who would be the Spirit of Truth ("When the Advocate comes, whom I will send to you from the Father, the Spirit of truth who comes from the Father, he will testify on my behalf" [John 15:26])—and if wisdom is the expression of divine truth made manifest in the creation, since wisdom aides one in differentiating between what is trustworthy and what is not, then ignorance and complacency are experiences of a lacking or corruption of divine truth and a lacking of the vision of the Spirit, of Truth, in creation. The True and the Wise are interchangeable names for the Spirit, cohering with Being Absolute. The more creation expresses the truth and wisdom of God, the more the creation produces the hopefulness and joyfulness of a community in relation to God. The enactment or bringing into being of such a vineyard requires the grace of enlightenment capable of producing attentiveness to and awareness of voices marginalized and silenced by systems as they stand, thereby eliciting reconciliation of broken relationships. The relative absence of Truth has resulted in degrees of ignorance and complacence. That which has no Truth and, therefore, no Wisdom in it, is absolutely deceptive. It lacks Being altogether: it is nothingness. Absolute deception cannot exist in creation—though that which lacks a high degree of truth and wisdom can be enormously powerful—approaching but not able to overtake the power of the Truth of the God who brought all that exists into being.

There is an immediate application of all of this to political realities in the here and now. If God is in some way to be identified with the Good, the Beautiful, and the True—if God is our heart's desire, if God is the one after whom our soul yearns until it finds its rest in the source of all Being[35]—is it not our intransigent injustice, indifference, and ignorance that prevent us from living as God would have us live: justly, compassionately, and wisely? And when we lack a sense for justice, compassion, and wisdom, do we not become violent, negligent, and complacent—disoriented states of being that oppose God's desire for us, created as we are by the Good, Beautiful, and True? Do we not violate God's intention for us by failing to resist political powers that disregard human rights, by lacking the courage to oppose the violent subordination of others, and by lacking the wisdom to overcome the greed and materialistic self-centeredness that is witnessed in our functioning consistently out of a model of scarcity and by our hoarding of the world's plenty? If the superabundant expression of the Good, Beautiful, and True is Love, how does our reception of divine Love through grace overcome such harmful and uncharitable tendencies? How is this cycle of our undoing to be undone? "Who will rescue me from this body of death? Thanks be to God through Jesus Christ our Lord!" (Rom 7:24-25). There is hope. Grace is present among us as it always has been, empowering us to resist varying forms of oppression, encouraging us to be in solidarity with those who suffer, and enlightening us to discern when reconciliation of broken relationships is possible without doing further harm.

According to this thought experiment, God is intimately present (albeit mysteriously and mystically so) to the creation that has its being in God's Being, in a God who is receptive to a creation that is curious to know the source of its origins. In my theological imagining, God is a divine mother, who is pregnant with creative activity, the creation still in gestation in her womb. Speaking metaphorically, God opens up a space in her very being for an evolutionary process to unfold. Within this womb of God, the universe is coming into being, with its requisite struggle for survival precisely because it is created. In terms of all being—animate and inanimate, organic and inorganic—every

---

35. Augustine, *Confessions*, 1.1.

individual atom is within God's being, bearing within itself the imprint, the divine fingerprint, of the very Source of its being. These atoms are emerging into what they are intended to be—each an integral part of a whole being that, when fully developed and in the fullness of time, will be born. At that moment, which we await in hopeful and expectant anticipation, *kairos* time (fullness of time from God's vantage point) and *chronos* time (linear time from humankind's vantage point) become one. Material being will be granted access to immaterial Being—to the very mind of God, in a grand union of being. Granted access to this beatific vision now veiled, the community coming into being by participating in the vineyard of just and right relations will be fully developed. Until then, we catch glimpses from time to time—fleeting experiences as short as a nanosecond (or longer if we are blessed)—of moments both perceptible and inviting, luring us to persist and not to lose courage, enabling us to see the first fruits of a vineyard already in God's mind green and lush. God is actively engaged in the world, exercising power in appropriate ways—enticing us with experiences of goodness, beauty, and truth, calling us to make these more vividly manifest in our own lives. "Seek the welfare of the city where I have sent you . . . , and pray to the LORD on its behalf, for in its welfare you will find your welfare" (Jer 29:7).

Language employed within this imagination is both analogical and metaphorical. Parenting and gardening metaphors open our imaginations to see in a way that is otherwise hidden from view. And transcendental analogies invite us to participate in a deeper way in the reality presently unfolding. There is a proportional relationship between transcendental categories and the ultimate reality in which they already exist. When humans call God "Love" because of our participation in the being of God, our words have some correspondence to God's reality. In this view, there is an intimate relationship between human language about God and God's Being because of the relationship between God and humanity more broadly. Because there are ultimately no sharp points of separation between our being and God's Being, we are bold to believe that the transcendental categories of being can participate in the Being of God. While our experience of love falls short of the fullness of Love that has its identity in the Being of God, our experience of love nonetheless points in a real way to the Love of God. This dance between the source of all existence and creation's experience of Being draws us more and more deeply into Love's Being. When by grace we respond to the Being of God, we are transformed into beings more and more like the Author of Life, more and more loving, just, compas-

Chapter 3

Beauty's Trace
On *Imago Dei*

In a world that is filled with anguish, memories of holocausts and apartheids and genocides still haunting, even as new ones are unfolding, is it possible even to speak of Beauty's trace—of a vestige of God still present among us, lighting our way through the darkness that closes in, night threatening to extinguish any glimmer of light still remaining? Some days, it would seem, it is easier to think so than others. But today— reviewing images by Samuel Bak (b. 1933), a contemporary artist who is one of the 250 or so survivors of a Jewish community once numbering in the tens of thousands from Vilna, a city in modern-day Lithuania—it is not so easy. The Nazis liquidated this Jewish "ghetto" in 1941. Among Bak's memories of those unspeakable days is one of his friend, Samek, who did not survive. Instead, Bak remembers his friend was left lying in a pool of his own blood, a warning to other Jews not to run, not to hide—a grim admonition that there was no escape.[1] After fleeing to a camp for displaced persons, Bak and his mother found their way by 1948 to Israel, a safe haven for Jews, they hoped, where together they could attempt to piece together their lives. Learning Hebrew and recognizing a gift for art, he left for Paris after high school to study painting.

Of struggling to find a visual vocabulary to express his inner world, Bak writes, "Mine was a story of a humanity that had survived two great wars and whose world now lay in shambles. Survivors were trying to repair the damage, to reconstruct what had been lost, to re-create

---

1. Danna Nolan Fewell and Gary A. Phillips, "Bak's Impossible Memorials: Giving Face to the Children," in *Representing the Irreparable: The Shoah, the Bible, and the Art of Samuel Bak*, ed. Danna Nolan Fewell, Gary A. Phillips, and Yvonne Sherwood (Boston: Pucker Gallery, 2008), 95.

something that would resemble in their eyes what was gone forever."[2] He continues, "A survivor myself, I observed and understood their need to reinvent life. Their story was my story. And in me it was also a story about a trauma that had been silenced for too many years."[3] Eventually, his young friend Samek would appear in Bak's paintings, taking the posture of the boy in the famous SS photograph from Warsaw. Present with allusions to these boys too, though, are haunting self-portraits, raising more questions still about the randomness of survival, about memory and tragedy, and about the monstrous depths to which the human being can sink. Bak insists that his images cannot be reduced to the historical context of the Shoah alone: "I am trying to express a universal malaise about our human condition,"[4] he writes.

> These representational paintings of mine depicted devastated land-scapes of ancient cities, urban constructions that seem to have been made of a child's building blocks. I painted figures that were half alive, and half contrived of bizarre prostheses. I imagined helpless and abused angels. Chess pieces were involved in games without rules. Huge fruit, mostly pears in various stages of reinvention, pears giving birth to other pears, pears made of stone, pears in the form of hovering planets, metaphors of a world without explanation. My paintings carried no answers, only questions.[5]

Sanctuary (1997), for example, using a palette of blues and greens and browns, is a painting of uncreation. Eden is undone. Trees and bushes indicate a landscape, conjuring memories of Eden, a garden that was once lush but is no longer. While some leaves in the foreground are green, even these are browning and wilting, becoming limp on tired branches. Hints of the cause of this garden's demise are discovered further in the distance, where tree trunks are scorched, eliciting memories of those fires, ever emblematic of death camps—but representing, too, fires other than these. Mountains climb in the distance, but storm clouds gather. Within this ominous setting is an altar of crumbling columns and bricks, of temples destroyed, of sanctuaries abandoned. Superimposed on the altar is the boy from the Warsaw ghetto, faceless in the foreground but emerging from behind with features of Samek—or Samuel?—survi-

---

2. Samuel Bak, "What, How, and When: On My Art and Myself," in Fewell et al., *Representing the Irreparable*, 6.

3. Ibid.

4. Ibid., 7–8.

5. Ibid., 7.

vors and victims entangled with an allusion to the crucifixion of Christ, the wounded hands bearing the imprints of nails—or are they bullet holes?—present in both representations of the child, above and below. In the deserted sanctuary, God too is implicated in the destruction, ensnared with the rest in the foliage, bearing witness to a breaking of the treaty, to an un-writing of the covenant, to a severing of relationship. The painting pulls us onto religious ground, where our questions are joined with Bak's own, none of them finding easy resolution—all of them remaining unanswered, unsettled, unsatisfied—all of them confronted by a silence finally only appropriate in the face of the horrors we create.[6]

Like Bak, Nobel laureates Elie Wiesel and Desmond Tutu have survived the atrocities of the twentieth century and have grappled with the question of what it means to be human. Their answers stretch the realm of possibility, from the angelic to the monstrous. Author, public intellectual, humanitarian, and survivor of the Shoah, Elie Wiesel opened the Yiddish version of his memoir *Night* with a reference to his tradition's belief in the inherent goodness of humankind: "We believed in God, trusted in man, and lived with the illusion that every one of us has been entrusted with a sacred spark from the Shekhinah's flame; that every one of us carries in his eyes and in his soul a reflection of God's image. That was the source if not the cause of all our ordeals."[7] In these painful sentences, Wiesel attributes his community's vulnerability to the Nazi campaign of extermination to an anthropological stance. Because they believed in the presence of the *imago Dei* in all persons, he writes, the Jews were vulnerable to the evils conducted at the hands of the Nazis. If only his people had not believed in the inherent goodness of humankind, he suggests, members of his community would never have stepped onto those trains.

Wrestling too with the profound human capacity for atrocity, South African activist and Anglican Archbishop Emeritus Desmond Tutu, after citing episode after episode of torture and murder under apartheid in his book *No Future without Forgiveness*, arrives at a different anthropological position.

---

6. In writing this, I resonate with Theodor Adorno's sentiment that "to write poetry after Auschwitz is barbaric." See Theodor Adorno, "Cultural Criticism and Society," in *Prisms*, ed. Shierry Weber Nicholsen and Samuel Weber (MIT Press, 1983), 34. At the same time, I recognize Adorno's update, "Perennial suffering has as much right to expression as a tortured man has to scream." See Theodor Adorno, *Negative Dialectics* (New York: Bloomsbury Academic, 1981), 362.

7. Elie Wiesel, *Night*, trans. Marion Wiesel (New York: Hill and Wang, 1958), x–xi.

> This and more was the kind of testimony that devastatingly made me
> realize that there is an awful depth of depravity to which we all could
> sink, that we possess an extraordinary capacity for evil. . . . This
> applies to all of us. There is no room for gloating or arrogant finger-
> pointing. . . . Those guilty of these abuses were quite ordinary folk.
> They did not grow horns on their foreheads or have tails hidden in
> their trousers. They looked just like you and me.[8]

These men, who have witnessed the depths to which humans can
plunge, are struggling with age-old questions. Who are we, by nature?
Do we carry in us a divine spark—the *imago Dei*? Is its light diminished
by the power of sin or made more radiant through a sanctifying transformation? Or are we, finally, all of us monsters and monstrous—carrying
in us, given a certain configuration of circumstances, an untold capacity
for cruelty, barbarity, and savagery? Are we then monsters and monstrous by nature—or is this monstrous capacity only a potential within
us, only sometimes realized? Do we even share one common nature?
Do our ethnic differences, cultural distinctions, and inherited particu-
larities negate commonality? If we do not share one common human
nature, does it open the way for one "race" or "class" of people to be
said to be intrinsically superior to another? If we do share one common
nature, how can we describe it? Can we go beyond words of a shared
vulnerability out of which we sometimes act in fear and violence and
sometimes out of courage and generosity of spirit?

What, indeed, is it, to be human? If we believe and live into the
imagination that we are "original blessings," will we respond to human
beings and being human differently than if we lived with the imagination that we are originally sinful?[9] If we believe and live into the
imagination that we possess a "deep, wicked, abominable, inscrutable,
inexpressible corruption of our entire nature, in all its powers," will we
respond to human beings and being human differently than if we lived
into the imagination that we are, as Wiesel laments, created in the divine
image?[10] Was Wiesel right? Was it the misapprehension of the nature
of humankind that led to the ordeal for the Jews? Or was Tutu right

8. Desmond Mpilo Tutu, *No Future without Forgiveness* (New York: Doubleday,
1999), 144.

9. Matthew Fox, *Original Blessing* (New York: Putnam, 2000).

10. See the "Solid Declaration of the Formula of Concord," (SDFC) in *The Book
of Concord*, ed. and trans. Theodore G. Tappert (Philadelphia, PA: Fortress Press,
1959), 510.

to recognize that we all have a capacity for monstrosity that we must never underestimate? Is it possible that both are right?

These are among the questions that will concern us as we turn to the nature of the human person in the present and subsequent chapter. In these pages, I am examining, first, Beauty's trace in a meditation on varying interpretations of the *imago Dei*, then Beauty's veil in a consideration of the impact sin has had on humankind's ability to relate to God—an impact that I am suggesting partially obscures our moral vision, thereby blinding us from living with integrity in relation to the presence of the Good, the Beautiful, and the True within us. This is the *imago Dei*, the gift of divine life that is known within the mind of God and shared with us, whispering still in a small, barely audible voice, coaxing us all to lives of deeper engagement in the world.

The first chapter of Genesis records an ancient understanding of human nature:

> Then God said, "Let us make humankind in our image, according to our likeness; and let them have dominion over the fish of the sea, and over the birds of the air, and over the cattle, and over all the wild animals of the earth, and over every creeping thing that creeps upon the earth." So God created humankind in his image, in the image of God he created them; male and female he created them. God blessed them, and God said to them, "Be fruitful and multiply, and fill the earth and subdue it; and have dominion over the fish of the sea and over the birds of the air and over every living thing that moves upon the earth." (Gen 1:26-28a)

This passage speaks of the *imago Dei*—the image of God. The English word "image" is a translation of *imago*, which Jerome translated into Latin from the Greek Septuagint. In Greek, the word *eikon* denotes "likeness, image, or portrait" etymologically from *eikenai*, meaning "to resemble, to be like, or to look like." Inheriting this etymology, theologians began to ask, What does it mean to resemble, to be like, or to "look" like God? In what way or ways, precisely, are we like God? Are we portraits of God? Does this resemblance have less to do with physicality and more with spirituality—with the human mind, heart, will, soul, spirit, or some combination thereof perhaps? Maybe "image" pertains instead to the manner in which we relate to our loved ones and neighbors, or to the capacity that humankind possesses to relate to God and to others in the first place. Or is it a function of our dependency—that we are creatures of God with the task instituted from the dawn of time to have dominion, or to be good stewards of the earth and its resources, cocreating with God by caring for the creation and by populating it? On what basis can conclusions about the meaning of *imago Dei* be made, given our distance from the culture and the authors who first inscribed these words onto tablets and scrolls for the ages?

The concept of being created in the image of God is a significant one in both Jewish and Christian traditions. One Jewish teaching, traced to Rabbi Joshua ben Levi (ca. 250 CE), maintains that thousands of angels go before every human person, rejoicing, "Make way for the image of God."[11] Likewise, Rabbi Judah (second century) writes famously in the Mishnah about how witnesses in cases of murder were to be admonished with the *gravitas* of their task, recognizing that to take a single life—to put out an *imago Dei*—is to eliminate all the life that might have emerged from it. To kill is to destroy an entire world.

> In capital cases both the blood of the man put to death and the blood of his descendants are on the witness's head until the end of time. For thus we find in the case of Cain, who killed his brother, that it is written: "The bloods of your brother cry unto Me" (Genesis 4:10)—that is, his blood and the blood of his potential descendants. . . . Therefore was the first man, Adam, created alone, to teach us that *whoever destroys a single life, the Bible considers it as if he destroyed an entire world. And whoever saves a single life, the Bible considers it as if he saved an entire world.*[12]

Within Christianity, the *imago Dei* has, over time, been interpreted functionally, relationally, or substantially. Given the situation of the phrase in Genesis, in the midst of God giving humankind dominion and within the context of instructing humankind to multiply, some interpreters have understood *imago Dei* to have a *functional* meaning. Humans are cocreators with God, maintaining and continuing the creation as God's representatives.[13] Others have understood the term *relationally* to mean that just as God establishes a relationship with humankind so do humans respond to God and to one another by nurturing their relationships. Thus, we are said to be made in God's image.[14] The dominant

---

11. *Midrash Tehillim* 55.3 (146b).

12. *Mishnah Sanhedrin* 4.5, emphasis mine. See also Y. Michael Barilan, "From *Imago Dei* in the Jewish-Christian Traditions to Human Dignity in Contemporary Jewish Law," *Kennedy Institute of Ethics Journal* 19, no. 3 (September 2009): 231–59.

13. See, for example, J. Richard Middleton, "The Liberating Image? Interpreting the *Imago Dei* in Context," *Christian Scholars Review* 24, no. 1 (1994): 8–25.

14. See Dominic Robinson, "'Imago Dei': The Historico-Theological Background," in *Understanding the 'Imago Dei': The Thought of Barth, von Balthasar and Moltmann* (Burlington, VT: Ashgate, 2011), 5–44, for a helpful overview of the tradition. The

interpretation within Christianity, however, stretching back to the age of Augustine, through Thomas, and into the modern day, maintains that *imago Dei* is best understood *substantially*. The image of God is to be understood as an essential dimension of our being. Our capacity to reason, to exercise free will, to empathize with the pain of others—these things are demonstrative of the *imago Dei* within us, according to this line of thinking.[15]

Augustine shared the view that *imago Dei* coheres with the essence of our being and is among the first to articulate how the mind, heart, and will and their requisite reason, empathy, and freedom have been diminished as a result of sin. After the "fall" into sin, though he believed humans still bore the *imago Dei*, he understood human nature to have been severely limited, or compromised, in its ability to conduct itself in ways pleasing to God.[16] In other words, ever since humankind's first transgression, so thought Augustine, it has been natural to desire that which is self-centered rather than that which is God-centered. This orientation, proclivity, or tendency toward the self and its own will rather than toward God and God's will became known as the doctrine of original sin, and the location of this stain was thought to be on the *imago Dei*, i.e., the mind, heart, and will, each corrupted to a degree by sin and each restored through baptism.[17]

Systematized by Thomas, the medieval doctrine maintains that there is a remnant of the *imago Dei* in humankind that is capable of goodness.[18] This ability is itself an effect of grace, since nature is, itself, never devoid of grace.[19] Once restored by the waters of baptism, when the "stain" of

---

author treats Irenaeus, Augustine, and Thomas particularly well. While he misunderstands Luther, writing for example, "We are either free in our acceptance of our righteousness or we are slaves to the sin of rejecting this" (19), his treatment on the whole is useful as an overview of perspectives throughout the ages.

15. Ibid.

16. Augustine, *On Original Sin*, trans. Peter Holmes and Robert Ernest Wallis, rev. Benjamin B. Warfield, in *Nicene and Post-Nicene Fathers, First Series*, vol. 5, ed. Philip Schaff (Buffalo, NY: Christian Literature Publishing Co., 1887), chap. 2.

17. Ibid.

18. Thomas Aquinas treats the *imago Dei* in ST, I, q. 93., a. 1-9, respectively, asking: Is the image of God in man? Is the image of God in irrational creatures? Is the image of God in the angels more than in man? Is the image of God in every man? Is the image of God in man by comparison with the Essence, or with all the Divine Persons, or with one of them? Is the image of God in man, as to his mind only? Is the image of God in man's power or in his habits and acts? Is the image of God in man by comparison with every object? The difference between "image" and "likeness."

19. Ibid.

sin is washed away, the image is equipped into such a condition that it is increasingly able to cooperate with God's grace.[20] Since it remains initially in a state much like an infant, however, it requires the church and its sacraments in order to strengthen and mature it. All the same, the image has the potential to be transformed into a nature that is righteous before God, ever increasing in the degree to which it more perfectly reflects God's image by the extent to which it habituates cooperation with the mind, heart, and will of God rather than resistance to God and God's offer of actual graces.[21] Such an image is a sanctified image—a saintly image. On the last day, God will look at humans and will see the degree to which the individual has been transformed into a Christlike image through the work of the church, and all so transformed will be reconciled and will be granted the vision of God.[22] According to Thomas, this is that in which the hope of the Christian resides.

Because such a view requires the support of a fair amount of Platonic and Aristotelian philosophy with its requisite application of reason, Luther and the reformers after him deferred to these words attributed to Paul: "See to it that no one takes you captive through philosophy and empty deceit, according to human tradition, according to the elemental spirits of the universe, and not according to Christ" (Col 2:8). The mantra *sola scriptura* suggested to Luther that the Catholic conception of the human person as possessing a nature that was merely damaged by sin was insufficient. When he read verses like this one from Paul's letter to the Romans, Luther concluded that sin's damage was more extensive than his Catholic Church was suggesting:

> We have already charged that all, both Jews and Greeks, are under the power of sin, as it is written:
> "There is no one who is righteous, not even one;
>   there is no one who has understanding,
>   there is no one who seeks God.
> All have turned aside, together they have become worthless;
>   there is no one who shows kindness,
>   there is not even one."
> "Their throats are opened graves;
>   they use their tongues to deceive."
> "The venom of vipers is under their lips."
>   "Their mouths are full of cursing and bitterness."

20. Ibid.
21. Ibid.
22. Ibid.

"Their feet are swift to shed blood;
    Ruin and misery are in their paths,
  and the way of peace they have not known."
        "There is no fear of God before their eyes." (Rom 3:9-18)

Although he agreed with Augustine that humans are "originally sinful," meaning that people are born with a stain of sin that compromises their ability to do consistently what is God pleasing, Luther disagreed as to the degree of damage that sin had wrought. Whereas Rome defended the perspective that there is still some degree of the original nature left that enables people to desire in ways that align with God's mind, heart, and will, Luther and the Reformers opposed the optimism of the Catholic perspective. Luther's view was that human nature is entirely alienated from God. It is enslaved to the power of sin. Even after baptism, the human nature remains in a desperate state, entirely dependent on the grace of God to cover it and, in nature's stead, to perform good works through the person. The *imago Dei*, in other words, was left in a state unable to respond to grace by the fall into sin.

The Council of Trent clarified the Catholic doctrine against the Reformers, saying that as much as it had been damaged by sin, human nature had been in no way destroyed by the fall into sin. "[The] free will, *weakened* as it was in its powers and downward bent, was *by no means extinguished* in them," is the official language from the Council of Trent—a statement that hints at how Catholics understood Luther's view of the human person.[23] This definition from Trent defends the view that humans in a postlapsarian state remain inherently love worthy in their very being. They understand this love worthiness to be already a grace, or a heavenly gift, from God. In short, Catholic doctrine asserts the view that human nature itself is an expression of God's grace, no matter how compromised the human capacity to please God has become as a result of sin's disorienting power. Affirming the Augustinian and Thomistic traditions, the council located this weakened capacity in the will, associated with the *imago Dei*. In other words, the *imago Dei* itself was weakened by sin.

In spite of certain passages in the *Book of Concord*,[24] Trent's understanding that Luther was arguing that the goodness of human nature had been entirely destroyed (and with it, therefore, the *imago Dei*) is

---

23. Council of Trent, Session 6, chap. 1, emphasis mine.

24. As, for example, the Solid Declaration's description of the "deep, wicked, abominable, bottomless, inscrutable, and inexpressible corruption" of the entire nature and all its powers, as quoted above, SDFC, 510.

not entirely accurate. Rather, Luther thought that no good work that a human person performs is in any way salvific. For the contemporary situation, perhaps the title of Luther's own work on the subject, *The Bondage of the Will*—as well as one version of the Lutheran confession which has the people say, "We are in bondage to sin and cannot free ourselves"—provides a careful nuance.[25] For the Lutheran, then, it is more that the will, encapsulated by the phrase *imago Dei*, is in bondage to sin, rather than that the will has been obliterated or, in the words of Trent, "extinguished" by sin.[26] In either case, Luther understood human nature and its ability to be righteous before God to be entirely debilitated by sin. A slave is not free but is bound to a master. Therefore, if the will ultimately reflects the image of God, and if the will is bound to sin, humankind requires a Redeemer to save human nature from self-destruction and from inflicting harm on the neighbor. Thus, whereas Augustine read Paul to say that there is an orientation or a tendency toward sin that requires Christ's rectification, Luther read Paul and Augustine after him to say that because humans are entirely bound to sin, they are incapable on their own of righteousness in God's sight, and so they require a Redeemer. In a clearly anti-Jewish move, Luther taught that the first covenant is absolutely insufficient to save because no one is capable of living up to its demands.

> Meanwhile it is to be noted that the whole Scripture of God is divided into two parts: precepts and promises. The precepts certainly teach us what is good, but what they teach is not forthwith done. For they show us what we ought to do, but do not give us the power to do it. They were ordained, however, for the purpose of showing man to himself, that through them he may learn his own impotence for good and may despair of his own strength. For this reason they are called the Old Testament, and are so. For example, "Thou shalt not covet," is a precept by which we are all convicted of sin, since no man can help coveting, whatever efforts to the contrary he may make. In order therefore that he may fulfill the precept, and not covet, he is constrained to despair of himself and to seek elsewhere and through another the help which he cannot find in himself; as it is said, "O Israel, thou has destroyed thyself;

25. See Martin Luther and Erasmus, *Free Will and Salvation*, Library of Christian Classics (Louisville, KY: Westminster John Knox Press, 1995). See also the *Lutheran Book of Worship* (Minneapolis, MN: Augsburg Fortress, 1978), used now primarily by the ELCA, for the Lutheran Church-Missouri Synod published its own *Lutheran Worship* (St. Louis, MO: Concordia Publishing House, 1982), which uses a different confession: "We confess we are by nature sinful and unclean."

26. Council of Trent, Session 6, chap. 1.

but in Me is thine help" (Hosea xiii.9). Now what is done by this one precept is done by all; for all are equally impossible of fulfilment by us.[27]

Thus, bound to sin, the enslaved, if not extinguished, *imago Dei* was dependent on the liberating act of a Redeemer to rescue it from its condition. This truth was operative for all human beings as all descend from Adam.

Luther understood God to send Christ into the world in order to redeem the world—and in this recognition that "God so loved the world that he gave his only Son" (John 3:16) is rooted the dignity of the human person. For Luther, humanity's love worthiness is rooted in God's desire to bring humankind into being and, once it had fallen into sin, to save it. Human dignity is grounded in God's will and, as such, ought to be viewed as inviolable. But this becomes conflated with Luther's anthropology. When Luther taught that baptism covers or "seals" Christians with an entirely new image—one of Christ's righteousness (*imago Christi*, for at baptism Christ takes up residence in the human heart)—he drew a sharp line of contrast between baptized souls and unbaptized ones. Thus, for Luther, the "good works" humans do are attributable to Christ, but these are in no way salvific for it is by "grace alone" (*sola gratia*) that humans are saved. While the sinful things humans do are attributable to them and to their sinful natures, the good works they do are attributable to the presence of Christ residing within them. The baptized are saints and sinners simultaneously. The unbaptized cannot do any works that are righteous in God's sight. Thus, Christ alone enables humans to live righteously. On the last day, God will look at humans but will see the image of Christ and all so marked will be reconciled. This, at any rate, is that in which the hope of the Lutheran resides.

All of this is to say that Luther maintained that the *imago Dei* and the human capacity for goodness is in bondage to sin, leaving humankind in a state of total alienation from God and in a state of complete dependence on God's grace, whereas the Council of Trent maintained that the *imago Dei* has been damaged by sin, leaving human beings still able to participate in the mind, heart, and will of God in a postlapsarian state to a lesser degree than they would have been able to in a condition prior to the fall of humankind. In either case, these Christians are in agreement that, as a result, humans are more apt to desire that which is self-centered than that which is God-centered. By their official statements, Catholics and Lutherans alike agree that humans are not able

---

27. Martin Luther, *Concerning Christian Liberty: With Letter of Martin Luther to Pope Leo X* (Fort Worth, TX: RDMc Publishing, 2007).

to live as Christ lived, and thus they require a divine intervention in order to be justified, or "to be made right" again, in God's sight. They agreed, in the ancient formulation, that there was no salvation outside of the church, suggesting that God the Father finds love worthiness only in souls saved by the redemption of Christ and sanctified by the Holy Spirit rather than in all souls that God brought into being.[28]

These models are helpful not because they are the only two possible in the realm of imagination about *imago Dei* but because they outline the dangers of the question before us. Both are locating sin's damage in the ontology of the *imago Dei* itself. Damaged or destroyed, weakened or in bondage—the damage has been done to the divine image. Does this lead ultimately to the conclusion that those who are unbaptized are lesser beings, lesser humans, in some way? Implicit in these teachings, is there a dehumanization of those who are unbaptized? In dehumanizing the "Other," does it open the way for genocide? Does such a view explain how the holocaust was able to take root in a country where much of the population had been taught that the value of the Jewish soul was diminished in God's sight, and that God's preference was decidedly for the baptized?[29]

Acknowledging the theological developments that took the doctrine about the *imago Dei* in many divergent directions, J. Richard Middleton, a professor of biblical worldview and exegesis at Northeastern Theological Seminary, a seminary in the Wesleyan tradition in New York, argues convincingly that the author or authors behind the primeval accounts in Genesis 1–11 understood the *imago Dei* as a *"royal function or office of human beings as God's representatives and agents in the world, given authorized power to share in God's rule over the earth's resources and creatures,"*[30] an interpretation around which, Middleton claims, there is "virtual consensus among Old Testament scholars."[31] In writing about

---

28. This doctrine was revisited by the Catholic bishops during the Second Vatican Council. See especially chap. 2, "On the People of God," in *Lumen Gentium*, which argues that other Christians are "linked" to the church and that practitioners of religions other than Christianity are "related to" the church and can hope to attain to salvation by allegiance to truths they share in common.

29. Michael Robert, *Holy Hatred: Christianity, Antisemitism, and the Holocaust* (New York: Palgrave Macmillan, 2006); Johannes Wallmann, "The Reception of Luther's Writings on the Jews from the Reformation to the End of the 19th Century," *Lutheran Quarterly*, n.s. 1 (Spring 1987): 72–97; and Lucy Dawidowicz, *The War Against the Jews, 1933–1945* (New York: Bantam, 1975, repr. 1986).

30. Middleton, "The Liberating Image?," 12.

31. Ibid., 11. Middleton shares that Claus Westermann is one significant dissenting voice. See Claus Westermann, *Genesis 1–11: A Commentary*, trans. by John J. Scullion from the 1974 German ed. (Minneapolis, MN: Augsburg, 1984), 142–61.

the biblical context, Middleton attempts to change the trajectory of discourse about *imago Dei* in order to foster a healthier interpretation. Given the degree of agreement among scholars about its meaning, it is an opportunity, too, for the churches to find common ground and to build up ecumenical relations among them.

Middleton draws on the text's sixth-century authorship (BCE) to argue that the Babylonian exile was prompting Israel to differentiate its creation myth from those of Babylon and to assert "Israel's unique insight about being human, in the process (as numerous scholars have noted) 'democratizing' the ancient Near Eastern royal ideology, by applying it to all human beings, male and female."[32] Middleton concludes, "Thus, far from constituting an oppressive text, Genesis 1 (and the *imago Dei* as rule) was intended to subvert an oppressive social system and to empower despairing exiles to stand tall again with dignity as God's representatives in the world."[33] He is quick to explain that true kingship, as demonstrated by Christ, was "to exercise power not . . . [by] lording it over one another, but in serving each other."[34] In other words, kingship properly understood entails "the right use of power"[35] which is "not oppressive control of others, but their liberation or empowerment."[36] Middleton justifies his Christian reading of the Hebraic text:

> What ties together this whole trajectory from Genesis 1 to the New Testament is the consistent biblical insight that humanity from the beginning . . . is both gifted by God with a royal status and dignity and called by God actively to represent his kingdom in the entire range of human life, that is, in the very way we rule . . . the earth. . . . Humanity created in God's image . . . is called and empowered to be God's multi-sided prism in the world, reflecting and refracting the Creator's brilliant light into a rainbow of cultural activity and socio-political patterns that scintillates with the glory of God's presence and manifests his reign of justice.[37]

Despite this present consensus among biblical scholars, the insight of the historical meaning was lost for a time, with profound impact on doctrines expounding belief in humankind and in human dignity. In what is human dignity rooted? Is it something that humans inherently

32. Ibid., 21.
33. Ibid., 21–22.
34. Ibid., 23.
35. Ibid., 23–24.
36. Ibid.
37. Ibid., 24–25.

possess and that is inviolable—and therefore should be recognized, acknowledged, and honored in every human person without exception? Is human dignity something that simply is? Or is dignity something that is affiliated with these interpretations of *imago Dei* as variable in each human person? Is dignity vulnerable to damage and alienation from God—either diminished, in bondage to, or extinguished by sin? Is dignity increased by one's cooperation with grace or by one's receipt of the gift of faith and the healing waters of baptism? Does human dignity fluctuate, then, according to the degree to which the human life imitates or participates in the life of God? If Christian theology proposes that human dignity is rooted in the *imago Dei*, then it matters what we are saying. The implications are profound. These issues demonstrate how anthropological questions are truly matters of life and death. Blood has been spilled over these questions.

The Augustinian model suggests our *imago Dei* is damaged by sin. Does that mean our dignity is damaged? Does that mean that those who are "holier" (the saints and those more advanced on the path to saint-hood) deserve to be treated as more "worthwhile" and of higher value than those not so sanctified? The Lutheran model suggests our *imago Dei* is entirely in bondage. Does this open all of humankind to be treated in the way that the powerful treat their slaves? When Calvin adopted many of Luther's ideas, he articulated that the human being was totally depraved.[38] Does this mean that at birth no one has inherent value and worth as a human person—and that only those who are baptized, and who have Christ "taking up residence" in them, are worthy, as only they are in possession of the *imago Dei*, in which inherent value and love worthiness are grounded?

Not only are these models with a *substantial* understanding of *imago Dei* insufficient but they are also dangerous. If we believe that the image itself increases or decreases, is made holy or is extinguished, then we have identified a measure of the inherent worth of the human person—with sometimes dire consequences. Such a view could be, and has been, used to determine who is worthy of receiving the limited resources of the church and state. From debates about allocations for the homeless to expenditures for pharmaceuticals to assist those living with HIV/AIDS, issues of worth, merit, and deservingness inevitably come to the fore. Some Christian doctrines have understood the faithful to be intrinsi-

38. John Calvin, *Institutes of the Christian Religion* (Philadelphia, PA: Westminster Press, 1960), 1.15.4, where Calvin writes that the *imago Dei* "was so corrupted that whatever remains is frightful deformity."

cally more valuable than those who go unbaptized. More pointedly, the holocaust of the Jews can be traced, at least in part, to a dehumanization that occurred in the Christian imagination, which considered Jewish life less valuable due to the nonreceipt of baptismal graces. Therefore, whatever is said about *imago Dei* must be carefully deliberated, for the stakes are very high.

Drawing, therefore, on the royal model outlined by Middleton and the tradition that developed within Judaism, I would like to offer a modest proposal in the Trinitarian imagination as outlined in the previous chapter. If we consider the concept of the *imago Dei* from the vantage point of a theological aesthetics informed by the Catholic tradition, and if we draw on the tradition that has dared to utter the Good, Beautiful, and True as names for God, each indwelling the other, we could imagine humankind to be crafted by and to reflect still, to whatever degree material nature can, the Good, Beautiful, and True nature of the Holy One from whom all existence derives its being and on whom everything depends for existence. Understood from within a Trinitarian framework, the Goodness, Beauty, and Truth that each one possesses inherently, yet imperfectly, transcends the material, much like the mind transcends the brain. The glory of this first Goodness, first Beauty, first Truth, made manifest in every human being bearing its image, is limited only by the ability of the human mind and imagination to visualize that which is infinite.

Imago Dei is the Good, Beautiful, and True radiating within us, just as light radiates from the flame of a candle, burning in us as perfectly as it is possible for material nature to reflect that which is divine. *Imago Dei* is our truest nature. As God's Beloved, with both an origin and a destiny in God, *imago Dei* is grounded first and foremost in God's imagination and has its ontological perfection or authenticity there. *Imago Dei* is God's image of us, possessing God's perfect vision of who we are, will be, and in some sense always have been. In that rootedness within God's imagination comes our dignity. But God's image of us is truly within us, having been gifted to us when we were conceived. In the *imago Dei*, we embody God's own Goodness, Beauty, and Truth shaped in God's mind to a degree proper to materiality and made unique by our genetic distinctions as these distinctions interact interpersonally with familial and cultural influences.

As material beings, our existence is naturally limited. As we emerged from simpler forms of life, it was natural for us to protect our own, whether our own family or our own group. We have evolved biologically, intellectually, and technologically; survival is wedded now to seeing and honoring our interconnectedness—and to seeing the whole as one tribe, one race, one humanity. The potential for making errors in judgment is implicit in a limited nature. When humans "fall," we fall not from perfection but from innocence. We emerge into consciousness—of an awareness, or a deeper knowledge—that we sometimes behave in ways contrary to what is holy and right. When we came to this awareness, we experienced shame. Yet, even still, the image created in us calls us to live with a higher degree of integrity in relation to God's imagination of who we really are and can be, and ultimately in union with the nature of the Good, Beautiful, and True Nature that is our source.

This first conscious act of violating God's good and holy will for us, an act contrary to the *imago Dei* within us, is symbolized in the story of Adam and Eve. As representatives of human beings, both male and female, Adam and Eve represent the moment that humankind emerged from a state of innocence into a state of self-awareness. Their distrust and disobedience demonstrates a coming into consciousness of a law higher than one's own. In the story, these two begin to recognize how actions have impact beyond themselves. When people act against this inner light, against their conscience, a sense that is individualized yet rooted in God's own mind, they set more destruction into motion and introduce obstacles, such that it becomes harder and harder to live with integrity in relation to one's inner compass, which nonetheless radiates within us, its light issuing from God's own. As the story goes, sin spirals out of control already in the first generations as relationships of violence escalate. Cain kills Abel. Lamech kills another man just for wounding him (Gen 4:23). Sons of God have intercourse with the daughters of human beings (Gen 6:1-8). It becomes so horrendous that God wishes to take it all back and sends the flood (Gen 6–9). All of this reflects how the human authors of Genesis were grappling with what it means to be human—with what it means to live contrary to one's highest aspirations, cognizant as we are of a higher standard and in relation to which, the authors convey, it is very difficult to live with any degree of integrity.

Before he became Pope Benedict XVI, then-Cardinal Joseph Ratzinger preached a series of homilies on the book of Genesis. Distancing himself from Augustinian understandings of sin passed from generation to generation through the act of sexual intercourse but nevertheless wrestling with the reality of an inherited nature of sin, he suggests in these homilies that we are all born into a sin-damaged world that has been impacted by a relationality that is inherent in our nature.[39] When we think and act in ways contrary to our true nature, we damage ourselves,

---

39. Joseph Ratzinger, *In the Beginning . . . : A Catholic Understanding of the Story of Creation and the Fall*, trans. Boniface Ramsey (Grand Rapids, MI: Eerdmans, 1995), 72–73.

our relationships with others, and the larger web connecting us all. In my mind, this damage obstructs our ability to see the divine nature of the Good, Beautiful, and True still radiating within us. Sin veils our vision to varying degrees. It partially eclipses our ability to see as God sees and to respond to God and to neighbor in a way that God wills us to respond and to which the *imago Dei* always calls us. This obstructed vision is born in us, stretching back, as it does, to our primordial past. Veil after veil is piled one upon the next, making it more and more difficult for us to live into God's imagination of who we are meant to be. The wombs that develop us are tainted with poisons; homes are violent; societies are intolerant; and the resources of the globe are inequitably distributed. From the moment of our conception, there is a distinction between God's imagination of who we are intended to be and who we are. The light of the *imago Dei* always shines within us, calling us to integrity, to wholeness of being, to union between our being and God's vision. Our purpose is to live, with the assistance of divine grace, into God's imagination of who we are. This vision is always present in the *imago Dei* burning brightly within us, even when these obstacles we create hinder its light, blocking it from view. The *imago Dei* calls us to live with greater and greater degrees of integrity until our being is absorbed by the Source of all Light, until we have union with God.

Despite the veils that partially eclipse our ability to live with perfect integrity into the vision God has shared with each of us—some veils inherited personally, others learned socially, and still others engineered structurally—these veils never block the view of the *imago Dei* from God's vantage point. And the light of the *imago Dei* itself is never diminished—only diminished is an ability to see it from a human vantage point. *Imago Dei* is not the nature of mind, heart, or will that are alternately diminished or extinguished by sin. Rather, vision and imagination are impacted by sin. It is the capacity of the human person to see both one's own and one another's Goodness, Beauty, and Truth—the reflection of God, or the Shekhinah's flame, to adopt the Yiddish phrase—that radiates perfectly and always within all of humankind—Jew, Christian, Buddhist, pagan, and atheist alike. If God has an imagination about each of us and about our potential, this imagination resides perfectly and always in God's mind, our lives in actuality either veiling to a greater and greater degree the divine life within us or unveiling and conforming to, with greater and greater integrity, the divine image of God's imagination shared with us.

Cardinal Ratzinger, once wrote of this potential, using the vocabulary of humankind as "God's project."

In the human being heaven and earth touch one another. In the human being God enters into his creation; the human being is directly related to God. The human being is called by him. God's words in the Old Testament are valid for every individual human being: "I call you by name and you are mine." Each human being is known by God and loved by him. Each is willed by God, and each is God's image. Precisely in this consists the deeper and greater unity of humankind—that each of us, each individual human being, realizes the *one* project of God and has his or her origin in the same creative idea of God. Hence the Bible says that whoever violates a human being violates God's property (cf. Genesis 9:5). Human life stands under God's special protection, because each human being, however wretched or exalted he or she may be, however sick or suffering, however good-for-nothing or important, whether born or unborn, whether incurably ill or radiant with health— each one is God's image. This is the deepest reason for the inviolability of human dignity, and upon it is founded ultimately every civilization. When the human person is no longer seen as standing under God's protection and bearing God's breath, then the human being begins to be viewed in utilitarian fashion. It is then that the barbarity appears that tramples upon human dignity. And vice versa: When this is seen, then a high degree of spirituality and morality is plainly evident.[40]

A flame reflective of God's own Goodness, Beauty, and Truth burns radiantly, despite veils that are imposed over it—veils that the monotheistic religions of the world term "sinfulness." These veils of personal, social, and structural sin obstruct vision, so that the Good, Beautiful, and True are partially eclipsed, influencing one's own ability to see beautifully, generously, and hospitably, and to be seen by others properly in the same sense. Sometimes, however, vision is so obscured by personal, social, and structural dimensions of sin that the Good, Beautiful, and True in oneself and one's neighbor are entirely eclipsed, blocked out in a kind of imaginative blindness, as when Nazis dehumanized Jews; and when Afrikaners dehumanized Africans; and when Americans dehumanized indigenous peoples; and so on. Sometimes, this blindness is attributable to an individual sense of greed or envy that distorts how we see ourselves and imagines that we are detached from a shared humanity, the whole of which we depend on for our own survival. It causes us to function out of a model of scarcity rather than a model of abundance and inspires us to hoard rather than to share resources needed by all. Sometimes, such blindness is due to cultural trends that condition how we see one another and place value on some over others: the rich and

40. Ibid., 44–45.

influential are privileged before the impoverished or addicted ones in our midst, for example, or the male is advantaged before the female, to give another example. Sometimes, this blindness is due to structural distortions that make complicity in structures of harm invisible from those most guilty of designing, implementing, and perpetuating them. We will turn to these matters in the next chapter.

Sanctification is the unveiling of vision, the lifting of the veils, one by one, degree by degree, until we arrive at a union between the vision of God and our own vision. It is then that the veils have been lifted, preparing us to see the Beatific Vision—to see God face-to-face. At that moment, veils no longer hide the countenance of God. This is when we will see one another, at long last, in the way that God wishes for us to see and to be seen—as we really are, and as God intends for us to be seen, with all memory of failure to live into the imagination of the Good, Beautiful, and True mystically and personally, socially, and structurally healed. Our task, if we are followers of Christ, is to develop by the power of grace a spirituality where we see beyond the veils, so to speak, as we increasingly develop a vision to see as Christ sees, as God sees, and to honor the image that is there, radiating within each one of us, murderer and saint alike. We are to develop in a way, guided by grace and the Holy Spirit, that enables us to see and interact with the addict as saints have worked with and seen addicted ones: as inherently Good, Beautiful, and True, as perfectly love worthy.[41]

The inviolable dignity of the human person ought to be grounded in this imagination of the *imago Dei*, reflective as it is of a vision grounded first in God. In this is the idea that every person, drug addict and saint alike, is beloved of God. In this is the idea that, in their very existence as human persons, all people deserve to have their worthiness acknowledged and protected. In this way, we can understand dignity as equally possessed by all, rooted as it is in God's imagination and genuinely shared with us at our conception, rather than in the corruptibility of our own personhood. People who are addicted to drugs have not relinquished their dignity, nor have the saints added to their dignity by doing all they do to contribute to the common good. And certainly, when humans serve their neighbors, they are not contributing to anyone's dignity though they might, in the process of such service, become more open to recognizing the dignity people inherently possess.

This vision of the *imago Dei* is an elaboration of the Second Vatican Council's articulation of dignity's location in God's call to humankind.

---

41. Dorothy Day, "Room for Christ," *The Catholic Worker* (December 1945): 2.

"Human dignity rests above all on the fact that humanity is called to communion with God. The invitation to converse with God is addressed to men and women as soon as they are born. For if people exist it is because God has created them through love, and through love continues to keep them in existence" (GS 19). The document goes on to proclaim:

> There is a growing awareness of the sublime dignity of human persons, who stand above all things and whose rights and duties are universal and inviolable. They ought, therefore, to have ready access to all that is necessary for leading a genuinely human life: for example, food, clothing, housing, the right freely to choose their state of life and set up a family, the right to education, work, to their good name, to respect, to proper knowledge, the right to act according to the dictates of conscience and to safeguard their privacy, and rightful freedom, including freedom of religion. . . . [Such a social order] must be founded on truth, built on justice, and enlivened by love: it should grow in freedom towards a more humane equilibrium. If these objectives are to be obtained there will first have to be a renewal of attitudes and far-reaching social changes. (GS 26)

If humans are created in the *imago Dei*, and if their dignity is rooted not in the individual instantiations of that image but in the prototype, then perhaps it would be fruitful to consider anew the possibility that the image in which we are created is this Beauty—a Beauty who Christians believe became incarnate in the person of Jesus Christ, a Beauty indwelled by what is Good and True. If this Jewish man from Nazareth, born in Bethlehem and crucified in Jerusalem, was an incarnation of Beauty Absolute, if he made physically manifest what Beauty "looks like," Beauty has as much to do with his life of compassion, literally "suffering with" humankind, as it has to do with Thomas's harmony, proportion, and clarity—though these things may be, as Plato indicated, rungs on a metaphysical ladder of sorts, drawing us ever deeper and deeper into knowledge of what is most really Real. If Christ is the incarnation of the Logos of a God of Love, and if Beauty is this Love made visible, then Christ embodies that Love in human flesh, living a truly human life with the highest degree of integrity to the divine image radiating within him, a Beauty that radiates within all of us. If we are truly his disciples, our lives ought increasingly to reflect such integrity, such justice, such divine Goodness, Beauty, and Truth active in Love.

If this is the Beauty we reflect as a sheer matter of our existence, then the transformative potential about which the gospels speak, and about which Christ might be referring when he is recorded to have said, "Go and make disciples of all nations, teaching them everything I have commanded" (Matt 28:19), is breathtaking. Perhaps he meant we are to make disciples, literally "students," of all nations—teaching them to discover the holy image within themselves and then to follow in the way of the Rabbi, our teacher. Maybe he meant that he hoped for a conversion of the mind, heart, and will to the Goodness, Beauty, and Truth of God, demonstrated by lives committed to justice, devoted to compassionate service and to a pursuit of spiritual wisdom, attentive both to God and neighbor. Jesus certainly was a contemplative who retreated occasionally from the world to nourish his spirit and to tend to spiritual matters. But at the same time, he was deeply engaged in his world, tending to those who had been marginalized: sustaining the widow, feeding the hungry, healing the sick, entering into dialogue with women and untouchables, playing with children. For the Christian, then, it is both/and rather than either/ or: action and contemplation, service and prayer. Perhaps Jesus intended for his students to follow him down this path—a way not easily followed.

In order to conclude this chapter on "Beauty's Trace: On *imago Dei*," let me shift gears, so to speak, and drive us into the township communities with which I am most familiar—those that lie outside of Cape Town. Driving into them from outside is, as has been noted by poets and lyricists alike, a startling exercise in contrasts. As border crossers leave Cape Town behind them, with its crowded promenade that runs along the ocean, bustling shopping centers, and active tourist industry, they encounter heavily concentrated areas where people formerly designated "black" and "colored" under the apartheid regime live in a variety of small homes: millions of government-issue houses, brick homes, and corrugated cardboard shacks jumbled on top of each other in a tangled network of neighborhoods built on every scrap of ground available between freeways offering limited access in and out of these poor but vibrant communities. The overwhelming sensation in the area is dryness: sand, dirt, concrete, and cardboard compete for attention; water taps and toilets are relatively few and are shared by scores of people. Sheets of metal form tin roofs and cardboard boxes become walls for shelters, all of which seem strung together with cables of wire in a complex and unsafe network of electrical power.

John de Gruchy, professor emeritus of theology at Cape Town University, writes about the striking disparity between Cape Town and the townships in this way:

> Cape Town is a city of contrasts, awesomely beautiful, tragically ugly. Lying beneath Table Mountain, which rises sharply out of the Atlantic Ocean, it is situated on a peninsula that is the heartland of one of the six floral kingdoms of the world. The southern tip of the peninsula has

been described as both the Cape of Good Hope and the Cape of Storms, depending on how it has been experienced by those who have sailed around its craggy sentinel. Cape Point represents the end of Africa, or its beginning, cleaving the icy cold waters of the Atlantic from the warmer currents of the Indian Ocean. Tourists are awed by what they see. Those who climb Lion's Head to watch the summer sun set over the Atlantic are stunned by the beauty. Yet the city and its environs are saturated with aesthetic and moral ambiguity, the co-mingling of exuberance and pathos, creativity and destruction. A city of many cultures and political persuasions competing for space and control, yet bound together as one in the need to shape a common destiny.

As a human construct of several centuries, Cape Town embodies beauty in its architecture and its gardens. But alongside this beauty, whether natural or constructed, lies another, ugly reality, much of it the creation of colonial and apartheid legislation and oppression, an architecture that reinforces alienation from social others and the environment. Natural beauty has been scarred by greed and racism; by highways that separate citizens from the sea and its beaches; and by public works that reflect modernity at its worst. The stylish homes of the wealthy often reflect a vulgar opulence rather than the beauty of the surrounding habitat. Not too far from them, though designed to be out of sight and sound, are conditions of widespread poverty. These have spawned street children, gangs, drug trafficking, prostitution, and violent crime. The contrasting worlds of Cape Town are no different from those of many other cities around the world where rich and poor live and work cheek by jowl. But there are few cities where the contrasts are experienced so keenly simply because the beauty of the city and its environment is so breathtaking.[42]

De Gruchy introduces a problem for anyone who wishes to take seriously the sacramental beliefs of the kind I have been outlining in *Beauty's Vineyard*. How is it that the striking beauty of the landscape did not prompt the white population to moral action? If God is present in all beauty, regardless of the form in which it is perceived, and if all true Beauty is indwelled by Goodness, then the beauty of Table Mountain, the oceanfront, and the rolling vineyards, surely truly beautiful, should have given shape to a population, both black and white, that was compassionate and just. In saying these things, in no way do I intend to isolate this historical example from others like it, including my own

42. John de Gruchy, *Christianity, Art, and Social Transformation: Theological Aesthetics in the Struggle for Justice* (Cambridge, UK: Cambridge University Press, 2001), 171–72.

complicity in racism plaguing my own North American context. Rather, the poetry of de Gruchy's description and this philosophical dilemma is genuinely one with which I wrestle. If Beauty is, as I have been talking about it, the presence of God, tugging us patiently but diligently to live compassionately and, ultimately, to act justly, why does it so often apparently fail? How is it that Hitler could demonstrate the capacity to love but implement the extermination camps, to give but only one other example among throngs of them throughout history? Do these examples betray the truth—that sacramentality is a lie, that there is no inherent beauty in the things of this world, that nothing points to a Beauty Absolute, and that absolutely nothing elicits moral beauty? Is Samuel Bak's image of the dying Eden, the exterminated children of broken stone and disintegrating dust, the reality that shatters the illusion and reveals it as just that—an empty wish, nothing but ash?

Perhaps. Nonetheless, I resist that answer with every fiber of my being. My only response is to return to the idea of multiple veils introduced in this chapter, veils obstructing Beauty's face and shrouding the trace of the *imago Dei* within us. For some, spiritual blindness prevents an ability to see the love worthiness of all humanity. In some historical epochs, the blindness has affected entire nations, enabling those functioning within them to behave monstrously—a potential that certainly is within all of us sharing the human condition, as Desmond Tutu articulated so well in his book *No Future without Forgiveness* with which I opened this chapter. Even within such cultures, however, people of great vision and spiritual insight have emerged—people like Dietrich Bonhoeffer and Oskar Schindler in Germany, the Dalai Lama and Thich Nhat Hanh in Asia, Gandhi and Mother Teresa in India, Oscar Romero and Ignacio Ellacuría in El Salvador, Martin Luther King, Jr., and Dorothy Day in the United States, and Desmond Tutu and Nelson Mandela in South Africa. People like these have lived with great integrity, though perhaps not all self-consciously, in relation to the image of God—the Good, Beautiful, and True image—aflame within them, demonstrating for us what it looks like to live with a high degree of integrity in relation to the *imago Dei* also within us.

Rabbi Judah, when reflecting on the glory of the *imago Dei*, contemplated the paradox that while each one is unique, nevertheless each one resembles his or her Creator who, in turn, wills each *imago Dei* into being: "[Humankind was created] to show the greatness of the Holy One, Blessed be He, for if a man strikes many coins from one mold, they all resemble one another, but the King of Kings, the Holy One, Blessed be He, made each man in the image of Adam, and yet not one of them resembles his fellow."[43] One commentator has written in relation to this Talmudic text, "It seems, that, since human eyes can see and imagine only particular bodies and faces, God's 'face'—for which every human face serves as a genuine icon—remains elusive to human perception."[44]

Each *imago Dei*, made holy and absorbed into the One Source from whom all things derive their Being, ultimately becomes One with God. God's face remains ever elusive because, from our vantage point, we cannot see all beings in all their holiness—not only all beings who live now but all beings who ever have lived and who ever will be. But if we could, we would see God as in a photomosaic—God's face becoming visible by the millions and millions of faces made in the *imago Dei*, giving dimension to God's own image. From the vantage point of *kairos* time, we will gain access to a perfected image of who God is—but even now, in *chronos* time, by recognizing the holiness in all the images around us and by listening carefully to every voice, knowing that all perceptions can be made yet holier still, we gain a better sense of the image that resides within us all, too, calling us to live with greater integrity, with greater purpose, with greater joy. Present in the flame within them all, and drawn ultimately into the mystical union of their Source, is God's face—reflective of the world's great diversity and radiantly lit by the light illumined from within their own.

---

43. *Mishnah Sanhedrin* 4.5.
44. Barilan, "*Imago Dei* in the Jewish-Christian Traditions," 243.

The Lamentation Over the Dead Christ (2008) by Kehinde Wiley. Oil on canvas; 131 x 112 inches. Courtesy: Sean Kelly Gallery, New York. © Kehinde Wiley.

Chapter 4

Beauty's Veiling
On Sin

In the imagery of northern Italy during the Renaissance, Christ was often depicted reigning over his kingdom from the heights of heavenly glory. Yet during the Renaissance, there was also a curiosity about Jesus' humanity, born of the ideal of the period's understanding of the universal man, *l'uomo universal*. Leon Battista Alberti (d. 1472) described how this ideal was realized in his generation of artists: "[The universal man] took extraordinary and peculiar pleasure in looking at things in which there was any mark of beauty. . . . Whatever was done by man with genius and with a certain grace, he held to be almost divine."[1] Schooled in this attitude toward nature and beauty's capacity to express the divine, painters of the Italian Renaissance turned frequently to the quintessential nature that was, by definition, both divine and human. Their vision provided fresh insights into *the* Divine Word made flesh. Perhaps no other biblical scene was as dramatic in its pursuit to explore Jesus' human nature than the dead Christ, his body anointed with oil in preparation for the tomb. And, arguably, no other depiction of Christ's dead body had the *pathos* of Andrea Mantegna's.

When Mantegna painted his *Lamentation over the Dead Christ* in the last quarter of the fifteenth century for his own funerary chapel (though it was sold shortly after his death to pay off his debts), he positioned the viewer at Christ's dead feet. Jesus' body is sharply foreshortened and is visited by a weeping and haggard Mary, who wipes away her

---

1. In J. B. Ross and M. M. McLaughlin, eds., *The Portable Renaissance Reader* (New York: Viking, 1953), 480ff; quoted in Horst de la Croix, Richard Tansey, and Diane Kirkpatrick, eds., *Gardner's Art through the Ages*, II (San Diego, CA: Harcourt, Brace, Jovanovich, 1991), 609.

tears with a handkerchief, and John, whose face is visibly etched with distress. With his head resting on a pillow and a simple drapery covering his lower body, Christ's flesh is still jagged and bloodied from the nails that had been so cruelly pounded into his hands and feet. The pallor of death permeates the canvas, its monochromatic scheme ashen, lifeless, and pallid. The burden of the weight of his body on the marble slab imitates the mood in the room, heavily anchored in the tragedy that had befallen this innocent man. For those three days, seemingly abandoned by glory, the body was visited by those who loved him best.

Knowing this image, it is all the more striking to see Kehinde Wiley's majestic canvas bearing the same title, with richly vibrant color spanning more than 90 square feet in area.[2] This dead Christ, an African American male still fully clothed in his cuffed jeans, white T-shirt, golden necklace, and colorful jacket, lies supine on a satin-covered slab, his head supported only by his fur-lined hood. A silk fabric inspired brocade, dense and lavish, encroaches on the body over a green ground, the ornamentation at once honorific and solemn. Painted with an expertise that rivals the skill of the Renaissance masters, this painting lacks the classical theological imagination of a God-man descended to earth to rescue a fallen humankind. Present, however, is a theological imagination still potent in its power. Wiley's painting depicts, perhaps, a critique of a tradition that has long offered songs of praise to Jesus even while his people perpetuated great injustices. It protests against a Christianity that too often fails to see the face of God in those who experience oppression today. Perhaps it calls for a savior who can bring redemption from complicity in structural racism that, too, has participated in the killing of this man, whose death is not marked by the tears of loved ones. By imitating on canvas the posture of Mantegna's Christ, Wiley offers a pointed critique of contemporary bourgeois Christianity while offering avenues too for faithful theological construction.

Here is the Body of Christ embodied in one who suffers an all-too-common and deeply unjust reality in modern-day America, where many laws no longer tolerate discrimination or segregation, even while more subtle but no less deadly forms of racism and classism persist. Did this Christ, like Trayvon Martin, an unarmed African American teenager who was shot by a neighborhood watchman in a gated community in Sanford, Florida, in 2012, get shot because he, with black skin, dared

2. Thelma Golden, Robert Hobbs, Sarah E. Lewis, Brian Keith Jackson, Kehinde Wiley, and Peter Halley, *Kehinde Wiley* (New York: Rizzoli, 2012).

to walk in a neighborhood that was predominantly white?[3] Or is his story similar to Terrance Wright's, the Chicago high-school student who was shot in the chest after being confronted by five assailants, perhaps because he was openly gay?[4] Or is his story like that of Laramiun Byrd, a twenty-year-old man who was the victim of a gunshot wound to the head in Minneapolis (and whose mother, remarkably, entered into relationship with the boy who wielded the gun, ultimately forgiving him, even becoming for him a mother)?[5]

The common threads weaving the larger tapestries of these stories are haunting. Each of the victims was a young African American man living in America, with his own unique stories, dreams, interests, and associations. Each of them was still learning how to navigate the world and its complexities, experiencing varying examples of human relationships gone wrong—in the first instance represented by segregation, in the second by heterosexism, and in the third by gangsterism. Finally, all of the young men were encountering larger social realities involving the interlaced realities of race and class in America. They were each killed by gun violence, a problem that disproportionately affects the African American community in the United States. They were victims of discrete acts of violence, the harm done to them further damaging relationships among people in their own communities, and in communities beyond their own, seeping into the very fabric of the structures by which we organize ourselves in human community. In Christian terms, in other words, they were victims of sin—personal, relational, and structural.

In relation to the vineyard on which this book is focused, Wiley's version of the *Lamentation* presents an opportunity to reflect theologically

3. "Trayvon Martin Case (George Zimmerman)," in the *New York Times*, http://topics .nytimes.com/top/reference/timestopics/people/m/trayvon_martin/index.html.

4. Terrance Wright, "Chicago Teen Killed in Armed Robbery, Family Suspect Homophobia," in *Your Black World* (October 21, 2012), http://www.yourblackworld.net/2012/10 /black-news/chicago-teen-killed-in-armed-robbery-family-suspect-homophobia/.

5. Byrd had attended a party and argued with Oshea Israel, who was sixteen years old at the time. Involved with gangs and drugs, Israel drew his gun and shot Byrd, killing him instantly. Israel was tried as an adult, and was sentenced to twenty-five years in prison. Daily Mail Reporter, "Woman shows incredible mercy as her son's killer moves in next door," in *MailOnline* (June 8, 2011; retrieved 25 April 2013, http://www.dailymail.co.uk/news/article-2000704/Woman-shows -incredible-mercy-sons-killer-moves-door.html). I wrote this chapter before the cases in Ferguson drove the story of racial profiling and police brutality to the center of the media's attention, and I am sending it to the publisher just as the curfew in Baltimore has ended. The painting only continues to become more prophetic the more American culture grapples with gun violence, racial profiling, and police brutality.

on the nature of human sinfulness. To Christian viewers, the painting invites the faithful to hope for Christ's resurrection in the body of believers who, by grace, become increasingly oriented to him and to his Beauty, expressed especially in solidarity with, and with compassion for, those who have been marginalized by systems as they stand. This Christ, as in his prototype, calls from the tomb for followers to transform the social structures of the world, to live Christ's Being into being in their individual lives and in their encounters with others in the community and in relation to the structures of our world, to live as ones changed by an encounter with his story—a story yet incomplete and still unfolding, albeit imperfectly, in a vineyard understood to be Beauty's own.

Because this book has been guided by Jesus' own first-century Jewish imagination of the kingdom of God as a community of people entering intentionally into a right relationship both with God and with neighbor, we will want to examine carefully what it means to be sinful. This chapter on sin will have moorings in the theology of Saint Augustine. But it will engage, too, with the writings of relational theologian Marjorie Hewitt Suchocki, whose concept of sin as that which violates well-being is instructive, even without requiring the turn to process thought she believes is necessary, or the shift from violation against God to violation against humankind that she suggests is needed.[6] In the way that I am conceptualizing it, sin is that which violates community. Because the community is understood to be in the here and now with an ultimate dimension in the hereafter, to be in opposition to community is, by definition, to be opposed to God. By reference to the owner of the vineyard and

---

6. Although I resonate with process theology and its emphasis on a deeply relational God, I do not see as necessary its collapse of the wholeness of God's Being. God can both fully Be and be in relationship with us. A Being, wholly existent, always Good, Beautiful, and True, can be relationally affected by our sinfulness in the unfolding of time, even when this is already restored in the fullness of time. There is an important distinction here between God's Being and our being, between God's time and our time. God's being remains whole despite our dishonoring of holiness. Our being is diminished by our rebellion against Goodness, by our deformation before Beauty, by our deception in the face of Truth. Our indiscretions are redeemed in time and are restored. In *chronos* time, time from the vantage point of human beings, Being desires reunion and restoration and actively engages in reuniting and restoring relationship with the whole of creation through the grace-filled giving of the covenants. If the Creator's immutability, that nature that is always trustworthy and reliable, is by nature in relationship with the created order, then God can be impacted by our sinfulness in *chronos* time (by willing otherwise, and always calling for repentance, from historical moment to moment), without losing integrity of Being, in which all already is, was, and will be, in *kairos* (or fullness of) time.

that owner's tenants and workers, so to speak, I will attempt to reclaim a first-century imagination of sin as that which violates the coming into being of this peaceable kingdom, which entails violations directed both earthward and heavenward, for violations against the Good, Beautiful, and True damage relationships within both spheres of being.[7]

By entering into such a perspective, we will want to examine sin's depths, recognizing its veiling capacity on the Beauty shared with the creation by the Being who left Being's trace in the *imago Dei*, that imagination of who we really are, grounded in the Goodness, Beauty, and Truth of God and shared with us in our very nature and which, in spite of sin's damage, desires integrity with its Source. Beauty is evident in the *imago Dei* in the predisposing grace that anchors us, ultimately, in the vision of God and enables our movement toward God in cooperation with Beauty's ultimate vision. Gradually, sacramental graces orient the will more securely to God and to the peaceable kingdom that is our aspiration, just as additional graces incrementally unveil divine Beauty to us. Grace demystifies and clarifies Beauty's vision in the world and for the world. When heaven and earth meet again, reuniting the heavenly Jerusalem with a restored Eden, Beauty's vineyard will be fully realized. Those who enter into it now receive a foretaste of its wine and other mystical delights by the kinds of beautiful relationships experienced within the vineyard's fences. Indeed, the capacity for Laramiun Byrd's mother to forgive her son's assailant, ultimately inviting him to be her son and to live next door, is a very earthly example of this kind of experience to which I am referring by reference to Jesus' imagery of branches, figs, and vines.[8] The vineyard is demarcated as a community that is concerned about justice for all of God's children and about peacefulness for all who share this planet as gift. In terms of a theological aesthetic of anguish and anticipation, sin's threefold

---

7. I am choosing to keep the language of the kingdom, even though I empathize with the kin-dom language of Ada Maria Isasi-Diaz, "Solidary: Love of Neighbor in the 1980s," in *Lift Every Voice: Constructing Christian Theologies from the Underside*, ed. Susan Brooks Thistlethwaite and Mary Potter Engel (San Francisco: Harper, 1990), 31–450, esp. 303–5. Because, in this work, I am attempting to situate the implications of an aesthetic imagination on the political realm, "kingdom" seems more pointed. If the gentle reader would, after each encounter with the word "kingdom," be reminded that the object is Beauty's vineyard, the peaceable kingdom of just relations, we will be reminded that such a kingdom is quite unlike the hierarchical, unjust, and oppressive relations typical of its earthly examples.

8. *People* magazine also shared their story. Margaret Nelson Brinkhaus and Lorenzo Benet, "How I Forgave My Son's Murderer" (September 12, 2011), http://www.people.com/people/archive/article/0,,20531391,00.html.

nature—at once personal as emphasized by Saint Augustine, relational as stressed by then-Cardinal Ratzinger, and structural as accentuated for our purposes by Suchocki—distances us relationally from Beauty by introducing veils that prevent us from being able to see or imagine possible alternative relationships, both with God and with neighbor, thereby further blocking the beautiful created order from achieving its Beautiful ends in God.[9] This veiling enters a degree of distancing in the relationship from God into nature that was not there by divine intention. It is undesired and undesirable but, once violations occur, further sin becomes inevitable and, in its inevitability, it becomes natural; it has become an aspect of our nature. Sanctification, then, will entail the Holy Spirit's work in healing these relationships, thereby lifting these veils, restoring nature even beyond its original condition, and removing the relational distance between creation's beauty and the Creator's Beauty. When vision is restored, holy ones will see God, and will see as God sees, a promise that is inherent in the Beatific Vision. But, by jumping to our redemption in Christ through the Holy Spirit's work in lifting the veils of our vision, we are getting ahead of ourselves. We must turn, first, to the reality of sin by examining the extent of its damage in its personal, relational, and structural dimensions.

Beauty's First Veiling: Personal Sin

In its personal dimension, sin is a violation against Beauty, for it limits the degree to which we are able, by nature, to participate in a right relationship with God, with Being, with Beauty. Sin obstructs our ability to see properly, and thereby it prevents us from being able to attain our *telos*, our ultimate end, which is an experience of the Beatific Vision, the vision of God, the vision of Beauty. It prevents us from living eternally with God face-to-face in the peaceable kingdom, for sin blocks the coming into being of the kingdom by making it harder for us to see what is right. Sin makes it more difficult to cooperate with God in bringing beauty about in the created order. Sin hinders us from tending to the garden, so to speak, and it affects the degree to which we are able to enter by our own volition through the garden's gates to experience the vineyard here and now. Sin is that which impedes us from experiencing Beauty's vineyard in its fullness, both on earth and in the hereafter.

---

9. Marjorie Hewitt Suchocki, *The Fall to Violence: Original Sin in Relational Theology* (New York: Continuum, 1995), 13.

This is the reality that St. Augustine articulated by opposing Pelagius in the fifth century. Disagreeing with the assertion that sin merely referred to the choices we make that violate God's divine law and will for us, Augustine asserted that sin is a condition of our being which subsequently impacts the decisions we make. A sinful state of being, he reasoned, is the precondition for sinful actions. Thus, sin is not merely an action or the violation of a law. Rather, throughout sinful existence, Augustine believed that humans have been born with an orientation away from God. In such a state, Augustine observed, we are inclined to please the self more than to do what is altruistic, generous, and God pleasing. Humanity's very nature is sinful. Thus, he said, we do not have the capacity to please God by living according to the law as dictated by Hebrew Scripture or by performing the rituals these Scriptures commanded. Instead, he contended, we required a savior who would come not only to forgive our sins once and for all but also to transform us beyond our created condition. The coming of Christ, in other words, enabled us to be transformed, he thought, from sinners into saints.

In his treatise *On Original Sin*, Augustine controversially articulated five premises against his opponent Coelestius, a disciple of Pelagius, whose teachings were circulating and, Augustine feared, were making redemption in Christ seem nonsensical at worst and unnecessary at best. In these debates, Augustine identified limitations we inherit from our first ancestors. We are, he declared, "originally sinful." Augustine, against his theological opponents, articulated four premises that we will want to remember as we construct Beauty's vineyard. Augustine understood Coelestius to teach:

1. "That a man . . . is able to live *anamartētos*, that is to say, without sin."[10]

2. "That Adam was made mortal, and that he would have died, whether he sinned or did not sin."[11]

10. In the text, Augustine acknowledges that Pelagius "rightly replied" (against Coelestius) that "a man by God's help and grace is able to live *anamartētos*, that is to say, without sin," making the statement acceptable to Augustine due to its emphasis on divine grace. In the list supplied here, I've dropped "by God's help and grace," in order to capture the sense of the position Augustine opposed. See Saint Augustine of Hippo, "Book II: *On Original Sin*," in *The Nicene and Post-Nicene Fathers*, V. St. Augustine: Writings Against the Pelagians (Edinburgh: T & T Clark, 1991), 240.

11. Ibid. Of course, evolutionary history is challenging Augustine's opposition to this premise, a reality to which theologians greater than I are going to have to grapple. It seems that it is quite natural for human beings to die, and that death is

3. "That Adam's sin injured himself alone, and not the human race."[12]

4. "That newborn infants are in the same condition that Adam was before the transgression," so "[that] we are procreated as without virtue, so also without vice."[13]

Augustine feared that, if Coelestius were correct, Christ was unnecessary. If we, by a mere act of will, could live without sin, and if death was natural for the human being, then the first covenant was sufficient to save humankind, thereby making Christ's incarnation and death superfluous.[14] Augustine understood the Christian covenant to fulfill and, indeed, to supersede the Jewish covenant—inscribing a decidedly anti-Jewish thrust into Christian history. Even so, Augustine maintained a position counter to Coelestius on every score. After a fierce debate, Augustine's views were approved at the Council of Carthage (418–419). Keeping the structure parallel to the articulation above, the doctrine can be summarized in this way:

---

introduced long before humans evolved to wreak disaster on the planet. This has obvious implications on our atonement theology, for Anselm believed that Jesus must be both fully human and fully divine in order to pay back a debt satisfaction incurred by human beings for dishonoring God. Anselm believed that Christ repaid the debt by accepting a death that was not owed God since, in Jesus, Christ had lived perfectly obedient to the demands of holiness and need not, according to the medieval imagination, have died.

12. Ibid.

13. Ibid., 241.

14. By this point in history, the break from Judaism was complete, and the anti-Jewish nature of what was being articulated doctrinally is evident. The apostle Paul was distraught that people were turning their backs on the offer of grace and freedom from the law that Christ represented, but Paul did not teach that the Jewish covenant could not save. Indeed, to the contrary, he wrote in his letter to the Romans, "The scripture says, 'No one who believes in him will be put to shame.' For there is no distinction between Jew and Greek; the same Lord is Lord of all and is generous to all who call on him. For, 'Everyone who calls on the name of the Lord shall be saved.' . . . I ask, then, has God rejected his people? By no means! . . . There is a remnant, chosen by grace. . . . If the part of the dough offered as first fruits is holy, then the whole batch is holy; and if the root is holy, then the branches also are holy. . . . So that you may not claim to be wiser than you are, brothers and sisters, I want you to understand this mystery: a hardening has come upon part of Israel, until the full number of the Gentiles has come in. . . . As regards the gospel they are enemies of God for your sake; but as regards election they are beloved, for the sake of their ancestors; for the gifts and the calling of God are irrevocable" (Rom 10:11-13; 11:1a, 5, 16, 25, 28-29).

1. Against the idea that we are able to live without sin, the Council of Carthage emphasized humankind's dependence upon grace:

    a. Canon 111: "That the grace of God not only gives remission of sins, but also affords aid that we sin no more."[15]

    b. Canon 112: "That the grace of Christ gives not only the knowledge of our duty, but also inspires us with a desire that we may be able to accomplish what we know."[16]

    c. Canon 113: "That without the grace of God we can do no good thing."[17]

2. Against the idea that Adam was mortal and would have died even if he had not sinned, the Council of Carthage decreed that Adam was immortal:

    a. Canon 109: "That Adam was not created by God subject to death."[18]

3. Against the idea that sin did not enter the entire human race, the Council of Carthage quoted Scripture:

    a. Canon 114: "That not only humble but also true is that voice of the Saints: 'If we say that we have no sin we deceive ourselves'" (1 John 1:8)[19]

4. Against the idea that newborns share the prelapsarian state of Adam, and so they are morally neutral at birth, the Council of Carthage argues that infants are originally sinful:

    a. Canon 110: "That infants are baptized for the remission of sins."[20]

The amount of ink that has been dedicated over the years to sometimes explicating and sometimes demonizing these teachings and their implications is enormous. Suffice it to say that I am making reference to these canons to retrieve a sense of our brokenness—a brokenness that in my experience and in my observation of the world has a personal

---

15. These canons are quoted from New Advent, "The Council of Carthage," http://www.newadvent.org/fathers/3816.htm.

16. Ibid.

17. Ibid.

18. Ibid.

19. Ibid.

20. Ibid.

dimension.[21] In these canons, I recognize how Augustine is battling with a perspective that suggests that we can do it on our own, and at the same time I worry about the anti-Semitic course the teaching has taken, which appears to nullify the everlasting covenant to the Jews—a course which the Second Vatican Council addresses and to which I will return in this book in the chapter on "Beauty's Incarnation" (see LG 2). Though we must repent this unnecessary direction in which Augustine's theology has taken us, I nevertheless resonate with the impulse here that recognizes a flaw in human nature that is not there by divine intention. In my own observations of human nature, it seems that, indeed, to use Paul's words, we know what is right, but we seem unable to live accordingly without divine grace, a grace that is operative within all who do what is right:

> I do not understand my own actions. For I do not do what I want, but I do the very thing I hate. Now if I do what I do not want, I agree that the law is good. But in fact it is no longer I that do it, but sin that dwells within me. For I know that nothing good dwells within me, that is, in my flesh. I can will what is right, but I cannot do it. For I do not do the good I want, but the evil I do not want is what I do. Now if I do what I do not want, it is no longer I that do it, but sin that dwells within me. So I find it to be a law that when I want to do what is good, evil lies close at hand. For I delight in the law of God in my inmost self, but I see in my members another law at war with the law of my mind, making me captive to the law of sin that dwells in my members. Wretched man that I am! Who will rescue me from this body of death? Thanks be to God through Jesus Christ our Lord! (Rom 7:15-25)

Augustine insists that we are personally dependent on God and God's grace. Goodness provides a gift to humans, by grace, with the capacity for goodness, a capacity that sin does not entirely overcome. Goodness surrounds us constantly with graces that empower us to do what is just, encourage us to be compassionate, and enlighten us to discern what is wise. By grace, when we surrender to the Goodness, Beauty, and Truth that constantly surround us and call us to participate in their holiness, we are revealed more and more vividly as the images of God we are, images partially veiled by sin yet constituting collectively the resurrected Body of Christ until our sinful nature is

---

21. I am grateful to Hamline professor Deanna Thompson for her courage and for the model she provides in confessing personal sin within the construction of a feminist theology. Deanna Thompson, *Crossing the Divide: Luther, Feminism, and the Cross* (Minneapolis, MN: Augsburg Fortress, 2004).

entirely overcome. This is to live the life God intends for us. Humans receive grace upon grace and increasingly participate in the Being of God until they are mystically united with the Source of their being.

Paul envisions that, by grafting Gentiles onto Israel's vine, Christ is breaking open the Jewish covenant, revealing a God who embraces not only those with Jewish ancestry but also the whole of humanity. God is, through Christ, expanding the covenant, revealing the covenant as radically inclusive, thereby opening salvation to the entire human race. This is the blessing promised to Abraham—that through his descendants, God would be made known to the nations. First, through exile and, Christians believe, also through Christ, God has been made known through the lineage of Abraham, the Jewish people, who "remain most dear to God."[22]

So, from Augustine, we retrieve the idea that we inherit a condition by being born into a sin-damaged world that is bent somewhat toward selfishness rather than generosity. We are naturally inclined away from God and toward ourselves. We remain forever dependent on grace. I can perceive in myself, and I can observe in those around me, an inability to respond to God entirely as we ought. Nevertheless, I can sense, too, Beauty's presence and Beauty's desire for relationship with me. But I am incapable on my own of living in relationship to God and to others as I sense Beauty wills for me to live. Certainly in the modern world, we have an expanded vocabulary for speaking of this reality. But it cannot be dismissed entirely by reference to psychology or neurology, for we can experience too grace's power to transform ways of being human in the world beyond what is possible with medications and therapies, as grace-filled as these things can be. Grace is evident when we are enabled to live as Beauty invites us to live, and when we witness Beauty's revelation in the lives of those who have lived beautifully by forgiving easily, acting justly, and living simply. They are a powerful group, this cloud of witnesses, who have walked this way before us.

Augustine grounded his assessment, to be sure, in a more literal reading of Genesis. In a more contemporary articulation, nonetheless in keeping with the Christian theological tradition, the story of Eden enshrines in a story the fleeting moment when, not yet conscious of the ways in which we defy Beauty's hospitable wish for us by our animalistic instincts and self-interested impulses, which cannot yet be considered sinful since they are committed prior to consciousness, humans evolve to become self-aware. Adam and Eve represent humankind emerging

---

22. Ibid.

from a state of moral innocence into a state of moral consciousness. They evolve, recognizing that there is a Being to whom they are in relation— a Divine Beauty who has revealed God's Beauty with a creation that continues to participate in divine life. Humankind fails to recognize until it is too late, however, that with our freedom, we can damage the whole of created being by committing even just one rebellious act, its damage having personal, relational, and structural repercussions, its ripples almost never ending. As a result, humankind's freedom ever after becomes restricted—to some degree, tainted—as it is by all the destruction that has come before. Nonetheless, the damage done to the whole of being can be repaired by habituating holy acts—acts that are always a complex dance between predisposing graces already in human nature responding to and cooperating with God's beautiful invitation. Although Christian theologians differ about the dynamics of nature and grace that make this repair possible, the Jewish imagination refers to this gradual healing of creation as *tikkun olam*, the repair of the world.

Among contemporary theologians who retain an understanding of original sin is Marjorie Hewitt Suchocki, who speaks less in terms of concupiscence, Augustine's term for "desire," typically for that which is ungodly. Suchocki speaks more in terms of an innate penchant for violence that she considers to be the root of our sinful condition. For Suchocki, sin is a "participation through intent or act in unnecessary violence that contributes to the ill-being of any aspect of earth or its inhabitants."[23] She describes its trifold structure as "a bent toward violence through our evolution, the interwoven relationality that creates a solidarity to the human race, and the temporal structures of intersubjectivity through which we inherit assumptions concerning how we interpret, value, and act in our world. Insofar as these presuppose the ill-being of any aspect of creation, then we are involved in support and perpetuation of that ill-being. We are sinners."[24]

But we need not make the theological moves Suchocki makes to a God in the process of becoming in order to protect a sense of divine relationality, on the one hand, and human accountability, on the other. Taken in light of the traditional metaphysics with which I have been working here, such a move introduces a Being who is not fully Good, Beautiful, and True and is, thus, to a degree—even if slight—evil, deformed, and deceptive. This is not a God to whom I wish to offer worship or praise. Rather, it is possible that a wholly Good, Beautiful, and

23. Suchocki, *The Fall to Violence*, 12.
24. Ibid., 13.

True God lovingly created the world in which we live and breathe and have our being, intending for us the peaceable kingdom. Built into the human being is a self-protective instinct, which is a good thing. It has enabled our survival. It is, fundamentally, a principle in defense of life. But often, prior to self-consciousness and extending into the phase of self-consciousness, protection of life for the continuation of the species has been accomplished by violence and aggression. Also available to humans has been the potential to share and to collaborate in order to enable the thriving of the entire community, including neighboring tribes. Self-consciousness made us aware that aggression was not the only way to be—that we had options available to us, including creative strategies to disarm an opponent without resorting to violence, a way that Christ demonstrated in his life. If we had exercised our newly discovered and self-conscious freedom in a holy way, that is, in a nonviolent manner, the peaceable kingdom could have been ours. Eden represents this possibility. We have chosen instead, however, to employ aggression—an aggression that was, in Suchocki's words, unnecessary and avoidable. Through it, we have harmed relationships both with God and with neighbor. We have violated life, turning instead toward evil and violence. This sinful way of being, aggressive and violent, has become normalized. It has become rooted in our nature, and we have attempted to justify it. In Suchocki's words, "We are by nature an aggressive species with a history of physical and psychic violence. Killing is violence; greed and verbal abuse are also violence. Violence has many forms existing along a continuum from obvious to subtle, but at its base, violence is the destruction of well-being. The capacity for violence is built into our species through aggressive instincts related to survival. When that violence is unnecessary and avoidable, it is sin."[25]

As beings possessing freedom, the potential for sinful aggression has been there always, to be sure. But, as Augustine articulated centuries ago, God is only accountable for the *potential* for us to exercise our freedom against God, a potential that is innate to any created being, for only an uncreated Being has no privation of Goodness, Beauty, and Truth. The actualization of that sinful aggression, however, and fault for it lies with humankind and in humankind alone—in us, who chose to normalize violence rather than holy strategies of nonviolence, choices with consequences that all humans still bear.[26] Holy choices, too, have been always available

---

25. Ibid., 85.
26. Augustine, *Anti-Pelagian Writings: On Original Sin* (Grand Rapids, MI: Eerdmans, 1971).

to us and have always been God's holy wish for us. But once aggression was chosen over its very possible alternative, "Our birthmark," says Suchocki, "is a common capacity for violence, or an aggressiveness written deep within the structures of our being. This heritage lies behind our universal ability to live and act in such a way that we violate the well-being of some aspect of creation. We sin."[27] Suchocki does not refer to the predisposing graces about which the tradition speaks but speaks instead of instincts toward bonding: "Instincts toward bonding are also primal within us, and self-transcendence through memory, empathy, and imagination makes it possible for bonding rather than aggressiveness to be our dominant mode of being."[28] Our nature, then, neither wholly sinful and violent nor wholly altruistic and peace loving, requires, in my words, divine assistance.

With these careful nuances, then, the situation remains dire. Whether described using the terms of self-centeredness about which Augustine spoke or the bent toward violence about which Suchocki speaks, we are shaped by the past, which impacts our future. Having internalized a way of self-centeredness and violence that seems to us nothing but natural, we live in fear, always vulnerable to the self-interest and violence of the other. As Suchocki rightly observes, "We threaten to destroy not only each other, and the whole species of other animal life, but even the planet itself."[29] She reappropriates Augustine's insights about selfishness and pride by noting that "anxiety emerges as a relationally based response to the pervasive effects of violence throughout the earth. Pride and self-centeredness are ways of coping with and covering our own sins of needless violence. . . . We continue to be prey to our own violence, the sin that so easily besets us."[30] Suchocki's perceptions about violence, restored within a view of God as relating to us from a perspective of Absolute Goodness, Truth, and Beauty enables us to reclaim Augustine's doctrine of original sin, recognizing its impact on us on a personal, that is, on an individual level.

If, indeed, the young African American man in Kehinde Wiley's *Dead Christ* was killed, as are so many, by gun violence in American culture, individual sinfulness is represented by the aggression of the one who freely pulled the trigger. The murderer has actualized a potential latent within all of us. Given the same circumstances, any of us might have done the same thing in a cycle into which too many are drawn. Disadvantaged

---

27. Suchocki, *The Fall to Violence*, 94.
28. Ibid., 95.
29. Ibid., 99.
30. Ibid.

by the normalization of a dominantly white male culture where black men are disempowered, and often born into homes coping with poverty, homes headed by single moms working more than one job to feed their children, too many African American males are unable to break into the workforce after receiving a substandard education in schools funded by tax codes that favor communities of privilege. Too many find themselves in situations where escape is sought through alcohol and drugs. These situations then spiral, accelerated by ready access to gangs, drugs, and guns. Systems of oppression intertwine with individual choices to create a living hell. Kehinde Wiley's painting suggests that, if Christ were incarnate through the scandal of particularity in today's culture, he would be in solidarity with those who are very often oppressed in America—with African Americans. Just as he lived among the poor and ostracized in his own first-century Palestine under Roman occupation—immigrants, lepers, widows, prostitutes, and Samaritans—so would he live among the poor and ostracized in urban America. Eventually, in our own context, someone would pull the trigger. Another would be shot and killed. This is the vigilante justice exercised on the streets of our cities—and it kills Christ, whom we are to see in the faces of every person we encounter.

But we are beginning to recognize the insufficiency of any account of sin as solely individual. We are beginning to recognize that sin's impact on each of us is not merely personal. As we relate to the world and to those around us, we are beginning to recognize that sin's damage has been more extensive than this treatment describes. Sin's havoc extends beyond the one who commits the crime. The one who murders, as in the present example, is not the only one who is harmed by the violation. Understanding sin as affecting us only individually, and understanding the harm done only in terms of the one who pulls the trigger, is incomplete. It is not only the murderer who requires redemption. For we live in community. We are communal by nature. We are not only damaged personally by sin and its violence but also relationally. It is to the second of these dimensions that we now turn.

Beauty's Second Veiling: Relational Sin

To use a simile, sin is like a cancer. It manifests itself in an individual person, more precisely in an individual person's imagination, and eats away at it, harming the spiritual health of the one bearing the illness. In this case, as in some cancers, the disease is genetic. Augustine thought that all of humankind inherited the disease from the generation before it. Augustine understood this cancer to manifest itself in a diseased will, disabling it from desiring what it ought to desire, namely, communion with God. Thus, the cure was conceived as a need to heal each individual will, just as treatments are individualized to target and to cure cancer. In terms of original sin, the cure was accomplished by receiving a number of medicinal treatments, if you will—an infusion of medicinal graces, beginning with baptism and then followed by a lifetime of additional sacramental therapies. All of these restore the will, even beyond its original condition of mere neutrality. It is shaped more and more into a will aligned with Christ's and thereby with God's own holy will, increasingly willing that which is purely good. A community of souls so transformed by grace is meant to constitute the church, even the Vineyard, a countercultural witness to the world in which we live our common lives, imperfect as they are.

The insufficiency of merely a personal understanding of sin is evident, though, by making a comparison. Let's imagine the sinful person is not diseased by cancer but by alcoholism. The disease of alcoholism damages the one who is addicted to alcohol, to be sure. But the damage does not end there. The alcoholism damages all of the afflicted one's relationships, especially those with whom the alcoholic is closest: the alcoholic's spouse, children, and colleagues. The alcoholic harms too the afflicted one's loved ones, who are not able to trust as they once were, maybe even extending the alcoholic condition to one or more in his household. This example reveals itself in a way that the cancer analogy cannot, because cancers for the most part are not contagious. Sin cannot be understood as merely individual, as something that affects only the one who is sinful. Rather, sin is something that damages individuals and communities bound by relationship. Sin, in other words, is both personal and relational—a sense that is captured by then-Cardinal Ratzinger, later Pope Benedict XVI, in his homilies on Genesis, as well as by Marjorie Hewitt Suchocki in her understanding of sin through human solidarity.

In his homilies on Genesis, Cardinal Ratzinger interprets the account of Adam and Eve, deriving from it the affirmation that human beings are the same—ultimately dust—whether kings or peasants. We are beings who are dependent on God for our very being, the future pope affirms. We are "God's projects," as God shapes us into the persons God intends for us to be.[31] Created in God's image and likeness, humans possess, Cardinal Ratzinger insists, an inviolable dignity: "Each human being is known by God and loved by him. Each is willed by God, and each is God's image."[32] Because each person emerges from the "same

---

31. Joseph Ratzinger, "The Creation of the Human Being," in *In the Beginning: A Catholic Understanding of the Story of Creation and the Fall*, trans. Boniface Ramsey, (Grand Rapids, MI: Eerdmans, 1990), 42–43.

32. Ibid., 45.

creative idea of God," human life is precious and sacred, and "stands under God's special protection."[33] This is because "however wretched or exalted he or she may be, however sick or suffering, however good-for-nothing or important, whether born or unborn, whether incurably ill or radiant with health—each one bears God's breath in himself or herself, each one is God's image."[34] As images of a Trinitarian God, who is an eternal *perichoresis* of the Father, Son, and Holy Spirit—or, in the terms to which we have been referring, an eternal relationship among persons who are Good, Beautiful, and True—to be human is also to be inherently in relationship. Cardinal Ratzinger affirms, "To be the image of God implies relationality."[35] And so, in this inherent relationality, we understand sin as not only personal but also relational.

The relational nature of sin is revealed in the creation accounts in Genesis. For then-Cardinal Ratzinger, the story of Adam and Eve explains not "how human persons come to be but rather what they are."[36] He writes, "We cannot say: creation *or* evolution, inasmuch as these two things respond to two different realities."[37] Thus, Adam represents the one who develops an evolved consciousness and thus signifies the one "with whom the history of sin begins."[38] Because "sin begets sin, . . . all the sins of history are interlinked."[39] Cardinal Ratzinger defends the doctrine of original sin by attempting to understand better the nature of the human person. According to Ratzinger, we are damaged not only personally by sin but also as an entire human race. His paragraph about this reality is striking, and so it is replicated here in full.

> Human beings are relational, and they possess their lives—themselves—only by way of relationship. I alone am not myself, but only in and with you am I myself. To be truly a human being means to be related in love, to be *of* and *for*. But sin means the damaging or the destruction of relationality. Sin is a rejection of relationality because it wants to make the human being a god. Sin is loss of relationship, disturbance of relationship, and therefore it is not restricted to the individual. When I destroy a relationship, then this event—sin—touches the other person involved in the relationship. Consequently sin is always an offense that touches others, that alters the world and damages it. To the extent that this is true,

33. Ibid.
34. Ibid.
35. Ibid., 47.
36. Ibid., 50.
37. Ibid.
38. Ibid., 71.
39. Ibid.

> when the network of human relationships is damaged from the very beginning, then every human being enters into a world that is marked by relational damage. At the very moment that a person begins human existence, which is a good, he or she is confronted by a sin-damaged world. Each of us enters into a situation in which relationality has been hurt. Consequently each person is, from the very start, damaged in relationships and does not engage in them as he or she ought. Sin pursues the human being, and he or she capitulates to it.[40]

According to Ratzinger, once humans sinned against God in our primordial past, the entire trajectory of the human race was affected. The human race inherited all of the relational damage that had been incurred. And while the damage was devastating, it was not entire, as Luther and the Protestant movement after him believed. Martin Luther believed in "the deep, wicked, abominable, inexpressible corruption of our entire nature, in all of its powers."[41] John Calvin maintained that we were, as a result of Adam's sin, "utterly depraved."[42] These theologies left no beauty in the human being with which the Holy Spirit could work, requiring John Wesley to develop a theology of regeneration. The Council of Trent, however, articulated a middle position between two extremes—between the total devastation enunciated by the Reformers, on the one hand, and the hopeful optimism enunciated by Pelagianism, on the other. The council articulated a position that humans retained a free will that "for all that it had been weakened and sapped in strength, was in no way extinct."[43] The freedom that the will retained was itself a grace, predisposing it to God, such that the human being could not claim even faith in God as a work credited to the self (Eph 2:8-9).

> The council further declares that actual justification in adults takes its origin from the predisposing grace of God through Jesus Christ, that is, from his invitation which calls them, with no existing merits on their side; thus, those who had been turned away from God by sins are disposed by God's grace inciting and helping them to turn toward their own justification by giving free assent to and cooperating with the same grace. Consequently, though God touches a person's heart through the light of the Holy Spirit, neither does that person do absolutely nothing in receiv-

---

40. Ibid., 72–73.

41. Theodore Tappert, *The Book of Concord: The Confessions of the Evangelical Lutheran Church* (Philadelphia, PA: Fortress Press, 1959), 510.

42. John Calvin, *Institutes of the Christian Religion*, trans. Henry Beveridge, Christian Classics Ethereal Library (2001); http://www.ccel.org/c/calvin/institutes/institutes.html.

43. Council of Trent, Session 6, chap. 1.

ing that movement of grace, for he can also reject it; nor is he able, by his own free will and without God's grace, to move himself toward justice in God's sight. Hence, when Scripture says, *Return to me and I will return to you*, we are being reminded of our freedom; when we answer, *Restore us to yourself, O Lord, that we may be restored*, we are admitting that we are forestalled by the grace of God.[44]

That the will retains this degree of power to give free assent to and to cooperate with God is itself a grace—alternately referred to in the tradition either as a prevenient or a predisposing grace in the nature of the person. This grace enables the will to respond to God, "inciting" and "helping" it to give assent to and cooperate with additional graces that continually hearken the will to align with God's Beauty. Thus, to have faith is not something we can credit to ourselves, even while maintaining that the faithful are not elected or predestined by God to have faith in the way that either Luther or Calvin spoke of it. If we understand God as Beauty Absolute, and if we imagine the impact of sin on us personally in an Augustinian sense (with relational damage as interpreted by Cardinal Ratzinger), we recognize that the beauty in our being, gifted to us by God, is veiled to a degree by our birth into a world already damaged by sin. As a result, we are not able to participate in the world as we ought, and we are dependent on grace for our redemption, a redemption that has both this-worldly and otherworldly realities, a redemption that cures us personally and relationally.

Marjorie Hewitt Suchocki grounds the relational dimension of sin in a human experience of violence that damages more than the one who commits the sinful act. She writes of our human solidarity. "We are individuals, but we are also participants in an organic whole much greater than ourselves, the human species. In an interrelated world, all things co-exist, and those things most closely related to ourselves in the vast scheme of things exercise a definitive impact on who we are and how we are."[45] Because of this "organic solidarity of the race, we are," she asserts, "affected by the sins of others, and our own sins likewise have an effect upon all others."[46] Indeed, she understands relationality as constitutive of what it is to be—thus, to be human is to be interrelated with the whole of humanity: "Relationships are constitutive of existence, and therefore through relationships all things are woven together."[47] The implications

---

44. Ibid., chap. 5.
45. Suchocki, *The Fall of Violence*, 101.
46. Ibid.
47. Ibid., 104.

are evident enough. "Evil anywhere is mediated everywhere through the relational structure of existence."[48] Suchocki also states,

> The internal nature of relationships means that what happens in one entity has an effect on all entities. When this effect is evil, that evil spreads until it touches all. It seeps pervasively through the ground, percolating from depths of original sin and personalized sin in ever-successive layers of pollution. And the effects are not simply external, like a stain that can be washed away. Rather, the effects are internalized within each affected entity, forming one aspect of how the entity experiences the world. The interrelationality of existence creates a solidarity of the race that involves each in the plight of all.[49]

Suchocki recognizes that we are, by our relationality, "bound up with one another's good, [and] woven into one another's welfare."[50] She maintains that "such a reality is easy to acknowledge at the personal level, but the deeper reality is that our relationality extends far wider than our consciousness is capable of handling. To live in a relational universe is to be affected physically and psychically by everything and everyone that exists."[51] Therefore, "we are bound up with one another throughout the earth, inexorably inheriting from each, inexorably influencing all. Our prized individuality exists through connectedness."[52]

> We participate in violence in many modes, at many levels, from economic deprivations of entire populations, to various psychic oppressions of many peoples, to the outright physical and mental agony inflicted on persons through wars, political tortures, and crime. And if through the solidarity of the race, we necessarily are affected by all violence everywhere, we must perforce respond to this violence, whether subliminally or consciously. And the subliminal response is simply anxiety.[53]

In other words, both Cardinal Ratzinger and Marjorie Hewitt Suchocki implore us to understand the nature of sinfulness as that which damages not only our individual souls but also the relational realm in which we live and breathe and have our being. Thus, when an African American man is shot, it is not just the one who pulls the trigger who is damaged by the sin of killing—though certainly the violation is manifested there first and foremost. The victim is harmed, as the victim's

48. Ibid.
49. Ibid.
50. Ibid.
51. Ibid.
52. Ibid.
53. Ibid., 108.

mother and father and siblings are likewise wounded, as is the entire community that can no longer continue with their lives as if nothing has happened. Individuals within the community live in fear. They might seek justice. And they might seek vengeance. Relationships of trust and forbearance are damaged. This is the situation into which the next generation is born, as distrust and cynicism become embedded. Many people respond in ways that are not necessarily life affirming. Some commit personal sins of violence against another, and the cycle of violence continues.

Yet even this description is an insufficient account of the situation in which we find ourselves. We are beginning to recognize that sin's impact on each of us is not merely personal and relational—it is also structural. As we engage in a world that is increasingly accessible to us not only locally and nationally but also globally, we are beginning to recognize that sin's damage has been even more extensive than an account of its personal and relational dimensions adequately describes. Sin's impact extends beyond the one who commits the crime and even beyond those who are relationally bound to the wrongdoing and its interior damage. The one who murders is not the only one who is harmed by the violation, nor are those who are in the social network of the one wronged by the crime the only ones who are violated. For we are persons who live in communities shaped by social structures into which sin has also penetrated. We are not only damaged personally by sin and its violence. Sin seeps not only into the relational levels of our existence but also into the structural dimensions of our world. It is to this dimension that we now turn.

Beauty's Third Veiling: Structural Sin

The account of sin as we have examined it thus far is incomplete, for it fails to take into account the systems we create that have been infiltrated by sin, structures that have been engineered to benefit some and disadvantage others by their relative distance from seats of power. In order better to understand the world's sinful structures, let's turn to the work of physician and scholar Paul Farmer.[54] He practices medicine in Haiti, among other places; half the year he also teaches medical anthropology at Harvard. Farmer's experiences in the poorest places of the world inform his scholarship. As a witness to the ways people in the inner cities of the United States, Peru, Mexico, Russia, and Haiti (where

---

54. A previous version of this section was published in Kimberly Vrudny, "Religion, Ethics, and AIDS," in *Religious and Ethical Perspectives for the Twenty-First Century*, ed. Paul Myhre (Winona, MN: Anselm Press, 2012), 112–39.

he has conducted most of his anthropological work) are challenged by poverty-related health problems in general, and with issues associated with HIV/AIDS in particular, he has written a number of books and articles attempting to help leaders in health and human rights understand the interrelationships between poverty and public health. These books include *Women, Poverty, and AIDS: Sex, Drugs, and Structural Violence*, as well as *Pathologies of Power: Health, Human Rights, and the New War on the Poor*, among others. These works will be instructive for us as we attempt to understand the nature of structural sin.[55]

Significantly, Farmer has not lost sight of the personhood of those with whom he comes face-to-face as both a doctor and an anthropologist. Farmer writes in *Pathologies of Power*,

> This book is a physician-anthropologist's effort to reveal the ways in which the most basic right—the right to survive—is trampled in an age of great affluence, and it argues that the matter should be considered the most pressing one of our times. The drama, the tragedy, of the destitute sick concerns not only physicians and scholars who work among the poor but all who profess even a passing interest in human rights. It's not much of a stretch to argue that anyone who wishes to be considered humane has ample cause to consider what it means to be sick and poor in the era of globalization and scientific advancement.[56]

Farmer's words are what theologians might consider prophetic. In attending to systemic causes of public health crises throughout the world, Farmer's words are received as an interruption to the status quo, potentially disturbing those from whom is often hidden the plight of men, women, and children most detrimentally impacted by the structures as they are engineered.[57] He writes,

---

55. Paul Farmer, *Pathologies of Power: Health, Human Rights, and the New War on the Poor* (Berkeley, CA: University of California Press, 2005), and Paul Farmer, Margaret Connors, and Janie Simmons, eds., *Women, Poverty, and AIDS: Sex, Drugs, and Structural Violence* (Monroe, ME: Common Courage Press, 1996). See also Tracy Kidder, *Mountains Beyond Mountains: The Quest of Dr. Paul Farmer, A Man Who Would Cure the World* (New York: Random House, 2004).

56. Farmer, *Pathologies*, 6.

57. "Interruption" is a term used within political theology. Coined by Catholic theologian Johann Baptist Metz, "interruption" points to the recognition that the "concerns of first world people are not like those of the third world." Bryan Pham describes Metz's theology by acknowledging that, "for the most part, we [in the first world] are not dealing with a population that is lacking in material goods. The concerns of the people of the first world are the concerns that deal with excess; we have entered a cycle of consuming too much [and we do not see] how destructive this

Human rights violations are not accidents; they are not random in distribution or effect. Rights violations are, rather, symptoms of deeper pathologies of power and are linked intimately to the social conditions that so often determine who will suffer abuse and who will be shielded from harm. If assaults on dignity are anything but random in distribution or course, whose interests are served by the suggestion that they are haphazard?[58]

Farmer goes on to ask a series of questions that anyone interested in becoming involved in public health ought to ask so that, first and foremost, he or she will abide by the axiom "Do no harm."

Can we identify the worst assaults? Those most at risk of great suffering? Among persons whose suffering is not fatal, is it possible to identify those most at risk of sustaining permanent and disabling damage? Are certain "event" assaults, such as torture or rape, more likely to lead to later *sequelae* than is sustained and insidious suffering, such as the pain born of deep poverty or racism? Are certain forms of insidious discrimination demonstrably more noxious than others? . . . By what mechanisms, precisely, do social forces ranging from poverty to racism become embodied as individual experience?[59]

Already in the 1970s, Johan Galtung, a Norwegian scholar who is credited with founding peace and justice studies as an academic discipline, coined the phrase "structural violence" to capture the reality that there is a cumulative negative effect on a person's ability to thrive in one's society based on one's relative distance from those with sociopolitical and economic power.[60] He also wrote about cultural violence, where

---

is to us and to our world; the results are always emptiness and destruction. Metz's interruption is aimed at waking us up from our dreamy world and [disrupting] our apparently comfortable lives by forcing us to look around our world and see how destructive we can be when we are blind to the suffering of those around us. Metz would say that we are then attentive to the 'other.' These kinds of disruptions can come as dangerous memories where we remember events of the past that question our consciences. Furthermore, Metz thinks that they have trapped us inside egotistic and ethnocentric mentalities; as a result, a political theology will interrupt us in our endless cycle of mundaneness of life and liberate us from consumption that in the end always leaves us not in fulfillment, but in emptiness of heart." See Bryan Pham, "Political Theology: Interruption," http://guweb2.gonzaga.edu/metz/theo.html.

58. Farmer, *Pathologies*, 7.

59. Ibid., 30.

60. Johan Galtung, "Violence, Peace, and Peace Research," *Journal of Peace Research* 6, no. 3 (1969): 167–91.

relative degrees of power are associated with one's race, class, gender, and so on, because of the way in which social systems are organized such that they benefit those most like the powerful, who are privileged by such systems, and such that they disadvantage those most unlike the powerful, who are underprivileged or disadvantaged by the social structures so established.[61] Thus, Galtung differentiated between direct violence, such as the violence of armed conflict, and cultural and structural forms of violence, that can simmer for a time in societies which are able to tolerate some degree of disparity. But there is a threshold, he theorized. When societies cross the line and the division between the rich and the poor, the privileged and the disadvantaged, becomes too great, unless there is a correction of course, it is only a matter of time until the situation boils over into direct violence.[62]

Regardless of the fault or guilt of the powerful persons or societies that initially shaped systems that benefit some to the disadvantage of others, these are systems into which humans are socialized and which are normalized over centuries. They are woven into the fabric of societal, religious, political, and economic expectation, causing even those experiencing their harshest impact to assume that this is just the way it is and always has been, and that there is nothing that can be done about it. As psychologists Deborah DuNann Winter and Dana C. Leighton have observed, "Direct violence is horrific, but its brutality usually gets our attention: we notice it, and often respond to it. Structural violence, however, is almost always invisible, embedded in ubiquitous social structures, normalized by stable institutions and regular experience." The authors go on, "Because they are longstanding, structural inequities usually seem ordinary, the way things are and always have been."[63]

Paul Farmer believes harmful structures can be dismantled, however, and that healthier designs can be developed and implemented, as he has demonstrated by founding Partners in Health, an organization "providing a preferential option for the poor in health care."[64] In terms of naming the problem, Farmer combines Galtung's categories and offers several definitions for structural violence as a means of explicating how the underprivileged are relatively more at risk, for example, for acquiring an HIV/AIDS infection than their more privileged counterparts.

---

61. Ibid.

62. Ibid.

63. Deborah DuNann Winter and Dana C. Leighton, "Structural Violence," in *Peace, Conflict, and Violence: Peace Psychology in the 21st Century*, ed. D. J. Christie, R. V. Wagner, and D. D. Winter (New York: Prentice Hall, 2001).

64. Partners in Health, http://www.pih.org.

All of these definitions share the idea that structural violence refers to a detrimental impact on human life as the result of socially engineered inequalities that constrain agency and brutalize populations negatively impacted by systems as they stand.

1. "I use [structural violence] as a broad rubric that includes a host of offenses against human dignity: extreme and relative poverty, social inequalities ranging from racism to gender inequality, and more spectacular forms of violence that are uncontestedly human rights abuses."[65]

2. "[Structural violence refers to] social and economic inequities that determine who will be at risk for assaults and who will be shielded from them."[66]

3. "Suffering is 'structured' by historically given (and often economically driven) processes and forces that conspire—whether through routine, ritual, or, as is more commonly the case, the hard surfaces of life—to constrain agency. For many . . . choices both large and small are limited by racism, sexism, political violence, and grinding poverty."[67]

4. "Social factors including gender, ethnicity ('race'), and socioeconomic status may each play a role in rendering individuals and groups vulnerable to extreme human suffering. . . . Simultaneous consideration of various social 'axes' is imperative in efforts to discern a political economy of brutality."[68]

Another way of conceptualizing structural violence is to look carefully at varying degrees of jeopardy any given sector of the population has in relation to those who occupy seats of power. In the United States, for example, a person's jeopardy is measured by degrees of separation from middle-aged, insured, able-bodied/minded, well-educated, native-born citizens who are affluent, Caucasian, heterosexual, and male Christians. Such a structure can be broken down into the following categories or systems of jeopardy, to name only the most prominent, alongside systems of privilege:

65. Farmer, *Pathologies*, 8.
66. Ibid., 17–18.
67. Ibid., 40.
68. Ibid., 42–43.

SYSTEMS OF JEOPARDY
(CULTURES AND STRUCTURES OF VIOLENCE AND PRIVILEGE)

Realm of Cultural Violence

SINGLE DEGREE OF JEOPARDY

Gender Disadvantage

Sexism: Female.

DOUBLE DEGREE OF JEOPARDY

Skin Disadvantage

Ethnocentrism/Racism: female person of color.

TRIPLE DEGREE OF JEOPARDY

Orientation Disadvantage

Heterosexism: (female) lesbian person of color.

QUADRUPLE DEGREE OF JEOPARDY

Age Disadvantage

Ageism: Elderly (female) lesbian person of color.

PENTUPLE DEGREE OF JEOPARDY

Religious Disadvantage

Anti-Semitism or anti-Muslimism (for example):
Muslim elderly (female) lesbian person of color.

Realm of Structural Violence

SEXTUPLE DEGREE OF JEOPARDY

Health-Care Disadvantage

Uninsured: Muslim elderly (female) lesbian person of color
who is uninsured.

SEPTUPLE DEGREE OF JEOPARDY

Physical and Mental Disadvantage

Ableism: Muslim elderly (female) lesbian person of color
who is uninsured and physically or mentally disabled.

OCTUPLE DEGREE OF JEOPARDY

Educational Disadvantage

Elitism: Muslim elderly (female) lesbian person of color
who is uninsured, physically or mentally disabled, and illiterate/
undereducated.

NONUPLE DEGREE OF JEOPARDY

Economic Disadvantage / Employment Status

Classism: Muslim elderly (female) lesbian person of color
who is uninsured, physically or mentally disabled, illiterate/
undereducated, and poor/unemployed.

DECUPLE DEGREE OF JEOPARDY

Citizenship Disadvantage

Xenophobism: Muslim elderly (female) lesbian person of color who is
uninsured, physically or mentally disabled, illiterate/undereducated,
poor/unemployed, and an unnaturalized citizen.

Realm of Cultural Privilege

SINGLE DEGREE OF ADVANTAGE

Gender Advantage

Gender: Male.

DOUBLE DEGREE OF ADVANTAGE

Skin Advantage

Ethnicity: Caucasian male.

TRIPLE DEGREE OF ADVANTAGE

Orientation Advantage

Orientation: Heterosexual Caucasian male.

QUADRUPLE DEGREE OF ADVANTAGE

Age Advantage

Age: Middle-aged, heterosexual Caucasian male.

PENTUPLE DEGREE OF ADVANTAGE

Religious Advantage

Religion: Christian, middle-aged, heterosexual Caucasian male.

Realm of Structural Privilege

SEXTUPLE DEGREE OF ADVANTAGE

Health-Care Advantage

Status: Christian, middle-aged, heterosexual Caucasian male
who is insured.

SEPTUPLE DEGREE OF ADVANTAGE

Physical and Mental Advantage

Ability: Christian, middle-aged, heterosexual Caucasian male
who is insured, mentally and physically able-bodied.

OCTUPLE DEGREE OF ADVANTAGE

Educational Advantage

Education: Christian, middle-aged, heterosexual Caucasian male who
is insured, mentally and physically able-bodied, and well educated.

NONUPLE DEGREE OF ADVANTAGE

Economic Advantage / Employment Status

Class: Christian, middle-aged, heterosexual Caucasian male
who is insured, mentally and physically able-bodied, well educated,
and wealthy/well employed.

DECUPLE DEGREE OF ADVANTAGE

Citizenship Advantage

Citizenship status: Christian, middle-aged, heterosexual Caucasian
male who is insured, mentally and physically able-bodied,
well educated, wealthy/well employed, and a natural born US citizen.

And so on . . .[69]

---

69. See Kimberly Vrudny, "Religion, Ethics, and AIDS," in *Religious and Ethical Perspectives for the Twenty-First Century*, ed. Paul O. Myhre (Winona, MN: Anselm Academic, 2013), 121.

Of course, there are many additional personal factors that can influence one's ability to attain even a modest level of economic security. These very often account for those rare but nonetheless present examples of people with many degrees of jeopardy operating against them who nonetheless beat the odds and find sometimes phenomenal degrees of financial success. What is the individual's marital status, if indeed marriage is legally available? How many steady sources of income does the household have—zero, one, or two? What burden of debt does one's household carry? Are there assets to inherit from previous generations? Are there dependents in the household? How many? Is there familial support, particularly to care for little ones when one is working, or to provide shelter in case of job loss? From what kind of family does the individual come? Is there an abusive background? Is there a history of addiction in the family? Was the individual longed for and loved—or was he or she frequently berated? What is the individual's intelligence quotient? What skills come easily to the person? Are these skills in demand or obscure? What kind of safety net does the family, community, or government offer in case of temporary setbacks? Will those setbacks remain temporary, or will they become permanent, internalized, and generational? Such factors, however, do not disprove the inertia that the systems of jeopardy can and do have on entire communities.

Indeed, a person's vulnerability to poverty, illness, and homelessness increases by the degree to which one is disadvantaged culturally and structurally by systems tolerated by society. This is not difficult to illustrate. Consider these two individuals and the opportunities before them. The first is a Muslim immigrant to the United States from Somalia, who is unmarried because she identifies herself now, deep into adulthood, as a lesbian, though she cannot reveal this in her community. Despite her orientation, she has one dependent daughter who was born from an arranged marriage into which she entered at twenty. Her husband died in the region's hostilities. Due to the unrest in her country, she fled to this country in the early 1990s with her daughter who was then a toddler. She was given assistance from an organization that was devoted to helping refugees find security in the United States, the country that had agreed to give her temporary asylum. Now lost in the system, she is in her early forties. She is beginning to struggle with hypertension and diabetes related to her diet, consisting of inexpensive foods easily accessible at a corner gas station and consisting mainly of empty calories, mostly from carbohydrates. She lost her job as a maid in a hotel several years ago when the economy took a downturn. Despite her broken English, the hotel had given her a job without checking to see her green card, which had long since expired. She struggles each day to support herself, as well as her daughter, who is now raising a baby on her own.

The second individual is a white man in his early fifties. He is heterosexual, married, and has two children. He has no disabilities and was born and raised in the United States by fourth-generation citizens from England who paid outright for his private elementary and secondary schooling, which prepared him to attend Harvard for both his undergraduate and law degrees. He works as the CEO of a multinational corporation. He practices Christianity and is well respected in his church and suburban communities.

Comparing these stories makes it surpassingly evident that, despite the fact that we live within the myth that everyone has an equal opportunity to succeed in America, there is a great deal of disparity in opportunity for this woman and this man. It is obvious that the Somali woman has many more obstacles to overcome in order to achieve economic security and relative stability than the Harvard-educated white man working in business law. She has ten degrees of jeopardy operating against her while he has none. Yet, the mythic imagination in the United States suggests that things are structured in such a way that, if she only worked harder, she too could have everything that he has acquired. When she loses her home, runs out of food, and the community no longer will support her, what choices will she have? Many women, faced with these kinds of circumstances, find themselves selling their bodies for a loaf of bread. Men and women in such situations frequently turn to drug and alcohol use as a means of escape. Indeed, the Somali woman has so few choices available to her that pointing to her freedom and condemning her for her choices is duplicitous at best—yet this is common practice, and often goes without challenge, even in America's religious communities.

When stories like these are shared, people often rationalize, thinking, "But this woman's situation is very rare." But it is increasingly common to find someone with multiple degrees of jeopardy—and the chasm differentiating the disadvantaged from the privileged in America is growing ever wider.

> As of 2007, the top 1% of households (the upper class) owned 34.6% of all privately held wealth, and the next 19% (the managerial, professional, and small business stratum) had 50.5%, which means that just 20% of the people owned a remarkable 85%, leaving only 15% of the wealth for the bottom 80% (wage and salary workers). In terms of financial wealth (total net worth minus the value of one's home), the top 1% of households had an even greater share: 42.7%.[70]

70. G. William Domhoff, "Wealth, Income, and Power," September 2005; updated January 2011, http://sociology.ucsc.edu/whorulesamerica/power/wealth.html.

Moreover, the top 1% leverages a great deal of political and corporate power, with enough influence to manipulate efforts toward leveling the playing field at state, national, and multinational levels.

Obviously, most people in the United States are somewhere in between the Somali woman and the Harvard-educated CEO. Nonetheless, it is evident that opportunity in America is engineered, it is structured to favor those who share more in common with the white man than with the immigrant woman. In neighborhoods with high concentrations of poverty, which are overwhelmingly occupied in the United States by people of color, school systems are often less effective, creating masses of people who are ill equipped to find meaningful work at a living wage, thus creating concentrated regions of poverty. Impoverished conditions can create an ethos of overpowering helplessness that drives despair to the point that escape is predictably sought through drugs and alcohol. Such use too often leads to abuse and dependence, which are often accompanied by physical and sexual violence. When arrests are made, sometimes after incidents of racial profiling, men spend time in prison. Family structures are destabilized. When women recognize that survival itself is in jeopardy, some will turn to sex work. When profiteers exploit the situation, there is human trafficking. Where there is poverty, drug and alcohol abuse, physical and sexual violence, sex work and human trafficking, there is HIV/AIDS. Paul Farmer's work is intended to help us to recognize what is happening, so that we can reimagine the systems and so that fewer are vulnerable to the structures of violence now harming us all.

Upon first exposure to these explanations, it is natural to want to hold architects of social systems accountable for planning the systems as they stand. Since most systems' histories stretch back centuries, however, and since their construction has been edified and reinforced generation after generation, establishing specific blame for their design and implementation is nearly impossible. Another common response upon introduction to theories of structural violence, particularly for students who are white and male, is instinctively to resist; they feel assaulted, as if theorists are blaming social problems on white men, and even on them in particular. Such a reaction is unintended, counterproductive, and dangerous: unintended because the systems have been standing for centuries, so assigning fault in any case would need to be traced to the remote past and to men who are long dead; counterproductive

---

For commentary, see Jeffrey D. Sachs, *The End of Poverty: Economic Possibilities for Our Time* (New York: Penguin, 2005).

because any potential solution requires men and women with power and privilege to be involved in reshaping how society is structured for the greater benefit of all; and dangerous because a defensive posture or retrenchment will only harm to a greater degree those persons who are already vulnerable. To the extent that people recognize systems of injustice, however, and to the extent that, upon recognition, people desire to see the systems transformed, there is a continuum of responsibility and accountability. On the negative side, such a continuum ranges from direct involvement in the further design, promotion, and implementation of unjust systems, to complicity in their perpetuation by adopting a fatalism that believes there is nothing that can be done to change the way things are. Also operating on the positive side is a continuum of resistance that ranges from the reordering and advocating for the overhaul of structures identified as violent to responding charitably and compassionately to alleviate suffering while new, more just, structures are being designed.

Marjorie Suchocki's treatment of the structural dimension of sin is again instructive. Referring to structural sin as a sin of social inheritance and considering it a third dimension of original sin, Suchocki speaks of it as institutionally oriented. "Through our social heritage the particular forms of sin that are embodied in a society's institutions to protect the privileges of a dominant group deeply influence the structures of consciousness and conscience of each new generation." Thus, "Institutional forms of cultural life play a strong role in the transmission of sin from generation to generation."[71]

Suchocki draws on the work of Walter Rauschenbusch to document how social institutions transmit a condition of sinfulness. Especially critical of capitalism, but also of militarism, racism, sexism, heterosexism, classism and, indeed, all such -isms, Suchocki explains that "we draw our ideas, our moral standards, and our spiritual ideals from the social body into which we are born; these are mediated to us by the public and personal institutions that make up the society. The problem," she goes on to say, "is that the social institutions that so form our values in a capitalist society are driven by a greed that readily exploits the laboring classes, and justifies the exploitation through an idealization of its evil practices. And this idealization of evil becomes the norm from which society fashions its moral consciousness."[72] In relationship to an inherited condition, Suchocki writes, "When that society inevitably infects its progeny with hypocrisies designed to hide the violence of the privi-

71. Suchocki, *The Fall of Violence*, 113.
72. Ibid., 114.

leged, then those who inherit such hypocrisies will themselves believe and indulge them. The societies will be the bearers of sin to which the children will adhere even before they have the means of assent."[73] She readily acknowledges the analogous relationship between this and the doctrine of original sin, which Augustine articulated as that which is inherited as a condition that unwittingly corrupts individuals without their consent.[74] Finally, she concludes that we are in a "sorry plight," indeed, for when "the institutions of society are organized around a purpose of maintaining privilege or profit . . . and when this purpose is rationalized through an idealization that renders the purpose normative, then these values affect not only those immediately participating in the institution, but in the society as a whole within which the institution is embedded."[75] Finally, she reasons that "individuals raised within such a society internalize the norms, thus supporting them and ensuring their continued perpetuation."[76]

The relationships between personal sin, relational sin, and structural sin are complex. The way one is personally sinful in one's relationships and in the structures of society is sometimes direct and sometimes indirect. The Christian tradition has long insisted that followers of Christ follow the Golden Rule: "Do unto others as you would have them do unto you" (Luke 6:31), and often liturgies invite the Christian faithful to confess not only sins of commission but also sins of omission. "I have sinned against you in thought, word, and deed, by what I have done, and by what I have left undone."[77] In a similar way, the concept of structural sin expands what constitutes personal sin by including complicity in systems that are doing harm as sinful. The systems are opposed to God's will for human thriving, so to perpetuate them by failing to resist them is to enable harm. Often, one is not directly sinful in the structure. Few actually participate in the torture campaigns of governments, for example. In the Catholic tradition, however, since torture is considered to be an intrinsic evil, it is never acceptable under

73. Ibid., 118.
74. Ibid.
75. Ibid., 126–27.
76. Ibid., 126.
77. This example is from the ELCA's *Lutheran Book of Worship*. The Anglican *Book of Common Prayer* is similar: "We have left undone those things which we ought to have done; And we have done those things which we ought not to have done." The Roman Catholic *Confiteor* has the penitent say, "I confess to almighty God and to you, my brothers and sisters, that I have greatly sinned, in my thoughts and in my words, in what I have done and in what I have failed to do."

any circumstances.[78] But insofar as the population tolerates the practice of torture, sometimes due to fear, and fails to band together to demand its end, the population enables it to persist. Unless or until members of the population actively resist the practice of torture, the population is complicit. As Desmond Tutu once said, "If you are neutral in situations of injustice, you have chosen the side of the oppressor. If an elephant has its foot on the tail of a mouse and you say that you are neutral, the mouse will not appreciate your neutrality."[79]

Defining the structural dimension of sin helps us to recognize our collective responsibility in relation to the murders of African American youth on the streets of our cities, men who have become emblematic in this chapter of all victims of structural oppression. It is not the one who pulls the trigger, alone, who is responsible for the crimes that are predictable and repeated night in and night out in communities not far from the suburbs where privileged folk live in a fragile bubble that provides a veneer of security until revolutions demand the extension of privileges to the masses. As relational sin has enabled us to see, all are made unsafe when a single life is violated. Communities respond in fear, further distancing us from one another in an attempt to provide a sense of safety and security that is illusory. It is not only the victims and families and friends of the victims, however, who are harmed. As we have seen, there are, as well, dynamics of power and privilege that preceded the individual decision to pull the trigger. The conditions that are present in our society that are putting people into situations like those faced by Trayvon Martin, Terrance Wright, and Laramiun Byrd are conditions for which we are all accountable, for we all perpetuate systems that privilege some and harm others. To the extent that we are embedded in and implicated by these systems, we are sinful; and to the extent that we fail to resist these systems, even unknowingly, we sin.

Kehinde Wiley's *Lamentation Over the Dead Christ* raises well the dimensions of sin this chapter describes. As embodied among the marginalized African American youth of modern-day America, this Christ has been tortured and killed, as are too many on the streets of our cities—presumably and perhaps stereotypically the victim of a gunshot wound. Awaiting his resurrection, his dead body is entombed. His death

---

78. For a helpful resource, see United States Conference of Catholic Bishops, "Torture Is an Intrinsic Evil: A Catholic Study Guide for a One-Session Workshop," http://www.usccb.org/issues-and-action/human-life-and-dignity/torture/upload/torture-is-an-intrinsic-evil-study-guide1.pdf.

79. Desmond Tutu, quoted in Robert McAfee Brown, *Unexpected News: Reading the Bible with Third World Eyes* (Philadelphia, PA: Westminster Press, 1984), 19.

demands accountability. Certainly, the individual who killed him is responsible. But it is insufficient to reason that the situation that leads to so many similar victims can only be overcome by converting individual souls in the community to a way of nonviolence when they are victimized by structures of violence that oppress them. If a more just world is to be realized, the damage that has been inflicted for generations and that has infiltrated the entire society—affecting all people of every color within a scaffolding of institutional disparity and interpersonal fear—will need to be undone by giving due attention to each dimension of harm: individual, relational, and structural. We live in the hope that the Holy Spirit is among us, transforming us individually into people who are compassionate and forgiving. But so too is the Spirit among us, healing damaged relationships, as demonstrated in the way that Laramiun Byrd's mother forgave her son's killer, ultimately, after a long process of reconciliation, inviting him to become her son and to share her duplex. And so, too, is the Spirit among us all, inviting us collectively to resist systems that oppress on the basis, for example, of skin color, gender, sexual orientation, and economic standing. In the words of novelist Arundhati Roy, "Another world is not only possible, she's on her way. . . . On a quiet day, if I listen very carefully, I can hear her breathing."[80]

80. Arundhati Roy, *War Talk* (Cambridge, MA: South End Press, 2003), 75.

Orphans (2008) by Sefedin Stafa. Oil on canvas; 80 x 60 centimeters. Courtesy of the artist.

Chapter 5

Beauty's Story
On Parables

You shall not abuse any widow or orphan.
—Exodus 22:22

Wash yourselves; make yourselves clean;
remove the evil of your doings
from before my eyes;
Cease to do evil,
learn to do good;
seek justice,
rescue the oppressed,
defend the orphan,
plead for the widow.
—Isaiah 1:16-17

Religion that is pure and undefiled before God, the Father, is
this: to care for orphans and widows in their distress, and to
keep oneself unstained by the world.
—James 1:27

Memories like this one haunt me. I was in Cape Town, South Africa, in December 2006, on a travel grant from my institution's international education program to design the course "AIDS, Apartheid, and the Arts of Resistance." The sky was growing darker as evening passed gently to dusk. The heat of the summer day gave way to the coolness of nightfall. As colleagues and I were walking leisurely back to our rooms after having enjoyed a gourmet pizza and a glass of wine for dinner at a quaint pizzeria at a corner café not too far from our hotel, we passed a child who sat, all alone, on the curb. He was no older than five or six. As in all the commercials and documentaries I had seen through the years, his eyes were large and dark. They followed us, tracing our steps as we passed him by, each one of us, my companions and I. Once in my room, having taken leave of my friends, I sat on the edge of my bed and held my head in my hands. I imagined my own six-year-old in his favorite pajamas at home in Minnesota, preparing to climb into his soft bed heaping with blankets. Too anxious to remain in this posture, I paced in the room, straining at the window from the height of my floor in the tower to see if he was still on the street down below. I imagined taking him by the hand, insisting that he could not be alone on the street overnight. I wished I had given him food or money at the very least, suggesting that we should go together to buy a decent meal. I lamented that I didn't know how to find the number for child protection services, or something. Anything. I was sorry that I was too—too what? Too worried about being accused of kidnapping or child endangerment, or too afraid of being robbed or hurt—to offer him a warm bed for the night? Was he among the unaccompanied AIDS orphans in South Africa about whom I'd read so much? Did anyone come by to take care of him that night? Where did he spend the rest of his nights? Where is he now? Is he alive? Is he hungry? Is he safe?

To see Sefedin Stafa's painting of two *Orphans* (2008) some time later, a painting inspired by a similar scene, though this time on the streets of Athens, was powerful. Two young girls sit on a curb, the older one, too young to be a mother but forced to mother nevertheless, leans in an exhausted posture against a stone wall, her weight, and the weight of their situation, pushing them against the building's inhospitable embrace. It is cold and damp, as is evident by hints of moss growing on the cement beneath them. The elder one holds her younger sister to keep her warm. The younger one is not interested in fussing with the doll that lies behind her, for she is probably too hungry to play. Her eyes, exaggerated in size as if to plead for help and certainly to elicit emotion, look into the eyes of the viewer, interrogating the one who walks by. A plate collects coins that are tossed charitably, or perhaps uncharitably, at the girls, perhaps alleviating the guilt of passersby, presumably absolving them of their guilt, for their complicity, at the very least, for perpetuating a system that produces such a scene.

Orphans are now estimated to be over 153 million in number worldwide; thus, this scene unfolds nightly in the streets of our cities, in the United States and throughout the world. The sisters are just two of these countless children. Without an education, shelter, or decent clothing, what choice will they eventually have if they want to buy bread and something to drink? Of his art, Stafa unapologetically writes, "The mission of art is to bring beauty, emotions, and truth to people," and of his religion, Stafa shares, "God is one and the same for all people and one day he will be back to bring only beauty and joy, even [for] the poor orphans."[1] His painting brings us onto religious ground, where those who are privileged by the systems as they have been engineered stand convicted. What does it mean to be holy in a world where orphans roam the streets at night?

My memory of this brief encounter in Cape Town, in combination with my response to Stafa's painting, is all the more troubling to me because the stories of these orphans are interwoven in my mind with stories from the Christian tradition I claim to hold sacred. In my mind's eye, I detected on that street in Cape Town threads from stories I have been told since I was a child—stories about Jesus sharing still more stories with his disciples in the form of parables: stories of a jarringly good Samaritan, of a unique host at a great wedding feast, and of a persistent widow, among others. These parables have shaped my imagination, providing me, now as an adult, with a framework for meaning and meaning making. The beauty of the life Jesus describes in these stories is challenging. In no uncertain terms, he asserts that material luxury often prevents people from growing close to God. Despite awareness of the world's deepest needs, when those who become too comfortable wish to protect their increasingly lavish lifestyles more than to sustain those who, too often, go without the basic material necessities of life, Jesus conveys that they have sinned against God. Religious people surrounded Jesus, their rabbi, and sought relentlessly for answers to questions that plagued and perplexed them about the divine truths he was revealing. They yearned to hear that God approved of how they were choosing to live their lives—to hear that they were righteous in God's sight. Knowing what they wanted to hear as opposed to what they needed to hear, Jesus understood that the best way to engage them was through storytelling. In the tales he spun, they were invited to find themselves and to discern the message he would have them take away. Through the presentation of the parables in the gospels, we are invited to discern meaning for our lives as well, in the same way as those who first heard them, guided now centuries later by scholarship that enables us to understand them in their original

1. Correspondence with artist, September 13, 2013.

context. When we have done so, his words will be as challenging to the privileged now as they were to the audiences first hearing them. As Aboriginal Australian artist and activist Lilla Watson has observed, "If you have come here to help me, you are wasting your time. But if you have come because your liberation is bound up with mine, then let us work together." The liberation of the privileged is bound up with the liberation of those disadvantaged by the social systems as they have been designed. By telling parables, Jesus seeks not guilt but transformation.

The Good Samaritan (Luke 10:30-37)

Jesus' parable of the Good Samaritan is rather straightforward: a Jewish scholar in the crowd asks Jesus how to inherit eternal life. When Jesus replies that the greatest commandment is to love one's neighbor, his interlocutor asks, "But who is my neighbor?" Jesus answers by telling him a parable. The story goes something like this: both a priest and a Levite notice but pass by a man who has been wounded by a robber and left for dead along the side of a road. A Samaritan, on the other hand, sees him, has compassion for him, and takes action to care for him. Jesus asks his scholarly interlocutor to identify which man, among the characters in the story, was a good neighbor to the man injured along the side of the road. When the scholar answered that it had been the Samaritan, Jesus instructs him to live similarly.

Contemporary commentary on the parable is earnest in its attempt to challenge anti-Jewish readings that have dominated interpretation of the parable of the Good Samaritan for centuries. Luise Schottroff identifies three places in the story in which Christian interpreters through the ages have read the parable in anti-Jewish ways.[2] First, she examines how the interpreter reads the motivation behind the Torah scholar's question to Jesus. Schottroff sees the interlocutor neither as a righteous Jew nor as a conservative who is challenged by Jesus' radical interpretation of the Torah. Neither does she see him as a provocateur who attempts to trap Jesus. Rather, she reads his question to be a genuine inquiry from someone who desires to learn about how Jesus understands ethical living.[3] Second, Schottroff is attentive to how interpreters are speaking about Jesus' teaching on love. She counters the idea that Jesus is teaching love for all of humankind over and against Christianity's slight against

---

2. Luise Schottroff, *The Parables of Jesus* (Minneapolis, MN: Fortress Press, 2006), 131–37.

3. Ibid., 132–34.

Judaism's supposed "love for people of one's own nation."[4] She writes, "The parable does not reflect at all on the ethnic relationship between the Samaritan and the victim. It does *not* say that the victim is a Jew, so that the Samaritan's love overcomes a barrier."[5] Third, Schottroff analyzes how interpreters are reading the characterization of the priest and Levite. She reads them more neutrally, as common figures—people who would best represent the audience, people with whom they would identify, simply people who pass by someone in need. She does not read them as an opportunity to attack Jews, or Jewish authority, as so many interpreters have done in the past.[6]

While I respect Schottroff's motivation to protect readers of the parable from interpreting it in an anti-Semitic light, I am not convinced that the characterization of the priest and Levite are happenstance. To be sure, when Jesus tells the parable of the Good Samaritan, he shocks his audience. When the scholar asks, "Who is my neighbor?" Jesus responds with a parable that reflects favorably on a Samaritan, a lower-caste Jew in Jesus' century. Rather than affirming his audience's assumption that a priest and a Levite would model what it is to be neighborly, Jesus lifts up a Samaritan as one who responds to the needs of a man left wounded at the side of a road. The Samaritan people were a marginalized sect within first-century Judaism. Theirs was a history that stretched back to the annals of the divided kingdom, when shrines were set up to YHWH in places like Bethel and Gilgal, when the temple in Jerusalem was understood by the powerful to represent the only place where true worship should be offered to God. Therefore, the Israelites in Jerusalem in those times believed those who purportedly worshiped YHWH in Samaria were, in fact, worshipping falsely. Moreover, they had intermarried. To be a Samaritan, then, took on negative connotations in the mainstream Jewish community—a prejudice that persisted through the centuries.

Jesus, desiring to challenge the mind-set of his audience, lifted up the Samaritan. He did so not only to make the point that to care for people when they are wounded is a demonstration of good neighborliness but also to shock his listeners by lifting up the Samaritan as a model for being a good neighbor—a revelation that would have astonished his audience. In other words, he challenged his listeners to expand their imaginations about what it means to be a good person in God's judgment. The despised Samaritan becomes a model of right living in

4. Ibid., 134.
5. Ibid.
6. Ibid., 135–37.

Jesus' example, whereas the priest and the Levite, the ones Jesus' audience would have thought embodied the ethic of good neighborliness *par excellence*, failed to respond in a good and neighborly way to a need that was literally presenting itself immediately in their path. He thereby challenged his listeners to recognize their own prejudices—and certainly in a way that would have stung.

Does such a reading violate the principles outlined by Schottroff? First, in this reading, there is no commentary on the scholar's motivation for asking the question, since there are no textual clues on which to base such conclusions. Second, this reading examines the teaching on love entirely within its Jewish framework. Recognizing first-century tensions between various factions within the Jewish community—i.e., tensions rooted in historical conflict between Jews in Jerusalem and Samaria—is no more anti-Semitic than acknowledging twenty-first century tensions between Sunni and Shi'a Muslims as anti-Islamic, or, for that manner, than acknowledging tensions between ELCA and LCMS Lutherans as anti-Lutheran or anti-Christian. Christians must conduct this work sensitively, to be sure—recognizing how Christian belief has indisputably contributed to violence inflicted against Jewish communities—but not by avoiding the historical realities Jesus himself was addressing as a Jew in his own Jewish community. Third, Jesus is certainly delineating a distinction between the righteousness of the priest and Levite, on the one hand, and the Samaritan, on the other. They represent different categories of response to the person who has been robbed. To bypass the roles of these characters within the context of first-century Judaism in order to avoid charges of anti-Semitism is to miss the point of the parable entirely. If his point were to differentiate simply between the character of Jerusalem-based Jews and Samaritan Jews, it would have been sufficient for Jesus merely to imagine that a common Jew passed by the one who was robbed in the street whereas a Samaritan stopped to tend to his neighbor.[7] Since he didn't—since he identified a priest and a Levite specifically within the Jerusalem hierarchy—his choice merits some consideration. Recognition of this point is not to legitimize in any way an attack against Judaism but to challenge assumptions about who might, and who might not be, righteous in God's eyes. In keeping with the prophetic tradition within his own Jewish practice, Jesus seems to say through the parable that righteousness has to do with who is being just and who is being unjust. The parable had the potential to sting

---

7. John Dominic Crossan, *In Parables: The Challenge of the Historical Jesus* (San Francisco: Harper & Row, 1973), 63–64.

Jesus' listeners, who recognized that they had something to learn from this rabbi who was challenging their biases.

John Dominic Crossan, a member of the Jesus Seminar and certainly no anti-Semite, believes the key to understanding the parable is to present two contradictory ideas side by side and to allow this presentation to have its effect on the parable's intended audience. Jesus' audience would have been shocked to hear that a Samaritan was modeling how to be righteous in God's judgment.

> When the story is read as one told by the Jewish Jesus to a Jewish audience, and presumably in a Jerusalem setting, this original historical context demands that the "Samaritan" be intended and heard as the socio-religious outcast which he was. As John 4:9 put it laconically: "For Jews have no dealings with Samaritans." Hence the internal structure of the story and the historical setting of Jesus' time agree that the literal point of the story challenges the hearer to put together two impossible and contradictory words for the same person: "Samaritan" (10:33) and "neighbor" (10:36). The whole thrust of the story demands that one say what cannot be said, what is a contradiction in terms: Good + Samaritan. On the lips of the historical Jesus the story demands that the hearer respond by saying the contradictory, the impossible, the unspeakable.[8]

The parable of the Good Samaritan has a powerful message when interpreted in our own age of anguish and anticipation. It would have been as shocking to its audience in its own day as it would be to read this parable in today's situation, for example, of HIV and AIDS.

> *A scholar asked Jesus, "And who is my neighbor?" Jesus replied, "Once, a man fell sick with AIDS. He stumbled into the hands of fearful people, who isolated him, abandoned him, leaving him half dead on the street. Now by chance a Franciscan friar happened upon him; and when he saw him, he passed by on the other side. So likewise a bishop: when he came to the place and saw him, he passed by on the other side. But a homosexual man while traveling came near him; and when he saw him, he was moved with pity. He went to him and nursed his sores, having poured medicine on them. Then he brought him to an inn and took care of him. The next day he took out generous amounts of cash and gave it to the innkeeper, saying, 'Take care of him; and when I come back, I will repay you whatever more you spend.' Which of these three, do you think, was a neighbor to the man who fell sick with AIDS?" He said, "The one who showed him mercy." Jesus said to him, "Go and do likewise."*

8. Ibid., 64.

While it would be possible in such a recasting of the parable merely to say that a Christian happened upon the man fallen ill in the street and passed him by, and then another, the effect of the parable is heightened by calling out those who have devoted their lives to religious principles. While I might identify with the friar's and bishop's behaviors of passing by the one fallen sick, the impact of the parable is greater by contrasting the ideals by which they live with one who might embody the antithesis in their eyes—in this case, the gay man. This telling is in keeping with the ethos of Jesus' initial parable. And, in an age of AIDS, the parable conveys a message about what God expects of God's people on the basis of the authority of Jesus' own teaching. Preachers might encourage believers to read the person living with HIV and AIDS as the man "wounded," having been robbed and left for dead. Certainly, in the early years but even still today, many "righteous" ones—like the friar and the bishop in my telling—have attempted to justify looking away. In such a case, who were the "Samaritans" in the United States but the gay men who mobilized in the early days to care for those who were falling ill?

In response to the scholar's question: "Who is my neighbor?" the answer is reframed by Jesus to challenge his listeners' preconceptions. The man robbed and left for dead on the street is his neighbor. But more than this, the Samaritan offers a model for how better to live the Jewish life as a good neighbor to those who are vulnerable. So in our day, the person living with AIDS, marginalized as such people too often are by stigma and shame, is our neighbor. But more than this, the homosexual man who responds by raising money to pay rent or to organize meals for the one who has become sick is a model for how better to live the Christian life. This is in contrast to some Christians who would justify passing by those living with HIV and AIDS, in the same way that some Jews would have justified passing by the man robbed and left for dead. This answer might be as shocking for us in the church as Jesus' answer was for his audience. People living with HIV and AIDS are our neighbors who ought to be cared for, just as the man who was wounded deserved care and attention. Homosexual men, in the manner in which they cared for lovers and friends who had fallen ill in the early days of the epidemic, demonstrate better what it is to live in such a way as to inherit eternal life than is often modeled by our religious leaders (and likewise all of us) who have shunned our responsibilities as human beings, just as the Samaritan better demonstrated what it is to live justly than the priest and the Levite in Jesus' parable. The righteous ones are those who care for those fallen sick by offering compassion and affection in a time of need, as Jesus reveals through his parable. He sends the scholar off to do likewise.

AIDS, of course, is not only a disease of gay men. At the time of this publication, 51 percent of the people in the world carrying the virus are women. This number is higher in sub-Saharan Africa, where 60 percent of those living with the virus are female. Tragically, only 40 percent of those living with the virus in South Africa are receiving the antiretroviral therapies that can extend lives and minimize suffering. In Africa, who is the Good Samaritan but the "mamas" who have cared for their children and their children's children? In Africa, it has been marginalized women who have responded—the "mamas" who nurse their sons and daughters through their illness and then take in their grandbabies as their own children. Even as they mourn the death of their own children, they care for the orphans left behind, all on the smallest shoestring of a budget. Privileged Christians, hearing such a parable in today's churches, might not find the image of a granny in Africa as shocking as the exemplar of the homosexual man as caregiver—but it functions in the same way. Elderly women in Africa are models of being good-neighborly, just as are the homosexual men in America, just as was the Samaritan in Jesus' day. Upon hearing of such models, the listener might see as in a mirror and contrast one's own moral posture by comparison.

Not too many of us in the pews on Sunday morning resemble people like Kevin Winge, the former director of Open Arms of Minnesota, who accompanied his friend during the early days of the epidemic in New York City and then greatly expanded a program for providing meals to those living with the virus in his own Minneapolis.[9] Nor do we look very much like Priscilla, a widow living in a shack in the townships of postapartheid South Africa who, on her monthly income of the equivalent of $100/month, adopted twelve orphans because she knew she could care for them and love them.[10] Next to these Good Samaritans, most of us would pale. But we are invited by the parable to imagine anew ways of being in the world, attentive to those around us.

For me, this is the power of Jesus' parable. Both by its ethical imperative as well as its shocking revelation, I am challenged to love more openly and more deeply, no matter my starting point. According to Crossan, the parable breaks open the meaning of the kingdom of God:

> The literal point confronted the hearers with the necessity of saying the impossible and having their world turned upside down and radically

9. Kevin Winge, *Never Give Up: Vignettes from South Africa in an Age of AIDS* (Minneapolis, MN: Syren Book Company, 2006).

10. Kimberly Vrudny, *30 Years / 30 Lives: Documenting a Pandemic* (Seattle, WA: CreateSpace, 2010), 16.

questioned in its presuppositions. The metaphorical point is that just so does the Kingdom of God break abruptly into human consciousness and demand the overturning of prior values, closed options, set judgments, and established conclusions. But the full force of the parabolic challenge is that the just so of the metaphorical level is not ontologically distinct from the presence of the literal point. The hearer struggling with the contradictory dualism of Good/Samaritan is actually experiencing in and through this the inbreaking of the Kingdom. Not only does it happen like this, it happens in this. The original parabolic point was the reversal caused by the advent of the Kingdom in and through the challenge to utter the unutterable and to admit thereby that other world which was at that very moment placing their own under radical judgment.[11]

Having reversed the people's expectations, the parable of the Good Samaritan challenges us, even still, to live a life more just, more compassionate, more wise. This was Jesus' vision of the kingdom of God. Just as people in Jesus' day were invited to bring it into greater being in the here and now, so too does the invitation remain ours today.

The Great Feast (Luke 14:16-24)

Several stories about "meal etiquette" appear in the Gospel of Luke, especially in chapter 14. The gospel opens with Jesus on his way to a Shabbat dinner at the home of a Pharisee. Tensions between them, whether historically accurate or reflected by the time of the author's writing, are indicated here, for the author writes, "[T]hey were watching him closely" (Luke 14:1), although apparently the relations were not so strained that Jesus would have turned down an invitation to dinner. Along the way, a man appeared before him with dropsy, and Jesus healed him despite the provision against work on the Sabbath. And then, finally arriving for dinner, when he "noticed how the guests chose the places of honor" (Luke 14:7), Jesus gave an instruction about humility. He told them a parable, indicating that those who exalted themselves by sitting in a place of honor at a wedding feast risk being humbled, and instructed them instead to sit in a humble position, that they might be exalted (Luke 14:8-11).[12] Jesus went on to give his second instruction, this

---

11. Crossan, *In Parables*, 65–66.

12. John Dominic Crossan reads this as an "example of situational reversal [which] shows how the Kingdom arrives so that one experiences God's rule as that which turns one's world upside down and radically reverses its normalcy. The Kingdom is not one's ultimate concern but that which undermines one's ultimate concern." Ibid., 70.

one about inclusiveness, by scolding his host for extending invitations only to friends, brothers, relatives, and rich neighbors. Jesus taught him, instead, that when he gives a banquet, he ought to "invite the poor, the crippled, the lame, and the blind," an action for which he will be eternally blessed (Luke 14:13). This advice elicited a response from one of the guests in the words, "Blessed is anyone who will eat bread in the kingdom of God!" (Luke 14:15). These words seem to prompt Jesus' third instruction, which comes in the telling of "the parable of the great dinner." The parable again provides a glimpse into Jesus' imagination about the kingdom of God and how it looks in the here and now. In other words, his story enables those listening to glimpse Beauty's vineyard.

In short, the parable is about a host who invites many to a great dinner feast. All of his guests, however, begin to make excuses about why they cannot come. One has just purchased land and chooses to go see his real estate rather than attend the banquet (Luke 14:18). Another has purchased some oxen and prefers to tend to them, so he sends his regrets (Luke 14:19). Another has just been married, and so chooses to spend time with his wife (Luke 14:20). The host becomes angry and asks his slave to "[g]o out at once into the streets and lanes of the town and bring in the poor, the crippled, the blind, and the lame" (Luke 14:21). When these do not entirely fill his house, he sends the slave to collect still more (Luke 14:23). The parable concludes with the host's words, "For I tell you, none of those who were invited will taste my dinner" (Luke 14:24).

These final words seem harsh when they are understood exclusively in terms of a final and eternal judgment. If the host is taken to be God, and the invitees human beings who are too caught up in earthly affairs like their real estate, livelihood, and spouses to take time for a dinner with God—an image that in our day has eucharistic overtones—and God condemns them by barring them from the eschatological banquet, from salvation, as it were, then the parable is severe indeed. But as we have seen, the kingdom of God is not, in Jesus' imagination, exclusively or even especially about an afterlife, though it has implications about that as well. Rather, the kingdom is primarily about God's will being done "on earth as it is in heaven" (Matt 6:10). This gives a different twist, then, to the final words of the parable. Those who reject the invitation to dinner, like those who do not enter the vineyard when called (Matt 20:1-16), will not taste the dinner or, for that matter, the sweet wine produced from the grapes collectively harvested.[13] If we understand this in terms of justice—if we do not accept the invitation to dinner, if

---

13. For a commentary on this parable, see the epilogue.

we do not accept the invitation to work in the vineyard, if we declare our right to persist in injustice—then we will not experience the banquet or the wine: a community of just relations where there is compassion and wisdom rather than ugliness and deception, peace rather than violence, solidarity rather than isolation in the midst of suffering, and a sincere effort to reconcile rather than to persist in an abuse of power when relationships have been violated.

Moreover, John Dominic Crossan points out two problems with interpretation about the host that need attention.[14] First, the host does not follow Jesus' injunction. He does not initially invite the poor and dispossessed; they are only his second choice when the first do not show up.[15] "Jesus said in [Luke] 14:12-14 not to invite the rich but to invite the poor in order to be rewarded by God not man. The parable, on the other hand, tells a story in which the rich are first invited, decline the invitation, and the poor are then invited in second place. The point is not quite the same."[16] When the invited snub the host, the host looks for guests to fill the seats at his table. Like the parable of the tenants with which we opened this book, this ought not to be read in an anti-Semitic way to suggest that God, the host, is rejecting the Jews in preference for the Gentiles. Instead, we might read this again to symbolize that justice and righteousness have been compromised, and so the host is open yet again to a community willing to live into God's expectations for them. They are invited into Beauty's vineyard, and they accept the invitation, taking their seats, so to speak, at the banquet. This is Beauty's imagination of the kingdom. Jesus believes the kingdom has to do with how we live life in the here and now—in solidarity with the oppressed, whether Jew or Gentile.

Second, according to Crossan, the host fails to give ample time to his potential guests, apparently putting out the invitation for dinner on the same day that his household is preparing the meal. This makes his anger at the guests seem inconsiderate in the extreme. In Crossan's words,

> A man decides on a sudden dinner that very day and sends out his servant to his friends as the dinner is being prepared. Because of the lack of warning each one finds he has a perfectly reasonable excuse. But the result is a meal prepared and a table empty. The host's reaction is to send the servant out to get anyone he can. There is no implication

---

14. In point of fact, Crossan is more pointed. He writes, "In itself it has to do with table etiquette and its motivation could be described at its most positive as utterly banal and at its most negative as rather immoral" (ibid., 69).

15. Ibid., 72.

16. Ibid.

that he is looking for riffraff. But one can appreciate the host's anger, probably as much with himself as with his friends. Can you imagine, asks Jesus, a situation in which all the invited guests are absent from a banquet and all the uninvited ones are present? This is fundamentally amoral and invites the hearers to recognize a situation of total reversal: the invited are absent, the uninvited are present. As parable it provokes their response to the Kingdom's arrival as radical and absolute reversal of their closed human situation.[17]

If we read the parable in the context that we have been indicating for Beauty's vineyard, however, there is yet another meaning inherent in the immediacy of the invitation. God's invitation for us to enter the kingdom, this vineyard of right relations, is always immediately before us. And although we have many excuses not to exercise justice today—whether because we want to tend to our real estate or to our occupations, or whether we say that it is more important for us to take care of our own families than the extended human family as if it must be one or the other, either/or instead of both/and—the situation is urgent. If not today, when? And if not me, who? Echoes of St. Teresa of Avila's words refrain, "Christ has no body now on earth but yours, no hands but yours, no feet but yours. Yours are the eyes through which to look out Christ's compassion to the world. Yours are the feet with which he is to go about doing good. Yours are the hands with which he is to bless [us] now."[18] The poor lack resources now such that they struggle day in and day out to survive. Widows and orphans are suffering now, hungry and potential victims of predators on the streets of our cities. Immigrants are in danger now, vulnerable to xenophobia and violence. Prisoners are lonely now, lacking human contact and demonstrations of decency, further compromising the cities where they live when they are released back into the community. The host is not required, then, to give us ample time to consider the invitation. The matter of the dinner is urgent, and hence so is the invitation.

Luise Schottroff's interpretation is, once again, instructive. She makes three points about the parable in her social-historical analysis of the story about what she calls "the snubbed host."[19] She writes of the story's radical politics, of the parable's implications for the gulf between the rich and the poor, and of Jesus' vision of the messianic community as described in the tale of the feast. The story's radical politics

17. Ibid., 73.
18. This prayer, attributed to St. Teresa of Avila, is not found in any of her writings.
19. Schottroff, *The Parables of Jesus*, 49–56.

are grounded, she interprets, within the larger context of the Gospel of Luke. These politics are not only relevant for Jews, she asserts, but also for the Gentiles who are becoming members of the Jewish community: "The Gospel of Luke proposes a radical social politics for Israel and for the Christianity drawn from among the nations."[20] These radical politics have financial implications: "People who are in a position to forgive debts should forgive debts and thus be prepared not only—as the Torah demands—to renounce interest, but even to renounce the payment of the principal (Luke 6:34, 35)."[21] This news comes as a gospel for the poor but as something quite else for the rich: "The gulf between rich and poor is described in the Gospel of Luke as a catastrophe for the rich, who are referred to the Torah for guidance (Luke 16:31)."[22] Lastly, "the meals with sinners celebrate messianic community."[23] For Schottroff, this means that "Jesus' feasts with sinners and the poor, the new meal practices of well-to-do people who follow Jesus, and the meal practices of the Christian communities (Acts 2:42-45; 4:32-35), including the Eucharist, signify the feeding of the hungry, the realization of solidarity within the people of God, and an experience of the kingdom of God."[24] Therefore, those who reject the dinner invitation reject God and God's justice, a rejection for which there are consequences. If these people do not taste the dinner, the entire community suffers, for injustice is perpetuated to the harm of the whole. She reads the parable, then, to mean that "the rich, in order to live according to Torah, must make the poor the center of their lives."[25] Moreover, "the parable as a whole, as a tale of real life, . . . opens the way to a meal community of well-to-do and poor in which the latter are not place-fillers but have a right to share in the joys of creation, food, and health."[26]

The meaning of the Lukan banquet is made still more comprehensible by a sermon titled "Banquet of the Dispossessed," written by James A. Sanders and recorded in his book *God Has a Story Too*.[27] Sanders believes God's will for humanity is particularly well expressed in Jesus'

---

20. Ibid., 50.
21. Ibid., 50.
22. Ibid.
23. Ibid., 51.
24. Ibid.
25. Ibid., 52.
26. Ibid., 56.
27. James A. Sanders, *God Has a Story Too* (Philadelphia, PA: Fortress Press, 1979), 80–89. See also Craig A. Evans and James A. Sanders, *Luke and Scripture: The Function of Sacred Tradition in Luke-Acts* (Minneapolis, MN: Fortress Press, 1993), 106–20.

teaching on banquet etiquette in Luke 14. Sanders's interpretation of the parable is especially profound for those who find themselves living in situations of privilege.

> When you give a feast, invite the riffraff, the beggars, the ugly, those who do not pull themselves up by their own bootstraps, those who seemingly refuse to better themselves because they are lazy, trifling, and undeserving. Mind you, here we sit at a fine banquet, honored guests of a fine leader of the community, and this Galilean teacher says we should fraternize with the very people who are a blight on our fine city, who live in and yet cause those slums which give our community such a bad name. You sell them a decent house and in two years it'll be run down and cancerous to the neighborhood around it. And this Galilean wants us to socialize with them.[28]

Sanders notes that the excuses given by the invited guests elsewhere in Scripture exclude people from the ranks of the faithful.[29] Those who attended to their daily routine without consideration for those around them, and for the destitute in particular, would never enjoy the messianic feast. Rather, the truly blessed, those who would dine at the messianic banquet once the long, hard day is over, would include—almost exclusively, as Jesus asserts in his parable—the dispossessed. And Sanders articulates with great skill the skeptical reactions that his parabolic teaching almost certainly elicited. Does his teaching not convict those of us who are privileged? How many of us are receptive to the idea that we should invite the homeless into our homes for dinner? And yet, according to Jesus, this is how the kingdom functions. This is what it looks like when we are living as God wants us to live. This is the holy life.

Once again, through his telling of stories, Jesus grants us access to his imagination about the kingdom of God. And it is not the way in which many of us have been taught to think of it. Indeed, Jesus' teachings have been domesticated, their radical nature tamed by delaying their realization to the afterlife. But without denying their eschatological dimension, they are much more profound if we understand them to pertain also to this world. The kingdom is near because, by grace, we have the ability to live into a community of right relationships here and now—and when we do, when we entertain beggars and prostitutes, when we dine with widows and orphans (not just throw coins at them)—we commune with Christ. We enjoy a foretaste of an everlasting, messianic banquet.

28. Ibid., 84–85.
29. Ibid., 89.

The Persistent Widow (Luke 18:1-8)

Another of Jesus' parables is likewise applicable to situations of unjust suffering being experienced acutely in the world of anguish today due to structural injustices that ensure that suffering and vengeance seeking will continue into the future. In the Gospel of Luke, some Pharisees had asked when the kingdom of God was coming, and Jesus had answered them, "The kingdom of God is among you" (Luke 17:21c). Perhaps sensing that his disciples were becoming restless, Jesus instructed them not to lose heart. He shared a parable about a persistent widow who presented her case time and again to a judge who had little regard for God, divine law, or fellow human beings (Luke 18:1-8). This unjust judge interpreted the law in a city where a widow repeatedly visited him to seek justice against her opponent. She was relentless. The judge, pushed to a point of exasperation if not exhaustion, freed himself of her by granting her justice, almost as if to dismiss an annoyance like a pesky fly. Jesus likened this to the power of persistence in prayer, suggesting that if even an unjust judge ultimately relents to the persistence of the widow, how much more will God respond "to his chosen ones who cry to him day and night" (Luke 18:7).

Set within a larger framework about the presence of the kingdom of God, Jesus assured his disciples that God heard their prayers. They mustn't lose heart, Jesus promised them, because the kingdom of God was already coming into being in their midst. Indeed, it was incarnate among them. A new reality, quite distinct from the oppression of the Romans over the Jews in Jerusalem and throughout Palestine, was emerging in a community that would embrace the covenantal promises sacred to Israel and its teachings on justice, even though they were not yet able to see it. The kingdom was inbreaking in the here and now, in time and space, making the presence of God manifest in new and radical ways—ways that would not be lost even when Jesus was killed by an empire that recognized in the movement of the impoverished masses accompanying him the makings of a revolution. The kingdom remains in our midst. We simply need to embrace it and to live into it.

This parable's lesson about not losing heart is as striking as the social situation out of which it emerged. Hebrew Scripture is filled with concern for the poor and economically disadvantaged. Indeed, the law code of ancient Israel mandated care of orphans, widows, and immigrants—people made vulnerable by the social structures of the ancient world where foreigners were distrusted, orphaned and abandoned children were largely on their own, and widows had no inheritance rights. In regard to the latter, the law specified that when a husband died, his brother was to care for his widowed wife. When there were no brothers, or when brothers abnegated their responsibilities, widows were left to the charity of the community, for they were not permitted to own property. While the Hebraic law code did not challenge the structure itself, there were inscribed into the Israelite tablets law codes that addressed how the society was to care for these susceptible ones in its midst:

> When you have finished paying all the tithe of your produce in the third year (which is the year of the tithe), giving it to the Levites, the aliens, the orphans, and the widows, so that they may eat their fill within your towns, then you shall say before the LORD your God . . . "I have neither transgressed nor forgotten any of your commandments . . . I have obeyed the LORD my God, doing just as you commanded me." This very day the LORD your God is commanding you to observe these statutes and ordinances; so observe them diligently with all your heart and with all your soul. (Deut 26:12-16)

Within this context, Jesus promised greater condemnation on those who pretended to be upholders of the law when, in fact, they were abusers of it. According to Luke:

> In the hearing of all the people he said to the disciples, "Beware of the scribes, who like to walk around in long robes, and love to be greeted with respect in the market-places, and to have the best seats in the synagogues and places of honor at banquets. They devour widows' houses and for the sake of appearance say long prayers. They will receive the greater condemnation." (Luke 20:45-57)

When Jesus told this parable about a widow who insisted that justice be served, Jesus asked listeners to consider a situation that would have been familiar to his first-century audience, thoroughly grounded as it was in the Torah's justice tradition. Listeners would have known the frequency with which widows were without protection, such that he need not even mention the particulars of this widow's case. The audience would have known that the character in Jesus' story was appealing to the court to intervene on her behalf—to demonstrate justice in relation to the Torah. Jewish Scriptures were clear that the judge was to rule in such a way as to protect and defend her. Jesus' audience would have comprehended that the judge failed to interpret the law in a godly way. That he failed to do so time and again enabled Jesus to convey something of God's nature by contrast to the unjust judge, assuring his listeners that if even such an unjust judge would ultimately relent, how much more so would God surely respond faithfully to those who are persistent in prayer?

Luise Schottroff explains, "In the Torah, widows and orphans are placed under the special protection of divine law. In the patriarchal societies of the ancient world they were structurally the first victims of economic and social injustice and of legal maneuverings, and they were the objects of treachery and attempts at exploitation."[30] She goes on to explain how the injustice enacted against this widow is twofold: "She has been victimized by a man who has infringed on the economic basis of her life, and against whom she seeks to defend herself with the aid of a judge. . . . But in addition, she becomes the victim of an unjust judicial decision that has no regard for her rights."[31] But she reads in this parable a model of resistance:

> The widow in the parable in Luke 18:1-8 resists by drawing the judge's attention to her rights, that is, to the Torah. Her obstinate persistence is possible because she knows that God's law is on her side. She also expresses her resistance by violating her social boundaries: She behaves loudly and aggressively in public; she may even scream and shout (v. 7 could be understood in this way). Women's resistance through public clamor and other violations of the boundaries that are placed around women, especially widows, is also attested in other sources. The judge's internal conversation reflects her transgression of boundaries: He can even expect this woman to attack violently, to hit him in the face. Attributing violence to women who exercise resistance is a sexist stereotype and a deliberate exaggeration. The woman and her action are at the center of the parable. The hearers are to learn from her. And so the interpretation of the parable, in the introduction and the conclusion, also refers to her alone, and not to the judge (vv. 1, 7, 8).[32]

In her persistent resistance to injustice, the widow appeals time and again for the powerful to hear her case. In my own imagination, I think of the women—grandmothers, no less—who gathered each week on Fifth Avenue in New York City to protest America's wars in Iraq and Afghanistan.[33] I think of the mothers of the disappeared (La Asociación Madres de Plaza de Mayo) who for decades have gathered weekly to

30. Schottroff, *The Parables of Jesus*, 191.
31. Ibid.
32. Ibid., 192.
33. Clyde Haberman, "On 5th Ave., a Grandmothers' Protest as Endless as the Wars" (*New York Times*, May 7, 2010), http://www.nytimes.com/2010/05/07/nyregion/07nyc.html.

appeal to the authorities for information as to the whereabouts of their sons and daughters who were taken and tortured and sometimes killed by the military junta that overtook Argentina between 1976 and 1983.[34] I think about the men and women in Tahrir Square who called for the resignation of Hosni Mubarak in Egypt—and the dawn of the Arab Spring.[35] And I think of the Zapatistas in Chiapas, among them widows and widowers in Acteál, who continue to resist the demands of the Mexican government which demanded they relinquish their land and their way of life to authorities operating under the globalized financial pressures of the North American Free Trade Agreement.[36] Gradually, and with justice on their side, these women and men contribute to the wearing down of their opposition—but sometimes at great personal cost. Even at risk of great harm, these protestors contribute to the resolution of conflict and the establishment of peace with an eye to the common good that ultimately will make the entire world more secure.

In such an age of anguish, when layer after layer of social injustice drives the situations that harm us all, the parable of the persistent widow who appeared time and again before an unjust judge ought to empower us and enliven us to be in solidarity with those who are put in jeopardy by the socioeconomic situation into which they are born or into which they find themselves. The privileged have power to make lasting change. By accompanying those so jeopardized, we can advocate for real and lasting social change; by encouraging cross-cultural engagement, we can overcome xenophobia; by reconfiguring national budgets to attend to educational, agricultural, and medical infrastructure and pharmaceutical accessibility, we can make life-prolonging education, food, and medicine accessible to all; by campaigning for women's rights, we can ensure the health and security of entire cultures; by championing the rights of vulnerable persons, we can protect elders and orphans; and by enforcing international laws against human trafficking and the illegal trade of drugs and by fighting corruption, we can trust that fewer girls will be forced to trade sex for money. All of these efforts are underway

34. Matilde Mellibovsky, *Circle of Love Over Death: The Story of the Mothers of the Plaza de Mayo* (Willimantic, CT: Curbstone Books, 1996).

35. Al Jazeera Online Producer, "Battle of Tahrir Square: Scenes of Violence as Anti-Government Protesters and Pro-Mubarak Supporters Clash in the Centre of Cairo," *Aljazeera*, http://english.aljazeera.net/news/middleeast/2011/02/20112391254 105223.html.

36. Teresa Ortiz, *Never Again a World Without Us: Voices of Mayan Women in Chiapas, Mexico* (Washington, DC: Epica Task Force, 2001).

and, in community, as disciples of Christ, we can tackle them all. It requires only our united will and our collective participation.

Jesus' parable of the persistent widow is set in a circumstance that resonates in the modern world. Like the disciples, we might become restless in our anticipation, in our longing for the kingdom of God. Remembering Jesus' assurance that "the kingdom of God is among you" (Luke 17:21c), we might be persistent, like the widow, in praying not "Come, Lord Jesus" but "Reveal yourself in us, Lord Jesus," thereby orienting us to embody God's answer to our prayers.

Stories like the ones Jesus told are stories in the best sense: they challenge, inform, and mold us to enact what is just, compassionate, and wise—what is good, beautiful, and true. Such narratives can give a structure to events in life that otherwise seem disparate and unrelated. They help us create worlds of meaning, whether in our families, in our political spaces, or in our religious traditions. By weaving our personal stories into these larger narratives, we identify as a community and can find a sense of belonging in an otherwise isolating environment. Storytelling enables us to relate to one another, providing points of connection and interrelation as we respond to one another's accounts and claim some of the stories as our very own. According to theologian Stanley Hauerwas, communities are identified precisely by their affiliation with narratives from the past and by their continuing efforts to find meaning in those narratives in the present. He writes, "Community joins us with others to further the growth of a tradition whose manifold storylines are meant to help individuals identify and navigate the path to the good. The self is subordinate to the community rather than vice versa, for we discover the self through a community's narrated tradition."[37]

South African theologian John W. de Gruchy writes poignantly, too, of the importance of stories.

> True story-telling, whether in the form of a parable, a novel, a drama, a film, a set of photographs, or shared personal experiences, is a reflection on or interpretation of life in its varied dimensions. Stories told with honesty, like all genuine works of art, break open realities, helping us to see things differently, to see ourselves differently and hopefully to live differently. Story-telling is dependent upon memory, and is itself a way of remembering essential to being and remaining human. That is why we keep diaries and treasure photographs of significant moments that document the stages on our life's journey, bringing into

---

37. Stanley Hauerwas, *The Peaceable Kingdom* (South Bend, IN: University of Notre Dame Press, 1991), 28.

focus people we love and respect, and recalling them in ways that help us savor the past in the present. That is why remembering the past rightly by a nation in search of a better future is so fundamental, and why the suppression of such memories is dangerous. Stories evoke hope, whether personal or communal, without which we cannot be truly human. Thus story-telling links memory and expectation in a way that helps make sense of the present.[38]

Each of the parables interpreted in this chapter is prompted by a question posed to Jesus about the kingdom of God. For centuries, the dominant lesson too many preachers communicated by reference to these parables was that they were primarily about a heavenly afterlife. They too often have gleaned from these teachings exclusively the lesson that God is gracious and patient, accepting humans despite their failed and feeble attempts at goodness. After all, when his disciples panic after hearing Jesus say, "Truly I tell you, it will be hard for a rich person to enter the kingdom of heaven" (Matt 19:23), and they ask him, "Then who can be saved?" (Matt 19:25), Jesus answers them, "For mortals it is impossible, but for God all things are possible" (Matt 19:26). These parables are surely about God's graciousness—but they are multivalent, expressing more about God than only this.

Each of the parables assembled here tells us about the kingdom of God as Jesus, as the incarnation of Beauty, imagines it. The kingdom is a community where outcasts such as Samaritans are recognized, too, for their innate dignity—for the goodness they demonstrate by caring for the vulnerable ones in their midst. The kingdom is a community where the dispossessed are not only welcomed to the table but also expected to take the seats of honor. The kingdom is a community where marginalized ones like widows are honored too. They belong in the community despite the presumptions of people who overlook their situations and thereby ensure their ongoing oppression.

According to Jesus, the heavenly kingdom is inbreaking here and now, in his own person, and in the community he is bringing into being. Failure to participate in the kingdom has implications for the next life precisely because, in Jesus' imagination, this world is not disconnected from the next. The chasm is not between heaven and earth but between the righteous and the condemned on the basis of whether or not they are contributing meaningfully to the kingdom of peace and loving-kindness and the bringing of heaven into being in the here and now,

38. John W. de Gruchy, *Confessions of a Christian Humanist* (Minneapolis, MN: Fortress Press, 2006), 7.

characterized by lives of justice. This is a point the gospel writers stress more than once.

> There was a rich man who was dressed in purple and fine linen and who feasted sumptuously every day. And at his gate lay a poor man named Lazarus, covered with sores, who longed to satisfy his hunger with what fell from the rich man's table; even the dogs would come and lick his sores. The poor man died and was carried away by the angels to be with Abraham. The rich man also died and was buried. In Hades, where he was being tormented, he looked up and saw Abraham far away with Lazarus by his side. He called out, "Father Abraham, have mercy on me, and send Lazarus to dip the tip of his finger in water and cool my tongue; for I am in agony in these flames." But Abraham said, "Child, remember that during your lifetime you received your good things, and Lazarus in like manner evil things; but now he is comforted here, and you are in agony. Besides all this, between you and us a great chasm has been fixed, so that those who might want to pass from here to you cannot do so, and no one can cross from there to us." He said, "Then, father, I beg you to send him to my father's house— for I have five brothers—that he may warn them, so that they will not also come into this place of torment." Abraham replied, "They have Moses and the prophets; they should listen to them." He said, "No, father Abraham; but if someone goes to them from the dead, they will repent." He said to him, "If they do not listen to Moses and the prophets, neither will they be convinced even if someone rises from the dead." (Luke 16:19-31)

On that night in Cape Town, the boy on the curb unwittingly became a part of my story. Yet in his story I became another blurred figure like all the others who walked by without offering so much as an acknowledgment. And each day, more threads unwind from the spool of my unfolding life, becoming interwoven with strings from the ancient and more recent past, revealing a tapestry not yet complete but coming into being in the still emerging religious tradition of which I am a living member. The tradition awaits still more strands that will entwine with those already woven in the days, weeks, months, and years ahead, interwoven, too, with all of humanity's evolving story. But the memory of my brief encounter with a boy I guessed was orphaned leaves a hole, a disconnected place in the tapestry, where I recognize a lacking of integrity, a failure to live up to the stories told by my rabbi, my teacher. I was not like the Samaritan who stopped to care for his neighbor lying along the side of the road. I was not like the host who opened his table to the poor. I was not like the widow who resisted injustice persistently by her relentless and active protest day in and day out. I was rather like the priest and the

Levite who walked by the man left for dead at the side of the road; I was like the ones too preoccupied to come for the feast; I was like the judge who swatted away at justice as if it were an annoying fly that would not leave the room. I was like the man who refused a guest at midnight (Luke 11:5-8). I was as stingy as the rich man who was condemned for failing to share with the one who begged for mercy and compassion at his gate (Luke 16:19-26). When I saw Jesus hungry and thirsty on the street, even in the being of a small child, I passed him by (Matt 25:31-46). While I recognize God's grace which nonetheless accepts me, forgives me, and embraces me, I also sense the Spirit's empowerment, encouragement, and enlightenment, prodding me to engagement.

Confessio

If Beauty is a name for Christ, parables are Beauty's narrative. Beauty discloses God's will for humankind in the form of parables. Through these stories, because of their multivalent nature, Jesus shares messages about life and life's meaning, pointing to implications for salvation both here and not here. Even the method of storytelling was ultimately not safe for Jesus. Finally, what he taught was too radical— and people sought to snuff out his life and, in it, to quiet the stories he shared, for they were dangerous stories. They were stories with revolutionary potential.

Three of the parables he shared with his disciples as recorded by Luke—stories about the Good Samaritan, the Wedding Feast, and the Persistent Widow—might be read with the intention of drawing from them hints about how God would have us live in an age of anguish—an age marked by AIDS, human trafficking, child soldiering, and orphaned children, to name but a few of the issues before us. The Good Samaritan, the consummate outsider considered the least righteous of all in the larger community, stopped to care for the man wounded on the side of the road. At the wedding feast, it was the destitute for whom the host laid out the luxurious banquet, shaming those who refused the invitation. The widow, the most vulnerable in her society, resisted injustice persistently, ultimately wearing down the unjust judge's resolve. When read with the backdrop of images of orphans roaming the streets of Cape Town and every town at night, of women and girls forced to sell their bodies to buy loaves of bread, and of children being drafted to kill in militarized zones, the relevance of these stories for our times resonates. The parables leave behind a textile with edges still undone, not finished until we pick up the strands and weave them mindfully and beautifully into our lives by living out a commitment to tend Beauty's vineyard.

personal

"Letter to My Father" (2005) from the CADAVERS series by Kukuli Velarde. Oil and markers on steel; 3 x 6 feet. Courtesy of the artist.

Chapter 6

Beauty's Incarnation
On Forgiveness

They sit for a portrait in formal black attire, but theirs is not merely another mother with child. Her knuckles taut, this woman's arms are wrapped protectively around her daughter (or is the woman protecting a younger version of herself?). Their facial features are bruised and bloodied. The younger one, with lips parted and teeth clenched, grasps a sheet of paper. Tears have streamed down their faces, but they are not crying. They stare back at the viewer, defying the gaze of onlookers who might, like the eyes covering the dingy wallpaper behind them, fix on the subject, scowling society's disapproval. Despite living through whatever terror they have just experienced, probably involving the anger of the man traditionally thought to be the head of their household, they are too often blamed for the violence that has been committed against them. Their eyes betray their exhaustion, their disbelief, and their bewilderment. But they are survivors. And they will confront whatever comes next.

Kukuli Velarde's self-portrait from the *Cadavers* series and titled "Letter to My Father" immortalizes a scene of domestic violence, capturing in a haunting frame an image both of defiance and resilience, a posture purchased at a high price.[1] Of Peruvian heritage, and working now in Philadelphia, Velarde is an artist whose work frequently offers a critique of colonization both cultural and religious. Of the painting, the artist has written, "'*Cadavers*,' my series of paintings on aluminum, are life-sized full body self-portraits while my self is an analogy for 'the other.' This 'other' is a minority: a woman, a person of Peruvian origin

---

1. Kukuli Velarde, http://www.kukulivelarde.com/site/HOME.html.

in the USA, or just a middle-aged woman."[2] Velarde writes eloquently of influences shaping her work: "The society I came from is, in my understanding, formed through the violent encounter between two cultural streams: the European and the indigenous world."[3] In many of her works, Velarde examines the violence against women that was intrinsic to the conquest and that "is replayed today in the sexual exploitation of powerless female workers in menial jobs" and in domestic spaces.[4]

Velarde often makes use of Catholic iconography explicitly, though the reference in images like the one treated here is subtle. Using the armature of the Madonna and child, this mother with her child are not adored but assaulted, thereby highlighting their distance from the idyll depicted in the traditional pairing. In this painting, the artist creates a sharp double entendre. She offers a critique of violence against women more universally even as she communicates this analysis using a Christian visual vocabulary, thereby criticizing the church's complicity in the subordination of women that constitutes a form of their abuse. Velarde's painting offers us, therefore, an apt visual metaphor to examine the violence that too often operates within the theologies of Christianity, a violence that manifests itself both politically and domestically in places where Christianity is dominant. Although many churches condemn the kind of domestic violence visualized in Velarde's painting, Christian theological positions themselves too often undermine an ethical posture in relation to acts of violence against women by conceptualizing God as both male and violent. If men emulate the God they worship, is it any wonder that so many become violent when so many understand their tradition to teach about a male God who justifies violence to achieve his ends?

According to a thought process that came to full flower in the Middle Ages, Christianity framed its grand narrative in terms of salvation history and promoted the notion that God justified the creation of the world by planning creation's redemption from the beginning of time.[5] Thus

2. Kukuli Velarde, "The Cadaver and the Aging Woman," http://www.nyartsmagazine.com/?p=8884.

3. Kukuli Velarde, "Kukuli Velarde's Work," http://www.hatchfund.org/showcase/kukuli_velardes_work.

4. Alice Thorson, "Vessels of Protest: Peruvian Kukuli Velarde Confronts Racism with Striking Ceramics Based on Historical Works," *Kansas City Star*, November 24, 2013, http://www.kukulivelarde.com/site/Reviews.html.

5. See Kimberly Vrudny, *Friars, Scribes, and Corpses: A Marian Confraternal Reading of* The Mirror of Human Salvation (*Speculum humanae salvationis*) (Leuven: Peeters, 2010).

God, knowing humans would fall into sin, saw to their creation and, in the best-case scenario, *foresaw* the crucifixion as the means of their redemption and *allowed* their demise so that humankind could be saved. In the worst-case scenario, God *designed* the drama of the betrayal and crucifixion as the means by which God would accomplish redemption and thereby undo the sin of humankind.

In his *Enchiridion*, Augustine describes sin as a "happy fault" (*felix culpa*): "For God judged it better to bring good out of evil than not to permit any evil to exist."[6] It is my contention, however, that a God who passively "permits" or "allows" evil to exist, even for a great end, is inherently problematic. The Paschal Vigil Mass *Exsultet* puts it, *O felix culpa quae talem et tantum meruit habere redemptorem*, or "O happy fault that earned for us so great, so glorious a Redeemer." By handing over his immortality, Jesus is thought, in some theories of atonement, to satisfy for sin by offering more than perfect obedience to God. By taking on the punishment humankind deserved, Jesus is thought in still other theories to substitute for the sin of humankind by offering up his life. In either case, according to these constructs, salvation history unfolded according to God's plan to such a degree that events described in the Old Testament were understood poetically to foreshadow incidents that would happen in the New. In other words, according to the perspective of salvation history, it is good that humankind exists and even that it sins so that Christ can come to bring about redemption. Christians are never to mind the image of God operating behind these theories, as one whose honor prevented forgiveness until due recompense had been paid, or as one whose wrath required that someone absorb the blows humankind so badly deserved. Both models are theologically problematic.

Increasingly, Christians are recognizing the inadequacies of the images of God the Father depicted in these theories.[7] If God the Father, knowing humans would fall into sin, justifies the creation of the world because a strategy for its redemption is also already firmly in place in God's mind, a strategy that requires crucifixion in order to accomplish salvation, evil has entered into the heart of God, and the Father is conceptualized as a monster. God the Father saves the many by requiring the murder of the Son. God the Father saves by resorting to violence. God the Father ends sacrifice by calling for sacrifice. God the Father redeems sin by committing sin. Such a God, then, is murderous, violent,

---

6. Augustine, *Enchiridion* 8.27.

7. See, for example, the compilation of essays in *Stricken by God? Nonviolent Identification and the Victory of Christ*, ed. Brad Jersak and Michael Hardin (Grand Rapids, MI: Eerdmans, 2007).

and sinful—an evil image, indeed. Yet this is the God to which many in the Christian churches are introduced each Lenten season when this divine drama is recounted, often with prayers that glorify the death itself, a death too often attributed to the hands of Jews once framed in the same liturgy as "perfidious."

It is worth noting that none of these theories have ever been indoctrinated into the church because they have, until now, not become controversial. Instead, one or more is dominant in any given epoch. But in the telling of satisfaction and penal substitution, and under the influence of this account of salvation history, violence is entered into the heart of God the Father and thereby into the very heart of Christianity by a process of theological reasoning that takes place over centuries. God the Father is portrayed as the mastermind behind the crucifixion, designing the divine drama from the beginning of time in order to justify creation. God can foresee that humans will freely choose to do what is evil. As the Creator, God the Father becomes in a satisfaction frame the uncompromising figure who refuses to forgive the debt until a death payment has been procured. In a substitutionary frame, God the Father becomes the wrathful deity who requires a scapegoat to bear the consequences for Adam's sin before forgiveness can be granted. In these models, the crucifixion has to occur if humankind is to be redeemed—and thus, the reasoning goes, because God desires redemption, so must God desire crucifixion. Judas, representing ultimately "the Jews," thus becomes both the protagonist and the foil. He carries through with the betrayal, an event that, according to this scheme, is necessary for the divine drama to unfold, but he is simultaneously ruined as the embodiment of the Christ killer. Jews after him are ever after persecuted, which is puzzling when, according to the mandates of salvation history, Christ's death is required as the necessary means by which God deigned to accomplish the redemption of the world. Jews have paid a heavy price for doing what Christian salvation history has claimed is necessary if redemption is going to unfold according to plan.[8]

Some contemporary theologians have shown how Christian theories of atonement have amounted to "divine child abuse," or "cosmic

---

8. I refer to this phenomenon as "the Judas complex," and I am grateful to the work of J. Denny Weaver, whose work on a nonviolent atonement theory validated what had bothered me since I asked a Sunday school teacher when I was in the third grade, "Why does Judas commit suicide if he was doing what God required?" Of course, I recognize where the story went awry in history now, but when I was a child, none of my teachers or pastors were able to help me make sense of it. See J. Dennis Weaver, *The Nonviolent Atonement* (Grand Rapids, MI: Eerdmans, 2001).

child abuse," as it was termed initially, contributing to the legitimization of other abuses, including domestic abuse.[9] Among the clearest more recent articulations of this argument is in a book coauthored by Rita Nakashima Brock and Rebecca Ann Parker called *Proverbs of Ashes: Violence, Redemptive Suffering, and the Search for What Saves Us*.[10] In their introduction, Parker recounts how a friend began a ministry for women. She opened their church as a sanctuary for women in situations of domestic violence. The friend observed how nearly "every woman who [has] come here for refuge has gone back to her violent husband or boyfriend. She thinks it [is] her religious duty."[11] This piety is loosely based in 1 Peter 2:18-25 (emphases mine):

> Slaves, accept the authority of your masters with all deference, not only those who are kind and gentle but also those who are harsh. *For it is a credit to you if, being aware of God, you endure pain while suffering unjustly.* If you endure when you are beaten for doing wrong, what credit is that? *But if you endure when you do right and suffer for it, you have God's approval.* For to this you have been called, because Christ also suffered for you, leaving you an example, *so that you should follow in his steps.*
> "He committed no sin,
>   and no deceit was found in his mouth."
> When he was abused, he did not return abuse; when he suffered, he did not threaten; but he entrusted himself to the one who judges justly. He himself bore our sins in his body on the cross, so that, free from sins, we might live for righteousness; by his wounds you have been healed. For you were going astray like sheep, but now you have returned to the shepherd and guardian of your souls.

Parker astutely processes messages of the faith through lenses of those experiencing domestic violence. She hears these lines through the ears of the abused: "Your life is only valuable if it's given away," "This is your cross to bear," "Jesus didn't turn away from the cup of suffering when God asked him to drink it."[12] She outlines the logic that abused women too often receive from the church: "A good woman would be willing to accept personal pain, and think only of the good

---

9. Steve Chalke and Alan Mann, *The Lost Message of Jesus* (Grand Rapids, MI: Zondervan, 2003), 16.

10. Rita Nakashima Brock and Rebecca Ann Parker, *Proverbs of Ashes: Violence, Redemptive Suffering, and the Search for What Saves Us* (Boston: Beacon Press, 2001).

11. Ibid., 17.

12. Ibid. Based on Matthew 16:25 and Mark 14:36.

of the family."[13] Women in these situations are trying to be good Christians, "to follow in the steps of Jesus."[14] Many internalize the message that things in life are structured according to God's will and therefore the oppression in this life should be accepted gladly, anticipating with joy the promise that "the last will be first" (Matt 20:16) in the life that is to come.

These are twisted understandings of biblical verses, to be sure—a point that Brock and Parker make through storytelling. But these are also common understandings in parishes throughout the world. Parker shares, for example, the story of a woman who feared for the safety of her children. The woman said, "The problem is my husband. He beats me sometimes. Mostly he is a good man. But sometimes he becomes very angry and he hits me. He knocks me down. One time he broke my arm and I had to go to the hospital. But I didn't tell them how my arm got broken."[15] Parker goes on to share the priest's counsel in this situation.

> The priest said I should rejoice in my sufferings because they bring me closer to Jesus. He said, "Jesus suffered because he loved us." He said, "If you love Jesus, accept the beatings and bear them gladly, as Jesus bore the cross." I've tried, but I'm not sure anymore. My husband is turning on the kids now. Tell me, is what the priest told me true?[16]

With Velarde's painting in the backdrop of our minds, viewers might imagine the woman in the portrait as the one receiving such advice from her priest. How much easier is it for her to believe her priest when she has heard for her entire life that everything happens for a reason, and that everything is a part of a divine plan? Is it any wonder that the violence of such a man would be protected when an image of God the Father as a murderous, scheming, torturous deity is entrenched so firmly in much of the Christian imagination? To put the argument succinctly: any God who redeems humankind by use of a deliberate and premeditated murder, even if the lamb goes willingly to the slaughter, is a monster, and belief in such a monster unleashes further monstrosity inevitably in those who become his disciples. If disciples are transformed into divinity, and divinity is conceptualized as inherently violent, is it any wonder that Christians have committed atrocities in the name of their religion? If the God Christians worship is violent, then

---

13. Ibid., 18.
14. Ibid.
15. Ibid., 21.
16. Ibid.

Christians too will legitimize the use of violence against one another. If God the Father sacrifices God the Son in a bloodbath in order to take God's wrath out on someone innocent whose death atones for the guilty, then a logical conclusion is that violence and torture, even murder, are permissible, a legitimate if utilitarian means of attaining a higher end.

Despite critiques of these theories, and despite convincing evidence that exposes the cross as the instrument of torture and execution it was, to question Christian understandings of atonement has for centuries been tantamount to anathema in our churches. Wayne Northey, in his contribution to the volume *Stricken by God? Nonviolent Identification and the Victory of Christ*, confirms, "The satisfaction theory has been seen as basic to Western orthodoxy and a non-negotiable pillar of evangelicalism in terms of its appropriation."[17] For the last few decades, however, increasing numbers of Christian theologians have been leveling critiques against these classical theories of atonement, wondering why Christians have been so willing to worship a God so violent that the Father would send His Son, intending him to accept a bloody, violent, and undeserved punishment, all in the name of love.[18] Such scholars suggest that, by laying out the atonement model in the way that they did, Christian theologians, Anselm and Calvin chief among them, Catholic and Protestant alike, admitted violence into the very heart of God—a violence that Catholics and Protestants have been too ready to emulate.

History is filled with Christians engaging in the world in precisely this fashion without questioning the presuppositions on which their behavior is based. The crusades of the Middle Ages; the pogroms of the early modern period up to the Holocaust; the apartheids of our own day—all of these have been justified theologically, a realization that truly ought to terrify and interrupt us.[19] If humans are so corrupt by

17. Wayne Northey, "The Cross: God's Peace Work—Towards a Restorative Peacemaking Understanding of the Atonement," in Jersak and Hardin, *Stricken by God?*, 356–77.

18. Derek Tidball, David Hillborn, and Justin Thacker, eds., *The Atonement Debate: Papers from the London Symposium on the Theology of Atonement* (Grand Rapids, MI: Zondervan, 2007).

19. "Interruption" is a term used within political theology. Coined by Catholic theologian Johann Baptist Metz, "interruption" points to the recognition that "concerns of first-world people are not like those of the third world." Bryan Pham describes Metz's theology by acknowledging that, "for the most part, we [in the first world] are not dealing with a population that is lacking in material goods. The concerns of the people of the first world are the concerns that deal with excess; we have entered a cycle of consuming too much and not see how destructive this is to us and to our world; the results are always emptiness and destruction. Metz's

nature that they are intrinsically disordered until they are cleansed by baptism, or until Christ covers their sinful nature through the seal that baptism offers, then it is only a short leap to the conclusion that those who remain unbaptized are intrinsically disordered; indeed, they are less than human. Some scholars of the Second World War have proposed that this theological trail leads directly to the Holocaust.[20] Atonement theologies, so say these critics, have given Christianity and nations operating under their presuppositions just theological cause to inflict all kinds of violence on humanity. The God behind the religion is, at the core, understood to be violent and full of vengeance, so those who aspire to be like this God are likewise going to be violent and vengeful.

In this chapter, I will interrogate the Christian doctrine of atonement that has, in some variations, suggested that if God were to extend mercy to sinners without exacting punishment, God's justice would be

---

interruption is aimed at waking us up from our dreamy world and disrupt our apparently comfortable lives by forcing us to look around our world and see how destructive we can be when we are blind to the suffering of those around us. Metz would say that we are then attentive to the 'other.' These kinds of disruptions can come as dangerous memories where we remember events of the past that question our consciences. Furthermore, Metz thinks that they have trapped us inside egotistic and ethnocentric mentalities; as a result, a political theology will interrupt us in our endless cycle of mundaneness of life and liberate us from consumption that in the end always leaves us not in fulfillment, but in emptiness of heart." See Bryan Pham, "Political Theology: Interruption," http://guweb2.gonzaga.edu/metz/theo.html.

20. See Christopher R. Browning, *Ordinary Men: Reserve Police Battalion 101 and the Final Solution in Poland* (New York: Harper, 1992, 1998). In his most recent edition, Browning addresses the scholarship of Daniel Jonah Goldhagen, whose PhD thesis was published as *Hitler's Willing Executioners: Ordinary Germans and the Holocaust* (New York: Vintage, 1997), and whose research was based in part on Browning's. They come to different conclusions, however, and Goldhagen's work is considered controversial. I am interested in how theological issues inform the debate. If a population is taught that a person is "enmity against God" unless or until he or she is baptized, as *The Solid Declaration of the Formula of Concord* puts it, how does that play out in a political space like the one created after World War I in Germany, when 69 percent of the population was Lutheran in 1939 (until Germany annexed Austria's largely Catholic population)? Does a theological assumption that all Jews are going to hell by their rejection of baptism lead to their dehumanization, thereby making it easier to kill, just as in Rwanda people killed those they referred to as "cockroaches" and in the military people are trained to kill "enemies"? The bibliography in this area is long. In this vein, however, see also Lucy Dawidowicz, *The War Against the Jews, 1933–1945* (New York: Bantam, 1975, 1986); and Johannes Wallmann, "The Reception of Luther's Writings on the Jews from the Reformation to the End of the 19th Century," *Lutheran Quarterly*, n.s. 1 (Spring 1987): 72–97.

collapsed. In other words, God's character is the issue. God's justice and mercy are in tension in one dominant Christian understanding of atonement—a theological problem that requires attention. Moreover, the Father and the Son seem to be at odds with one another when the Son requests the cup of suffering to be spared him, and when the Father appears to mandate he drink it. The scene leaves too many Christians under the impression that the Father wills the Son to suffer. In some ways, then, the issue before us is a Trinitarian one— and so I will turn to theological aesthetics to help Catholics through this dilemma. Christians ought not to abide conflict within the Trinity unless they are at peace with an eschatological vision still imbued with tension.

The issues outlined here develop already at the foot of the cross. So I will begin by considering the interpretations of the first followers of Christ as recorded in the Bible even as I attempt to retrieve the historical context in order to understand better what was happening on the ground in political terms on the night when Jesus was betrayed. Then I will contrast a restorative model of justice with retributive models in order to see how justice and mercy need not be understood to be at odds with one another, either politically or theologically. And finally, I will propose an understanding of the cross that situates the drama in a restorative framework. I will attempt to conceive of redemption in such a way that does not implicate God the Father in an act of torture, given that Catholic moral thought has understood torture, and the death penalty, to be intrinsically evil. And I will construct a way of thinking about the cross that is biblically sound, even as it is in keeping with the Christian theological tradition, albeit a thin tradition that has survived alongside more authoritarian and imperial models of the same. Such a rehabilitation of doctrine is necessary if Christians are going to reject the violence that has entered into the heart of their faith and if Christians are going to have integrity as a people of faith in calling for an end to violence, whether domestic, political, or structural.

Beauty and the Cross? Biblical Imaginations

Decades after his death, when the followers of Christ first began to record their understandings of what had unfolded in those hours when Jesus was arrested, tried, and tortured, they left behind, in writings later canonized as scriptural, three essential ways in which they were interpreting his death and resurrection. He was the High Priest, the Suffering Servant, and the Paschal Lamb. The author of the letter to the Hebrews, for example, situates Jesus' death in the context of the

Jewish celebration of Yom Kippur—the Day of Atonement. In this letter, the author refers to the practice of the High Priest sprinkling the blood of animals in the Holy of Holies to atone for the sins of the priest and of the people. In the letter to the Hebrews, Jesus is understood to be both the priest and the sacrifice. His blood purifies the Holy of Holies, and his death accomplishes forgiveness in a once and for all sacrifice to end all sacrifices (Heb 4–10, esp. 9:28).[21] The author of the Gospel of Mark, by contrast, opens with a quote from the prophet Isaiah, foreshadowing the suffering of Jesus from the beginning of his gospel. The author is building on the traditions of Isaiah (as well as other sacrificial language beyond that of Isaiah) to suggest, especially by his employment of the literary device of the messianic secret (he keeps Jesus' identity as a suffering messiah a secret until the end of the gospel) that Jesus is a suffering servant—one who suffers vicariously by bearing the cross, just as Isaiah had interpreted Judah to suffer vicariously on behalf of the nations of the world by enduring exile.[22] Likewise, the author of the Gospel of John interprets Christ to be the Paschal Lamb. Just as the Angel of Death had passed over the houses with doorposts marked by the blood of a lamb, so would the Angel of Death pass over those who became his followers. Already at the beginning of the gospel, John the

21. Harold W. Attridge, *The Epistle to the Hebrews: A Commentary on the Epistle to the Hebrews,* Hermeneia (Philadelphia, PA: Fortress Press, 1989). See also Craig Koester, *Hebrews: A New Translation with Introduction and Commentary,* Anchor Bible 36 (New Haven, CT: Yale University Press, 2001).

22. See William H. Bellinger, Jr., and William R. Farmer, *Jesus and the Suffering Servant: Isaiah 53 and Christian Origins* (Harrisburg, PA: Trinity Press International, 1998), and Adela Yarbro Collins, *Mark: A Commentary,* Hermeneia (Minneapolis, MN: Fortress Press, 2007). In response to an article that was published in the *Journal of Biblical Literature,* Adela Yarbro Collins writes, "Dowd and Struthers Malbon rightly conclude that the links between the Son of Man saying in Mark 10:45 and the Greek version of the poem of Isaiah 52:13–53:12 signify only that both the Servant and Jesus lost their lives for the benefit of many." Over against the idea that "ransom" refers to ransoming of captives (which she acknowledges is possible but unsupported), however, Yarbro Collins points to biblical passages that use "ransom" to speak of removal of guilt and the attendant possibility for reconciliation. In Leviticus, blood is poured out (as is Jesus' blood in Mark) for the expiation of sin. She concludes that Jesus' very human, very anguished death is made out to be, by the author of Mark, the way in which the plan of God is fulfilled—but this is in spite of the way Jesus died, not because of it. See Sharyn Dowd and Elizabeth Struthers Malbon, "The Significance of Jesus' Death in Mark: Narrative Context and Authorial Audience," *Journal of Biblical Literature* 125, no. 2 (Summer 2006): 271–97; with a response by Adela Yarbro Collins, "Mark's Interpretation of the Death of Jesus," *Journal of Biblical Literature* 128, no. 3 (Fall 2009): 545–54.

Baptist proclaims, "Here is the Lamb of God who takes away the sin of the world" (John 1:29).[23]

These biblical interpretations form the ground on which the doctrine of atonement will be constructed over the next two millennia. But it is important to recognize that these first-century interpretations of the cross themselves are the result of decades of theological activity—*Jewish* theological activity—as it was members of the Jewish community who first witnessed Christ's death and proclaimed his resurrection, and it was within the Jewish community that followers first struggled to understand what they had experienced. When they began to share the story, they interpreted it in terms that made sense to them. They drew on images and metaphors already in the Jewish imagination. And already these images and metaphors represented different, even competing models, each one saying very different things about the meaning of the cross.

Within the context of an evolving theological tradition, then, interpretations of the cross were becoming distanced from the actual historical and political events surrounding Jesus' death. Because early Christians certainly understood the political context of persecution, the cross became the site of a cosmic struggle between good and evil. This is something that the apostle Paul emphasizes in his letters (e.g., see Rom 6). But instead of understanding the cross to have very real and this-worldly political consequences, such that his followers should resist oppression as Jesus did, the cross was increasingly, especially after the fall of the Roman Empire, understood to have otherworldly implications. Instead of believing that followers should resist the evils of the world as embodied by unjust political orders, believers were taught to resist personal temptation for the spiritual salvation of the soul. The distance between the evolving Christian faith and the sociopolitical realities of what occurred on the night that Jesus was betrayed became so vast that many believers are now, two thousand years later, only vaguely familiar with the historical situation that led to Jesus' death. So I will sketch the contours of the historical events here in order to measure the distance between them and the interpretations about them that began in the years immediately following his death.

23. See Ernst Haenchen, *John: A Commentary on the Gospel of John*, Hermeneia (Philadelphia, PA: Fortress Press, 1984); Raymond E. Brown, *The Gospel According to John*, Anchor Bible 29-29A (Garden City, NY: Doubleday, 1966–1970); and Sandra Maria Schneiders, "The Lamb of God and the Forgiveness of Sin(s) in the Fourth Gospel," *Jesus Risen in Our Midst: Essays on the Resurrection of Jesus in the Fourth Gospel* (Collegeville, MN: Liturgical Press, 2013).

In the first century, Jerusalem was under Roman occupation. Headquartered in Caesarea at the regional level, Roman authorities considered treasonous any activity that undermined or threatened to undermine its sovereignty. They were suspicious of charismatic leaders in occupied lands who were gaining a widespread following, especially those speaking of other kingdoms, for they assumed that such figures were political revolutionaries. Figures suspected of resistance to Rome could expect to be arrested and tortured, perhaps even killed. The death sentence most often carried out in such cases was by public crucifixion in order to deter others from participating in political rebellion.

In Jesus' day, Rome greatly feared rebellion. This is illustrated through evidence that survives pertaining to the Roman governor of the region, Pontius Pilate. In a letter written by Agrippa I, reprinted in Philo's *Legatio*, the writer indicates that Pilate was "a man of inflexible disposition, harsh and obdurate."[24] Moreover, Pilate treated Jewish customs with contempt. He ordered the Roman garrison to enter Jerusalem with their ensigns (flags, etc.) bearing the image of the emperor. When protestors gathered to demand their removal, Pilate acquiesced, which gave the appearance of weakness. He later ordered the offerings to the temple to be applied to the building of an aqueduct. Protesters again gathered in Jerusalem, where they met the force of Pilate's soldiers, who "lashed into the people without mercy."[25] Galileans also lost their lives in such events. Although these specific incidents are not attested elsewhere, according to Luke 13:1, "At that very time there were some present who told him about the Galileans whose blood Pilate had mingled with their sacrifices." And according to the Gospel of Mark, others too lost their lives in an insurrection recorded in Mark 15:7, "Now a man called Barabbas was in prison with the rebels who had committed murder during the insurrection."

In fact, the historical record indicates that Pilate was so cruel that ultimately his own "recklessness caused his downfall."[26] A few years after Jesus' death, Pilate brutally executed respected and distinguished members of the community during an attack of Samaritans who were gathered on Mount Gerizim for purposes entirely religious, not revolutionary.[27] After this act of cruelty, Roman officials recognized that Pilate was a threat to long-lasting security in the region. So in the year 36, the

---

24. Emil Schürer, *The History of the Jewish People in the Age of Jesus Christ* (London: T & T Clark, 2000), 1.384.

25. Ibid., 1.385.

26. Ibid., 1.386.

27. Ibid., 1.383–39.

Syrian official Vitellius deposed Pilate and handed the administration of Judea to Marcellus. Fourth-century church historian Eusebius of Caesarea indicates that Pilate committed suicide within the next five years.[28] Pilate may come off looking genteel in the gospels of the New Testament because the first-century authors wanted their biographies of Jesus to circulate without provoking the outrage of Romans who continued to occupy Jewish lands.

All of the evangelists writing after the fall of the temple are reacting to the rejection within their own community of the proclamation that Jesus is Messiah. The exoneration of Pilate then serves to place greater responsibility for Jesus' death on fellow Jews with whom the authors of the gospels are increasingly antagonistic. The first readers would comprehend the author's motives when they encountered this sympathetic figure, Pilate, whom the authors portray as refined by admitting that he would execute, instead of Jesus, the "notorious prisoner" (Matt 27:16) Barabbas, also called a rebel "who had committed murder in the insurrection" (Mark 15:7 and Luke 23:19), and who would wash his hands of all responsibility for Jesus' death (Matt 27:24). Pilate's cowardly and unjust stance would not have been lost on the first readers, though, who knew him as murderous. In the same way, one might circulate messages in Syria today by saying only kind things about President Bashar al-Assad. If intercepted, officials might read these communiqués and consider the senders allies, when in fact they are rebels calling for an insurgency. This kind of a reality operating behind the New Testament texts is more evident to those who have lived through periods of political unrest in our own times but is all but invisible to those who have not.

Jesus traveled the countryside at a time when Romans were tightening the stranglehold on the Jews to prevent a rebellion, even as agitation for revolution was simmering within the Jewish population under occupation. Within this tense situation between the Romans and the Jews, it is clear that the Roman authorities would have been aware of Jesus of Nazareth, a charismatic leader gaining a large following in an area acquired by the empire. They were surely attentive to the fact that he was teaching about another kingdom. They would not have been interested in the theological intricacies of his teachings—only that, in teaching about a kingdom other than Rome, he was a threat to the empire.

---

28. Eusebius, *Historia Ecclesiae* 2.7. Historians know of no historical basis for Eusebius's statement about Pilate's supposed suicide. For a discussion, see Robin Jensen, "How Pilate Became a Saint," in the Biblical Archaeology Society's Online Archive, http://www.basarchive.org/sample/bswbBrowse.asp?PubID=BSBR&Volume=19&Issue=6&ArticleID=2#BSBR190614.

In the midst of all this, the information about the conspiracy around Jesus' arrest must be understood in political terms. In the Gospel of Luke, for example, the chief priests and crowds appealed to the sense that Jesus was a political revolutionary by accusing him with the words, "We found this man perverting our nation, forbidding us to pay taxes to the emperor, and saying that he himself is the Messiah, a king" (Luke 23:2), and that "he stirs up the people by teaching throughout all Judea" (Luke 23:5). These are political accusations in order to appeal to the Romans who would have had little interest in the religious disputes arising within the first-century Jewish community.

Understood within such a context, the Jewish authorities had a problem on their hands. If Jesus continued to foment rebellion by teaching of another kingdom, Jewish leaders feared that he would bring the wrath of Rome onto Jerusalem. The situation was particularly tense around feast days, Passover, Shavuot, and Sukkot, when the Jewish law dictated that "all your males shall appear before the LORD your God at the place that he will choose: at the festival of unleavened bread, at the festival of weeks, and at the festival of booths. They shall not appear before the LORD empty-handed" (Deut 16:16). At these times in the calendar year, Roman soldiers intimidated the Jews by moving in on their temple. Within this setting, it is easier to empathize with Jewish authorities' fear of Roman retaliation against them because of Jesus, as is testified in the Gospel of John:

> So the chief priests and the Pharisees called a meeting of the council, and said, "What are we to do? This man is performing many signs. If we let him go on like this, everyone will believe in him, and the Romans will come and destroy both our holy place and our nation." But one of them, Caiaphas, who was high priest that year, said to them, "You know nothing at all! You do not understand that it is better for you to have one man die for the people than to have the whole nation destroyed." He did not say this on his own, but being high priest that year he prophesied that Jesus was about to die for the nation, and not for the nation only, but to gather into one the dispersed children of God. So from that day on they planned to put him to death. (John 11:45-53)

Again later, the Gospel of John reads, "Caiaphas was the one who had advised the Jews that it was better to have one person die for the people" (John 18:14).

It is within this political milieu that Judas betrayed Jesus to the authorities. According to the Gospel of Luke, "[Judas] went away and conferred with the chief priests and officers of the temple police about how he might betray him to them. They were greatly pleased and agreed to give him money. So he consented and began to look for an opportunity to betray him to them when no crowd was present" (Luke 22:3-6). In exchange, then, for some pieces of silver, Judas eventually betrayed Jesus' location to the authorities. Desperate for money, desperate people will do desperate things. This is akin to community members who betrayed the location of resisters of the government in South Africa under apartheid. Many of these later committed suicide, feeling guilty for what they had done. Still others faced the practice of "necklacing," an expression of the oppressed community's anger after a betrayal. Back in Jesus' day, according to the Gospel of Mark, Judas kissed Jesus in order to identify him to the Romans (Mark 14:43-45). By the time of John's telling, Jesus stepped forward to identify himself, as he was by then understood to be on a divine mission (John 18:1-9). Jesus was arrested and, after a trial, he was handed over to the Romans, who crucified him among other political prisoners (Mark 15:27), alternately depicted as thieves, robbers, bandits, rebels, or revolutionaries.

It is not hard to imagine how difficult it was for his followers to process Jesus' death. Americans might remember the assassination of Martin Luther King, Jr.; El Salvadorans the assassination of Oscar Romero; Indians the assassination of Gandhi; and so on. These too were charismatic religious leaders involved in the public sphere, whose lives were ended all too abruptly because they, like Jesus, were working for justice for the oppressed. The story with Jesus is different, however, insofar as his disciples proclaimed his innocence as well as his resurrection and ascension. Paul proclaims the risen Christ and testifies to his appearances before the apostles:

> Now I would remind you, brothers and sisters, of the good news that I proclaimed to you, which you in turn received, in which also you stand, through which also you are being saved, if you hold firmly to the message that I proclaimed to you—unless you have come to believe in vain. For I handed on to you as of first importance what I in turn had received: that Christ died for our sins in accordance with the scriptures, and that he was buried, and that he was raised on the third day in accordance with the scriptures, and that he appeared to Cephas, then to the twelve. Then he appeared to more than five hundred brothers and sisters at one time, most of whom are still alive, though some have died. Then he appeared to James, then to all the apostles. Last of all, as to one untimely born, he appeared also to me. (1 Cor 15:1-8)

In the face of all of this, the community struggled to understand what had happened. They struggled to go on without him and to carry on his work. Already within two decades of Jesus' death and resurrection, the apostle Paul interpreted Jesus as the Paschal Lamb, killed as he was during the season of Passover: "Clean out the old yeast so that you may be a new batch, as you really are unleavened, for our paschal lamb, Christ, has been sacrificed" (1 Cor 5:7). After Paul, probably writing in the second half of the first century, the author of the letter to the Hebrews interpreted Christ as the high priest as well as the sacrificial offering (Heb 4–10). Around the time of the destruction of the temple in 70, the author of Mark draws on the idea of vicarious suffering, "For the Son of Man came not to be served but to serve, and to give his life [as] a ransom for many" (Mark 10:45). And finally, by the turn of the century, Jesus as the Lamb of God was given greater theological sophistication by the author of the Gospel of John.

Less than understanding the drama in terms of a salvation history that was unfolding, predetermined from the dawn of time and foreshadowed by figures in Hebrew Scripture, a perspective that flowered fully in the Middle Ages, we have in reality a community struggling to make sense of an atrocity, the torturous murder and death of someone they knew to be righteous. In order to make sense of it, they were constructing a grand narrative on familiar scaffolding. The community was interpreting Jesus in light of Abraham, in light of Moses, in light of David. Proclamations about Jesus formed a phase in the development of Judaism, one that would never become dominant within the Jewish tradition itself. In the second half of the first century, these understandings of Jesus were being worked out among his followers even as the larger Jewish community itself was developing its own traditions, based on long-established practices and beliefs that were themselves being reinterpreted, especially after the destruction of the temple. The rift between the followers of Jesus and the larger Jewish community, begun in a splintering over the question of circumcision, became more pronounced over time, in part due to the influx of Gentile believers into the Jesus movement. Thus, a new religion was eventually born and, by the mid-second century, Christianity was venturing on a course entirely separate from Judaism.

Beauty and the Cross? Historical Imaginations

As Christianity and Judaism became increasingly divorced from one another, understandings about Jesus' death and crucifixion that were less obviously Jewish in nature took root in the Christian imagination. For the first millennium, an understanding of Christ's victory over evil, sin, and death reigned. Known in its various instantiations as "Christus Victor," this interpretation of the drama understood resurrection to be the moment of Christ's victory over the powers of evil that had put him to death. By raising Jesus from the dead, God proclaimed victory over the powers of sin, death, and evil that had killed him. By becoming baptized, followers of Jesus shared in the victory accomplished on that first glorious day.[29]

In the eleventh century, however, a different interpretation of the cross was introduced to the Christian world. And so it is in the eleventh century that I want us to begin tracking what happens to Christianity's image of God the Father, for my concern is that the theories that develop during the second millennium introduce a conflict into the heart of the Trinity between the will of God the Father and the will of God the Son. At this time, an image of God the Father as uncompromising and unforgiving deepens in the Christian imagination, an image often traced in an anti-Semitic way to the Hebrew Scriptures, so Christians need to be attentive to this pattern of thought. It is worth noting that our issue here is squarely with the image portrayed of God the Father. Our focus here is not on the Son. There is no question that Jesus made choices freely throughout the drama, and that this entails a sacrifice. But I will want to ask: What did he sacrifice? To whom was it sacrificed? And for what reason?

In the eleventh century, Anselm articulated what has become the dominantly held view regarding atonement within Catholicism, the "satisfaction" theory. This understanding was cast in terms that made sense to medieval Christians who were immersed in a feudal culture of honor and shame. In his *Cur Deus Homo* ("Why God Became Man"), Anselm articulated the theory that humans were reconciled to God by Jesus' death on the cross, which is a departure from earlier Christian belief in the resurrection as the locus of redemption.[30] It is in this model that theological problems develop, as Anselm introduces a conflict between God's justice on the one hand and God's mercy on the other. In this model, despite God's mercy that by its very nature desires to forgive humankind, God cannot simply forgive humans. God's honor had been violated by sin. Anselm thought it would violate God's justice for God the Father simply to forgive humankind without exacting a debt penalty. Therefore, a satisfactory payment is required. Note that it is God's *honor*

---

29. Gustaf Aulén, *Christus Victor* (New York: Macmillan, 1958).

30. Anselm, *Cur Deus Homo*, in *A Scholastic Miscellany: From Anselm to Ockham*, ed. Eugene R. Fairweather (Philadelphia, PA: Westminster Press, 1956).

that the satisfactory atonement or debt payment is intended to restore, enabling God to forgive without compromising God's justice. *Cur Deus Homo* is Anselm's dialogical attempt to understand how Jesus' actions on the cross could restore God's honor, and it unfolds in the form of an extended syllogism and as a conversation between Anselm and his fellow monk Boso. Because it is a syllogism, the entire argument collapses if one of the assertions can be sufficiently challenged.

Anselm begins with the assertion that whoever has a rational nature is created to love and choose the highest good supremely.[31] Since the highest good is God, whoever fails to render to God what God is owed is guilty of sin and, by sinning, dishonors God.[32] Because God is owed perfect obedience or, as Anselm explains, perfect "uprightness of will,"[33] those who dishonor God by failing to live with perfect uprightness of will owe a debt to God and must pay it back. It is already at this point in his argument that Anselm introduces a conflict into the heart of the Trinity by suggesting that it is not fitting for God merely to forgive the debt without exacting a penalty. Simply forgiving the debt would collapse God's justice. "It does not belong to [God's] liberty or compassion or will to let the sinner go unpunished who makes no return to God of what the sinner has defrauded him. . . . Therefore the honor taken away must be repaid, or punishment must follow; otherwise . . . God will not be just to himself."[34] And herein lies the problem. Forgiveness must be withheld until the debt is paid in order to maintain God's justice. According to Anselm, God's mercy and justice are understood to be at odds with one another until the debt is satisfied, at which time God's honor is restored. It is an argument imbued with Western notions of jurisprudence that are unequivocally retributive in orientation. Justice, according to this line of thought and by definition, means to punish the wicked and to reward the righteous. This is a presupposition that requires attention and to which I shall return shortly. It also dismisses the reality that, if historical, Jesus asked the Father to forgive those who were killing him before he died. This indicates that they were in need of forgiveness, which denotes moreover that Jesus believed they were doing something wrong. It also means that Jesus did not believe that forgiveness was forestalled until his death remitted payment for their sin. The implications of these points merit serious contemplation.

31. Ibid., 2.1.
32. Ibid., 1.11.15.
33. Ibid.
34. Ibid., 1.12–13.

Anselm's argument continues by asserting that whoever satisfies the debt must possess both a human and a divine nature—an argument that defends the church's doctrine of the hypostatic union, or the mystical marriage between the divine Logos and the human body and soul of Jesus. Regarding the necessity that a human pay the satisfaction, Anselm writes, "For, as it is right for man to make atonement for the sin of man, it is also necessary that he who makes the atonement should be the very being who has sinned, or else one of the same race. . . . It is therefore necessary that the man by whom Adam's race shall be restored be taken from Adam."[35] In other words, since a human being brought the downfall of the entire human race, a human being must be the one to pay back the debt owed to God.

Anselm goes on to argue that it must also be a divine being who pays the debt obligation. Anselm begins his explanation in this way: "You make no satisfaction unless you restore something greater than the amount of that obligation."[36] Here, Anselm reminds Boso that humans, in exchange for life, owe God perfect obedience, or uprightness of will. The debt is incurred when the human being sins against God. That is to say, Adam incurs the debt. Once sin has come, all humans continue to owe God perfect obedience in exchange for life. But due to the fall of Adam, they owe still more in order to compensate for original sin, in addition to their own personal sin: "When you render anything to God which you owe him, irrespective of your past sin, you should not reckon this as the debt which you owe for sin. . . . But what do you give to God by your obedience, which is not owed him already since he demands from you all that you are and have and can become?"[37] Since no mere mortal can give God more than one's own perfect obedience, and not even that given the stain of original sin they are already carrying, the one who restores God's honor must be more than human—in other words, the debt must be paid by a human being who is also a divine being. Therefore, "No man except this one ever gave to God what he was not obliged to lose, or paid a debt he did not owe."[38] This man, of course, is Jesus the Christ.

But how does Christ give more than perfect obedience to God, for he too, as a human, must be perfectly upright? Anselm addresses this quandary by stating his belief that "had man never sinned he never

35. Ibid., 2.8.
36. Ibid., 1.21.
37. Ibid., 1.20.
38. Ibid.

would have died,"[39] for "it is inconsistent with God's wisdom and justice to compel man to suffer death without fault, when he made him holy to enjoy eternal blessedness."[40] According to Anselm, human beings were created to be immortal—and they would have remained so in the garden had they never sinned. Since, however, "all have sinned and fall short of the glory of God" (Rom 3:23), and since "the wages of sin is death" (Rom 6:23), Christ makes atonement for sin by accepting an unmerited death—a death only a sinless, and thereby divine, being can offer. Because Anselm understands Jesus to be born of a virgin through whom he did not contract the stain of original sin, and because Jesus never committed a personal sin, he need never have died. "Therefore, he who wishes to make atonement for man's sin should be one who can die if he chooses."[41] According to Anselm, Jesus alone can save because he alone can offer his own immortality as a transaction to free those who share the human race from the debt of Adam. Since the atonement must be paid by one of the race of humankind, and since only a sinless being can offer such an atoning death, the offering must be made by one who is both fully human and fully divine. Despite his immortality, Jesus the Christ gives his life, and in so doing satisfies the debt owed to God once and for all, so that no one need ever lose eternal life. His death enables participation in a new life through faith.

This idea of reconciliation with God was pushed a step further during the Reformation. John Calvin, in his attempt to systematize Protestant doctrine in his *Institutes of the Christian Religion*, reinterpreted atonement theory by stressing that God's justice (rather than God's honor) required a punishment (rather than a satisfactory debt payment) paid by a human being. This theory, closely related to Anselm's *satisfactory* model of atonement, is known as the *penal substitution* model. According to Calvin, Christ was punished in Adam's place, thereby taking all of the guilt for Adam's sin upon himself. Calvin understood that "God, to whom we were hateful through sin, was appeased by the death of his Son. . . . [Just as] by the sin of Adam we were alienated from God and doomed to destruction, so by the obedience of Christ we are restored to his favor as if we were righteous."[42] The salvific work is located entirely in Christ's death on the cross. Calvin wrote in his

---

39. Ibid., 2.2.

40. Ibid.

41. Ibid., 2.12.

42. John Calvin, *Institutes of the Christian Religion*, trans. Henry Beveridge, Christian Classics Ethereal Library (2001), 2.17.3, http://www.ccel.org/c/calvin/institutes/institutes.html.

Institutes of the Christian Religion, "In short, we are admirably taught by the ancient figures what power and efficacy there is in Christ's death."[43] Calvin acknowledged that this indicates some interruption between the Father and the Son in the Trinity. He writes, "The Father is not said to have consulted the advantage of his Son in his services, but to have given him up to death, and not spared him, because he loved the world (Rom. 8)." Believing he was retrieving a more biblical faith, Calvin taught that Christ's sacrifice of his life on the cross accomplishes this propitiation, this restoration of God's favor:

> "Herein is love, not that we loved God, but that he loved us, and sent his Son to be the propitiation for our sins" (1 John 4:10). These words clearly demonstrate that God, in order to remove any obstacle to his love towards us, appointed the method of reconciliation in Christ. There is great force in this word "propitiation"; for in a manner which cannot be expressed, God, at the very time when he loved us, was hostile to us until reconciled in Christ.[44]

Defenders of these accounts of atonement want to say that there is no issue here because Jesus went willingly to his death. To his credit, Anselm wrestled extensively in *Cur Deus Homo* with the question of whether God compelled Jesus to die. Indeed, Anselm returns to the question so frequently in his dialogue that it gives the impression that the issue weighed heavily on his mind, and it is a line that Boso is driving in his interrogation of Anselm's position. In a clear response to Boso's question on this point, Anselm writes, "The Father did not compel him to suffer death, or even allow him to be slain, against his will, but of his own accord he endured death for the salvation of men."[45] Also to his credit, Anselm locates Christ's mission in his holiness, not in his death. In other words, Jesus was sent to be holy, and on account of his holiness, he was killed. He was obedient not to God the Father's death wish for him but to the call to be perfectly holy in every situation. According to Anselm, "God did not, therefore, compel Christ to die; but he suffered death of his own will, not yielding up his life as an act of obedience, but on account of his obedience in maintaining holiness; for he held out so firmly in this obedience that he met death on account of it."[46] This might be read in light of history, in the sense that other figures

43. Ibid., 2.17.4.
44. Ibid., 2.17.2.
45. Anselm, *Cur Deus Homo* 1.8.
46. Ibid., 1.9.

who have died for obedience to holiness can be identified: Oscar Romero in El Salvador and Martin Luther King, Jr., in the United States, to name only two. But Anselm equivocates on the issue of holiness. Is holiness constituted by Jesus' obedience to the Father's wish for him to die in order to achieve redemption of humankind, or is holiness constituted by Jesus' obedience to the Father's wish for him not to return evil for evil, and thereby to remain righteous in every moment of the drama? There are passages in Anselm where it appears to be the former rather than the latter.

According to Anselm, the Father did not order Jesus to be crucified and took no delight in his suffering. But Anselm's treatment of the matter is filled with tension, because God the Father wills redemption, and redemption can only come through the means established before the creation of the world. Therefore, God must will the cross. Indeed, as I pointed out earlier, the tradition's grand narrative suggests that God intended for Jesus to die on the cross from the beginning of the world, for God's goodness would not allow God to create the world knowing it would fall into sin unless God had conceived of redemption from the start. And since redemption apparently requires the cross of Christ, theologians deduced that Christ's death on the cross was God's intention from the beginning. Anselm's only protection of the integrity of the Trinity is to say that Jesus accepts that the crucifixion is the best way to reconcile humanity to God, and willingly concedes to the Father's wishes: "[Christ] preferred to suffer, rather than that the human race should be lost; as if he were to say to the Father, 'Since you do not desire the reconciliation of the world to take place in any other way, in this respect, I see that you desirest my death; let your will, therefore, be done, that is, let my death take place, so that the world may be reconciled to you.' "[47] Anselm does not criticize Jesus' rather bold resignation to fideism on this point. Instead, Anselm is careful to delineate how believers should be pleased by Jesus' choice to accept death for the greater good, while not taking pleasure in the suffering of Jesus itself: "Thus, when we see a man who desires to endure pain with fortitude for the accomplishment of some good design, though we acknowledge that we wish to have him endure that pain, yet we do not choose, nor take pleasure in his suffering, but in his choice."[48] In a similar vein, Anselm is careful to say that even the Father was not pleased by Christ's suffering, though God the Father certainly wished the Son to

47. Ibid.
48. Ibid., 1.10.

endure death for a greater end: "[Since God the Father] did not prevent him from choosing, or from fulfilling his choice, it is proper to say that *he wished the Son to endure death so piously and for so great an object*, though he was not pleased with his suffering."[49] Nonetheless, Anselm departs from the previous thousand years of Christian history with its focus on resurrection as the locus of redemption and locates the salvific work of Christ squarely on the cross. Although he recognizes it as problematic and turns to it time and again, the account Anselm provides suggests, as well, that holiness is bound up with the Father's will for Jesus to die, rather than with the Father's will for Christ to live a holy life that would evoke an unholy vengeance within a sinful humankind who wished to put such a man to death.

> It is also a fair interpretation that it was by that same holy will by which the son wished to die for the salvation of the world, that the Father gave him the commandment (yet not by compulsion), and the cup of suffering, and spared him not, but gave him up for us *and desired his death*; and that the Son himself was obedient even unto death, and learned obedience from the things which he suffered.[50]

Indeed, for Anselm, Jesus' death supplicates the Father, indicating that there is something in the Father's heart that requires pacification: "And, by the names of Father and Son, a wondrous depth of devotion is excited in the hearts of hearers, when it is said that the Son supplicates the Father on our behalf."[51] Sentences like these are leading many theologians today to agree that Anselm enters something sinister into the very heart of God—a problem that he himself seems to recognize as he returns to it repeatedly throughout *Cur Deus Homo*. He also indicated that because parts of the argument were circulating, he rushed to finish it.[52] Perhaps he would have ironed out this matter if he had been granted the luxury of time.

Modern writers have drawn attention to how both of these models of atonement—Anselm's and Calvin's—imagine God to devise the entire scheme from the beginning of time. From before all time, God, in God's omniscience, foresees that humans will, by their freedom, transgress the divine order. Therefore, God designs a means by which to reconcile humanity to God. According to both dominantly held views,

49. Ibid. Emphasis mine.
50. Ibid., 1.10. Emphasis mine.
51. Ibid., 2.18.
52. Ibid., preface.

the scheme requires a bloody sacrifice. Indeed, both models require the death of God's own Son. The sacrifice of a fully divine and fully human life was necessary, God plots, in order to repay the debt to restore God's honor. One must accept the penalty to appease God's justice. Now freed again to become holy, Christians are fully transformed into saints through the process of sanctification and may hope for acceptance into the company of heaven by God, making it possible for them to enjoy eternity in the immediate presence of the Holy One. For God, knowing from before all time that this end—the blessedness for which humans were created—would be achieved, the ends justify the means. God becomes the mastermind behind the entire drama, and Jesus the Lamb goes willingly to his slaughter. And this is where Anselm's syllogism falls apart—for the conflict that was introduced at the beginning of the syllogism has now played out, requiring God to desire the death of a human being in order to enable forgiveness. It is a monstrous image only magnified if the torture of the Son to death is imagined as the necessary means to accomplish redemption. A different theological approach needs to be recovered from the tradition and reintroduced to the people of God if Christians are going to have any hope of having integrity as people of peace, hope, and love in contrast to the violent ways of the world.

Beauty and the Cross: Nonviolent Imaginations

The violence at the heart of these theories of atonement, and therefore at the heart of the Christian image of God the Father, is a problem that Mennonite theologian J. Denny Weaver takes seriously as he struggles to understand the meaning of the cross. Author of *The Nonviolent Atonement*, Weaver examines the gospel accounts and concludes "there is no indication of any kind that the death of Jesus in this story satisfies anything."[53] Contrasting the political history of Jesus' death with the development of theories of atonement, Weaver writes,

> Stated another way, nothing about [the narrative of the cross] turns it into a death needed by God to satisfy a divine need whether that need is punishment demanded by divine law or restoration of honor to an offended God, or restoration of distorted order of creation in God's universe, or restoration of worship that was wrongfully withdrawn from God. Those elements, lifted from some of the several satisfaction

53. J. Dennis Weaver, "The Nonviolent Atonement: Human Violence, Discipleship and God," in Jersak and Hardin, *Stricken By God?*, 316–55.

atonement theories, are simply not there when we rehearse the narrative of Jesus as given in the Gospels. These requirements of satisfaction are composed in some other paradigms and brought from somewhere else and placed on—imposed on—this story from outside.[54]

At the same time, Weaver is not satisfied to think that Jesus comes merely to demonstrate how to live—an account which Catholics would consider to be Pelagian and therefore heretical in its simplest articulation because it would suggest that humans could simply imitate Jesus, something that original sin prevents them from doing. Weaver, too, understands the drama to entail more than a mere demonstration of holiness. He believes Jesus' life and resurrection to have salvific power. In order to construct a nonviolent theory of atonement, Weaver examines the gospel accounts of Jesus and notes four critical points related to the reign of God as just and nonviolent.

First, Weaver emphasizes that Jesus' ministry had a strong social component, which was oriented to caring for the poor, the widow, the orphan, the prisoner, the immigrant, and the sick. Weaver argues, "Jesus carried on an activist mission whose purpose was to make the rule of God visible," which was a ministry that had "confrontational components."[55] Second, Jesus' actions provoked opposition.[56] Ultimately, this opposition called for his death. Christ's death was a result of human bloodlust—not God's. Third, "Jesus' way of confronting injustice and uplifting the poor rejected violence as a way to alleviate suffering."[57] Jesus taught his disciples strategies of nonviolent resistance, such as turning the other cheek and loving the enemy.[58] He also forbade his companions to defend him with swords.[59] And fourth, this mission to make the reign of God visible "encompasse[d] the created order."[60] In other words, salvation not only entails a heavenly afterlife but also is situated in the here and now. Weaver understands that the "struggle between reign of God and rule of evil occurs not in the cosmos but on earth, where the life and teaching of Jesus as a whole engage the struggle."[61]

54. Ibid., 323.
55. Ibid., 321.
56. Ibid.
57. Ibid., 322.
58. Ibid. Based on Matthew 5:39 and Matthew 5:44. For a reading of turning the other cheek as resistance, see Walter Wink, "Jesus' Third Way," in *The Powers That Be: Theology for a New Millenium* (New York: Random House, 2010).
59. Ibid., 322. Based on Matthew 26:52.
60. Ibid., 321.
61. Ibid., 324.

In no uncertain terms, Weaver understands the cross politically. According to Weaver, the Roman Empire used violence to kill a man they perceived to be a threat: a revolutionary, either potential or real. Jesus resisted what was demonic in them by using what scholars in justice and peace studies would today refer to as strategies of nonviolent resistance, but he was eliminated nevertheless in a brutal execution. To believe that God the Father is behind it, as classical theories articulate, makes God a conspirator with those who killed him. Such a belief makes God the Father a friend of Rome and an enemy of Christ—a twist that mires the story, and God's involvement in it, in utter confusion. Pinpointing this aberrant logic, Weaver writes,

> The various figures who conspire to kill Jesus—the mob, some religious authorities, Pilate, the Roman occupation force, obviously oppose the rule of God. After all, they kill the one in whom God is present on earth. But on the other hand, in satisfaction atonement, Jesus' death is needed as that which satisfies the offended honor of God. As a result, those who kill Jesus are actually acting according to the will of God.[62]

Weaver's approach extricates God the Father from the political conspiracy to kill Jesus. But Weaver maintains that there is metaphysical resonance to what unfolded in Jerusalem during that tumultuous week two thousand years ago. For Weaver, there are cosmic implications to the story: "One sees the nonviolence of Jesus when observing the story of his life, but one can also note the intrinsic necessity of nonviolence in the manner in which the reign of God confronted evil," Weaver writes.[63] "The triumph of the reign of God depends not on God's capacity to exercise either retributive violence or the greatest violence, but on the power of the reign of God to overcome in spite of and in the face of the violence of evil."[64] In short, Weaver locates the story's metaphysical import of the victory of goodness over evil not on the cross but in the resurrection.

> The victory of the reign of God over the forces of evil symbolized by Rome that killed Jesus, occurs through resurrection. Of particular importance for the moment is to point out that this victory through resurrection is a nonviolent victory, that is, a victory without divine violence. . . . Dealing death to Jesus exposes the fundamental, mutually exclusive means between the forces of evil, symbolized by Rome, and the reign of God made present in the life of Jesus. The ultimate

62. Ibid., 338–39.
63. Ibid., 330–31.
64. Ibid., 331.

weapon of the forces of evil is death, which is an act that annihilates existence. . . . It is this denial of existence that the reign of God overcomes through resurrection.[65]

Classical atonement theories were premised on the argument that whoever violates God's will must somehow remit a compensatory payment for what was taken in order to restore or repay what was dishonored or violated. Anselm's theory was rooted in medieval feudalism, a political system in which vassals pledged loyalty to an overlord by serving in his stead during times of war in exchange for rights to farm a plot of land. If the overlord's honor was violated as a result of the agreement, the overlord levied his expectation of a satisfactory payment. Anselm interpreted this in a metaphysical framework and developed his theory. A few centuries later, Calvin, trained as a lawyer, applied the conceptual framework and vocabulary with which he was familiar—that of sixteenth-century criminal law—to atonement theory. In either case, these assumptions, derived from the feudalism of medieval Europe or sixteenth-century jurisprudence, were steeped in Westernized frameworks, infused with retributive and punitive notions of justice. These systems presumed that a violation merited some kind of penalty, whether a willful sacrifice of immortality or the undergoing of a death penalty on behalf of someone else. Regardless, salvation was located in death.

From the eleventh century onward, the cross was understood to be the instrument by which God desired to save the world. Instead of a tool used by the enemy to kill Christ, the cross became understood in Christian history as the instrument used by God to redeem the human race—a shift that has had disastrous consequences theologically, politically, and personally: theologically, by giving Christianity an image of God the Father as cruel and violent; politically, by giving Christianity a divine foundation for the idea that the ends, even the ends of torture and capital punishment, justify the means; and personally, by providing a theological foundation to support the use of violence to achieve a higher end, including too often in domestic spaces, when a husband or father resorts to violence in order to "correct" the behavior of a wife or child.

In order to construct a theory of atonement that abides harmony within the Trinity, that sees no tension in the relationship between the justice of the Father and the mercy of the Son, and that opposes violence intrinsically, let us look to Africa. In the philosophical traditions

NB

---

65. Ibid., 330.

of sub-Saharan Africa, there is a concept that was made more widely known throughout the world by Nelson Mandela in leading his country's "long walk to freedom" from the tyranny of apartheid. *Ubuntu* is the Zulu word that expresses the understanding that we are human through other people. It expresses the idea that "I am because you are." We are dependent on one another for our very being and survival. According to the thinking of *ubuntu*, we are all born into an intricate, luminous, and radiant web of interconnectedness, in such a way that when the being of one is diminished, all are diminished, and where the being of one is nourished, all are nourished.

The philosophy of *ubuntu* underlies South Africa's truth and reconciliation process. Of the philosophical principles grounding the commission over which he presided, Archbishop Emeritus Desmond Tutu contrasts Western with African ideals of justice:

> One might . . . say that perhaps justice fails to be done only if the concept we entertain of justice is retributive justice, whose chief goal is to be punitive, so that the wronged party is really the state, something impersonal, which has little consideration for the real victims and almost none for the perpetrator. We contend that there is another kind of justice, restorative justice, which was characteristic of traditional African jurisprudence. Here the central concern is not retribution or punishment. In the spirit of *ubuntu*, the central concern is the healing of breaches, the redressing of imbalances, the restoration of broken relationships, a seeking to rehabilitate both the victim and the perpetrator, who should be given the opportunity to be reintegrated into the community he has injured by his offense. This is a far more personal approach, regarding the offense as something that has happened to persons and whose consequence is a rupture in relationships. Thus we would claim that justice, restorative justice, is being served when efforts are being made to work for healing, for forgiving, and for reconciliation.[66]

Based on Africa's traditional legal practice of resolving conflict by finding "justice under a tree," where those locked in conflict met with the elders of the community to find a resolution that satisfied all parties, perpetrators and victims alike, African ideals of justice emphasize restoration of the parties to peaceful relations in community with one another. Rather than concerning themselves primarily with the punishment of wrongdoers, African elders in the ancient world desired to prevent

66. Desmond Tutu, *No Future without Forgiveness* (New York: Doubleday, 1999), 54–55.

further fragmentation of the community. And it is on this philosophy that a process of truth and reconciliation is based.

When Glenda Wildschut, one of South Africa's seventeen Truth and Reconciliation commissioners, describes the work of the commission's practice of restorative justice, she speaks at length about the philosophy of *ubuntu*.[67] She explains how *ubuntu* is all well and good when humans are behaving themselves. She observes, however, that it becomes somewhat more difficult when humans betray the public's trust. Whereas most people who have been influenced by European ideas of jurisprudence would feel more comfortable with criminals being locked up behind bars for the rest of their days, the philosophy of *ubuntu*, she explains, recognizes the criminal's dignity and humanity as well. The philosophy of *ubuntu* is concerned about the one against whom a violation has occurred—and how properly to redress the anguish borne of violation, just as it is concerned with the rights and well-being of the wrongdoer. Therefore, *ubuntu* prompts members of the community to ask what can be done to recompense adequately those who have been violated, as well as what can be done to restore those who have transgressed the social order back into community. *Ubuntu* requires the community at large to ask: What can be done to heal our society, so that all within our community can flourish again? How do we move from here to a place where the entire community—survivors and perpetrators alike—can be restored to wholeness? Is such a restoration possible, particularly when the devastation is complete and there has been a loss of life? What options are available to a community practicing restorative justice in such cases?

Because families of victims desired knowledge of what had happened to their loved ones, the Truth and Reconciliation process in South Africa was intended to facilitate the stabilization of civil society by offering the public a disclosure of truth so the rift that had developed between communities on the basis of skin color could be closed. The process was conceived in the hope that, by offering forgiveness in the context of a public confession of wrongdoing, the hearing of truth would begin the process of healing for the South African society by removing the thirst for vengeance in the wronged and by requiring of the wrongdoer a very public statement of accountability. The survivors were told the truth about what had happened to their loved ones, providing them

---

67. Glenda Wildschut has come as a guest lecturer to our course, "AIDS, Apartheid, and the Arts of Resistance," which has been offered in Cape Town and Guguletu in 2008, 2011, and 2015.

with the sense of closure that so many needed to grieve and to move forward. Forgiveness was contingent on neither the receipt of an apology nor on the expression of truth, although apologies were sometimes offered and truth was often uncovered. The commission hoped that the receipt of such grace would inspire *metanoia*, a change of heart in the perpetrator, creating a will to contribute to the common good. Of course, not everyone was offered forgiveness. And not all were granted amnesty. Most offenders were thought by the commission unfit to live in community, and they were sentenced to jail. But even so, many survivors offered a word of forgiveness and some perpetrators were granted amnesty. Skeptics say that some people got away with murder. Advocates argue that the process prevented a civil war and the creation of more atrocities still. Still others think it is too soon to tell.

Two principles at the heart of the commission's work are forgiveness and reconciliation. These concepts, so central to the Christian religion, are variously understood. Many Christians flounder when asked, "What does it mean to forgive?" "Forgetting" is soon offered half-heartedly as a definition, so thoroughly connected are the two in the Western Christian imagination—and thus many Christians feel like failures for their inability to forget wrongdoings. But the mind does not work in this way. The memory holds all things, even repressed memories, so to feel a failure for an inability to forget is an interiorized abasement that is both destructive and counterproductive. Moreover, it is rooted in a shallow understanding of what it means to forgive.

Miroslav Volf confronts the definition of forgiveness squarely in his profound book, *The End of Memory: Remembering Rightly in a Violent World*. He treats the issues of memory and forgiveness by openly acknowledging that memories, particularly memories of wrongdoing, cannot be simply stamped out at will. Volf probes the role of memory especially in cases of trauma, applicable certainly to the thousands who experienced torture in South Africa and the millions who lived in fear under the apartheid regime. He accepts that the issue of forgiveness in relation to memory is rather more complicated than mere erasure, which is impossible at any rate. Volf searches for approaches to the question of how one ought to remember *rightly*.

> Today the association of forgiveness with the letting go of memories strikes us as immoral, unhealthy, dangerous—to top it off, impossible. The association seems immoral because giving up on such memories breaks faith with victims and white-washes perpetrators; unhealthy because memories of evils suffered and committed are deemed essential to our identity, and it is claimed that their disappearance would wreak

even greater havoc on our psyches than their painful presence; dangerous because the absence of the memory of misdeeds leaves no deterrent
for future perpetrators and seduces potential victims to let down their
guard; and finally, impossible because major events in our lives remain
indelibly inscribed in our memories and continue to be operative in sub-
conscious memory even if they disappear from conscious memory. . . .
Given how central memory is to human identity, the question cannot
be whether we *should* remember our past or forget it. The interesting
questions are rather: *What* should we remember? *How* should we go
about remembering? Should wrongs be remembered *eternally*?[68]

One key to understanding forgiveness and "remembering rightly"
in the South African context is an insight shared with me by Richard
Cogill, a South African Anglican priest whose family was forcibly removed from Simon's Town in 1973. His family was relocated to a township near Cape Town called Ocean View. We became friends when he, by
a circuitous route, enrolled at Gustavus Adolphus College in the United
States. We subsequently attended seminary together and met up again
when I began the process of bringing students to South Africa in 2006. As
he was introducing me to his country and its history, he talked with me
about distinctions between forgiveness and reconciliation. Even though
the two are often collapsed into the same moment in the Western Christian imagination, he told me that, for Africans, the two are related but
very separate movements of a process working toward restoration. They
are not synonymous with one another. Finally, he told me, forgiveness is
about power and empowerment. Forgiveness is a dispensation, he said,
over which I as an individual in relationship have control. Forgiveness
is something one who has been wronged in relationship has the power
to grant or deny. Moreover, forgiveness is a spiritual discipline, not a
one-off event. When hurt, anger, and resentment bubble again to the
surface, the violated ones practice forgiveness, even seventy times seven
times (Matt 18:22). And, in South Africa, forgiveness remains distinct
from reconciliation. Reconciliation requires the building of trust between
individuals or communities when a relationship has been damaged or
even severed. Reconciliation can be a slow, arduous, and sometimes long
struggle to restore trust and friendship again after a wrongdoing has
been committed. Reconciliation often requires an apology and works
of restitution. Forgiveness together with reconciliation constitutes a
restored relationship.

68. Miroslav Volf, *The End of Memory: Remembering Rightly in a Violent World*
(Grand Rapids, MI: Eerdmans, 2006), 143, 148.

In the context of postapartheid South Africa, Cogill explained (and here I ask for the reader's indulgence as I oversimplify the complex language of race), the black majority could choose individually and as a community to forgive individual transgressions and the white minority as a whole for crimes against humanity. They could choose to do this in order to achieve their own empowerment. To forgive would enable the community to let go of the attempt of the Afrikaner to colonize them and their minds. Forgiveness would enable them to move forward in peace without being forever controlled by memories of violations that occurred, both personal and corporate, and without fostering feelings of vengeance, which would only enable the cycle of violence to continue. Leaders mentored the population through the process, reminding the people of principles of *ubuntu* and explaining that to wait for an apology from the other side was to give the power over peace and the security of their future, both individually and communally, again into the oppressor's hands. To hang on to the anger, the hatred, the dreams of vengeance would be soul killing and would risk destruction of peace, both personal and collective. Forgiveness, by contrast, provided a way to free the imagination of a formerly oppressed people and opened a way into the future without the further destruction by civil war, violence, and bloodshed.

It is important to recognize that forgiveness was not intended to be a mechanism that would enable the white population to continue to oppress populations of color. It was not meant to enable the victimization time and again of the one who offered forgiveness. Rather, forgiveness was conceived as the first step on a longer journey to the restoration of community. Forgiveness opened the way to reconciliation. But it did not constitute reconciliation, as it is too often understood by Christians in the West. In order for two individuals or two communities truly to reconcile with one another, some degree of trust needs to be established between them, a process that takes time—and after trust, true friendship. Forgiveness opens the possibility for reconciliation to occur by creating a safe space for the one who has violated the relationship to extend an apology, which in turn creates a safe space for the violated one to reengage in relationship, and for the two to journey, ideally, together again to a restored relationship.

It might be said that in South Africa today there has been forgiveness, a dispensation granted not only individually during the hearings but also corporately by the nation itself through the process overseen by Archbishop Tutu—but not reconciliation. There is recognition, too, that reconciliation may not be the right word to encompass the complexity

of a situation in which the two populations never really enjoyed equal
and good relations in the first place. Much distrust remains in a country
where there has been development toward healthier relations, but where
persistent injustice and inequity threaten constantly to tear apart what
progress has been made.

Forgiveness and reconciliation are concepts at the very heart of the
Christian faith, though Africans have understood these ideas in ways
quite different from the manner in which Europeans, whose doctrines
initially energized missionary efforts on the continent, have understood
them. African concepts are restorative, whereas Western concepts of
both jurisprudence and atonement are rooted in a retributive or punitive understanding of justice. In the European Christian imagination,
someone needs to pay a satisfactory debt payment to restore God's
honor or to take the deserved punishment vicariously in order to appease God's sense of justice. These interpretations certainly have their
biblical moorings, but they construct an image of God that leaves much
to be desired in that all of them implicate God the Father in needing the
cross, an instrument of torture, to restore humankind to God.

Strikingly, in classical theories of atonement, God the Father bears a
stronger resemblance to the ones conducting apartheid than to the ones
opposing it nonviolently, so there was little of theological substance to
challenge the decisions that were being made by the Afrikaners, who
were primarily Calvinist in orientation. As I have said, if Christians want
to emulate such a God, they too will justify torture or violence for higher
purposes. Indeed, once the church was no longer persecuted by Rome
but married to it, it began to use torture or violence on the grounds of
crusading against disorder, saving souls, or behaving in "good neighborly" ways.[69] These atrocities betray the perverted logic at the root of
our theologies of atonement and demand theological disentanglement.
And it is in South Africa's process of truth and reconciliation that Christians might detect a way forward in constructing an understanding of
forgiveness in Christ without implicating God the Father in the brutal
torture and death of his only beloved Son.

As Weaver observed, to say that God wills Christ to die at the hands
of torturers makes God an ally of those who called for Jesus' execution,
as well as of Judas, who betrayed him, alongside the oppressive Roman
emperor, governor, and soldiers who carried it out—and it pits God

---

69. H. F. Verwoerd (1901–1966), who conceived and implemented apartheid, was
prime minister of South Africa from 1958–1966. He described his project as one of
"good neighborliness."

the Father, the Person of God I have been calling in *Beauty's Vineyard* Good and Just, against God the Son, the Person of God I have been calling Beautiful and Compassionate. Such a view characterizes God the Father as something of a monster. It is my contention that the conflict between justice and compassion emerges when justice is understood in the retributive and punitive frameworks of feudalism and criminal law that is the West's European Christian inheritance. The tension rather dissipates when justice is imagined in a restorative framework like the one demonstrated in South Africa, much closer to the communitarian understandings of first-century Israel. Such a structure opens the way to understanding God's forgiveness and reconciliation with humankind squarely through the incarnation and which locates atonement and the forgiveness of sin solidly in Jesus' life, not in his death. Most pointedly, South Africa's Truth and Reconciliation process, given its underlying restorative philosophy of *ubuntu*, sheds light on how Christians new to more traditional African forms of jurisprudence might think about the relation between God's justice and God's mercy—a point that classical theories of atonement leave locked in conflict.

NB

South Africa's history offers the world many significant lessons about forgiveness and reconciliation. For Christians, South Africa's history of struggle against apartheid invites the world to consider theological concepts anew and from an African perspective. By addressing directly memories that traumatized individual souls and devastated entire communities, many survivors forgave perpetrators of human rights violations under apartheid and navigated a way to a common future filled with hope and promise. South Africa's choice to confront the past rather than either to avenge or to evade memories of injustice and brutality provides a theoretical framework about forgiveness that ultimately transcends the country's political situation to provide insights into the deepest theological mysteries—insights into the nature of God, the natures of Jesus Christ, the relevance of his incarnation, and the drama that resulted in his death, for people of faith even still today.

Beauty and the Cross? A Restorative Imagination

How does the South African Truth and Reconciliation process inform atonement theology? I want to construct a theory of atonement that acknowledges the destructive potential in the doctrine the way it is too commonly understood today, that takes seriously the historical context of first-century Judaism, and that honors metaphysical principles at the heart of Catholic faith and doctrine, including the idea that

God can be known by the names Goodness, Beauty, and Truth, as well as the notion that these names can be appropriated to the Persons in the Trinity in such a way that there is always harmony between them. Moreover, such a doctrine will be informed by restorative rather than retributive understandings of justice. Articulated with the insights of theological aesthetics in mind, my construction has three divine, restorative moves and is grounded in a sacramental understanding of *creation*.

When the relationship between God and humankind is damaged by sin, the Goodness of God desires the relationship between God and the world to be healed. The Trinitarian God, who is forgiving by nature, repeatedly initiates attempts to heal the relationship with all of creation first *by establishing a covenant*, second *by becoming incarnate*, and finally *by spirating the Holy Spirit.* Restoration of the relationship with God is accomplished by the redemptive acts of God being made known first to the Jewish people through the establishment of their covenant. This restoration is then made known to non-Jews through incarnation. Through covenant and incarnation, then, all humans—Jews and Gentiles alike—are invited to participate in an ongoing process of reconciliation, a process that works to restore the relationship broken so long ago. The fruits of this healing process are experienced, by grace, through the advocacy of the Holy Spirit and are incrementally enjoyed in the here and now. Through an ongoing process, then, and until the final consummation, the universe in which we live and breathe and have our being is being restored. Let me say a few more words about each of these moments of this restorative theory of atonement, informed by theological aesthetics and in conversation with *ubuntu* theology, and then conclude by returning to the image by Velarde with which I began this chapter.

The Sacramental Ground: Understanding Creation

According to this restorative theory of atonement, God, who is Good, Beautiful, and True, brings the material world into being. Creation's goodness, beauty, and truth graciously participate in the life of God, bearing the divine fingerprint of the One who brought it into existence. God, the One Who Is, Existence Itself—a Being Good, Beautiful, and True—sees from before all time the depths our anguish will reach. Nevertheless, God wills to bring existence into being, for God anticipates that humans will, in the fullness of time, enjoy company in the immediacy of God's presence in the new Jerusalem, a restored earth in communion with heaven; indeed, for God, it is already so.

Just as a mother knows before she gives birth that her child will suffer and is nevertheless joyful beyond imagining at the moment of the child's birth simply because it is good that she exists, so does God open up a space within Being, within God's very Existence, and sets three-dimensional time and space into motion simply because it is good that creation exists. Creation is good. Genesis affirms this time and again. All of creation's existence is willed despite God's knowledge that humans will suffer terribly and sometimes unnecessarily at one another's hands. If God had created beings who, while lesser than God, did not have the capacity to fall to the extent that humans have, they would simply not be human.[70] To be human is to have the freedom capable of severely damaging divine and human relationships by a willing obstinacy; to be human is to be dependent on divine grace and God's mercy for healing, but not in such a way that dependence denies human freedom.

When the evolutionary moment comes, God graciously breathes self-consciousness into God's beloved children—all of humanity—bestowing on them minds capable of reason, hearts capable of contrition, life capable of immortality. This is the moment of their quickening, a moment ensconced in the story of Adam and Eve. They have evolved to become self-aware and are cognizant of themselves as one aspect of a larger creation. They perceive a divine law to be operative in the universe, and they quickly and freely choose to violate it, thereby damaging their relationship with God and with one another. It is a brokenness that will be inherited by their children, and by their children's children, and so on; it is a brokenness to which each generation will inevitably contribute, and in its inevitability is its original nature.[71]

In creation, however, God has provided all the grace that is necessary for the restoration of relationship. Grace has always been abundant. It is in the air that we breathe and in the DNA that structures our life, interweaving with the cellular structure of all existence. This grace, God's free gift of love and mercy, is evident whenever we perceive anything that is good, true, and beautiful. It is experienced in all instances of true justice, compassion, and wisdom. Wherever these are present

---

70. See chap. 2. Since God is understood in this construction to be perfect creativity, when God creates, God cannot bring another perfect creativity into existence, since one marker of perfect creativity is uncreatedness. In other words, God cannot create that which is uncreated. This does not collapse God's omnipotence, since potency pertains only to what is possible. Since to create that which is uncreated is a logical absurdity, the argument that this construction collapses a perfection of God can be dismissed. ST I., q. 25, a. 3.

71. See Joseph Ratzinger, *In the Beginning: A Catholic Understanding of the Story of Creation and the Fall*, trans. Boniface Ramsey (Grand Rapids, MI: Eerdmans, 1995), 72–73.

in the created order, they point back to their divine source in God, the source of all that is good, beautiful, and true. They point back to the divine artist, who through earthly expressions of goodness, beauty, and truth produces peacefulness, kindness, and hopefulness. These originate in Love and overflow in love. Grace draws us into God's holiness—a sanctification that is marked by increasing degrees of goodness, beauty, and truth enacted in our lives in community and present too in our individual lives, empowering us to live nonviolently, compassionately, and graciously, embracing all of humankind and all life on the planet we share as gift.[72] Without insiders and outsiders, the entire community of humanity is God's beloved, developing as one in God's womb, nourished when one is celebrated, diminished when one is humiliated.

The First Restorative Move: Establishing a Covenant

When humans evolved to have reason and conscience and first experienced shame for actions that in their former state would have been committed merely for survival and without guilt, they damaged their relationship with God by actualizing what had been only a potential— the power of sin. And when humankind actualized the power of sin, Goodness intervened so as not to leave the relationship in ruins. By *establishing a covenant* with the Israelites, God made the first divine, restorative move, expressing God's desire to be in continued relationship with humankind. Conscious of their sinfulness, the Israelites prayerfully discerned how to reconcile their relationship with God and recorded laws they understood to be revealed by God concerning what constitutes a right relationship both with God and with one another. They also developed ritual sacrifices to atone for sin when their violations were thought to throw off the balance in their relationships.

Likewise, when humans violated their covenantal relationship with God by transgressing against the divine order, they perceived God's voice through utterances of the prophets. Through prophetic and poetic oracles of doom and hope, the prophets pleaded with Israel to repent, promising a renewal of the covenant upon a true turning again to righteousness and to justice.

The Bible in both testaments testifies to belief in a God of Love, a God who cherishes human beings despite their obduracy and continually intervenes in order to bring about right relations with and

---

72. Alejandro Garcia-Rivera, *The Community of the Beautiful* (Collegeville, MN: Liturgical Press, 1999), and *The Garden of God: A Theological Cosmology* (Minneapolis, MN: Fortress Press, 2009).

Women? [handwritten margin note]

among them. At the proper time, God revealed God's very Being to the Israelites, and they safeguarded the revelation down to this day. To Abraham, to Moses, and to David, God bestowed a promise, expressing that Israel would be a blessing—that through this chosen people, the Jewish people, God's will would be made known.[73] Among other utterances, the covenantal laws mandated care of the vulnerable. And the prophets, disclosing the word of God for each generation, reminded humankind of its obligation to care for the ones disadvantaged by the economic structures of the world.

The Second Restorative Move: Becoming Incarnate

By becoming incarnate, Beauty, the prophetic Word, the Logos of God, took on flesh, providing the second divine move in this restorative approach to atonement. The rift that had developed in the relationship between all of humankind and their God was overcome by God, with the Jews by covenant and with the Gentiles by incarnation. Through Christ, Gentiles were grafted onto the Jewish vine (Rom 11). By living among us and by calling humankind to reconciliation with God, Jesus expressed God's forgiveness. This is not counter to divine justice but is intrinsic to the divine essence. God did not hand the power of forgiveness over to the violators, the sinful ones, by waiting for an apology; God the Father did not forestall forgiveness until after the crucifixion. Rather, forgiveness was and is in God's very nature, and Jesus, the incarnation of the Logos, Beauty incarnate, shared the Father's forgiveness with those with whom he came into contact throughout his entire life. Certainly, he expressed it from the cross when he said, "Father, forgive them, for they do not know what they are doing" (Luke 23:34).

NB [handwritten margin note]

Through the incarnation, Jesus expressed God's compassion for humankind—a compassion that, like forgiveness, is not at odds with God's justice. By becoming human, Christ communicated God's compassion for humankind—all humankind. God's embrace of humankind

---

73. Without such a revelation of God's law, or God's will for human thriving, God cannot be considered just. One dimension of justice is an expression of expectation. Even children recognize injustice when parents discipline them for violating rules previously undisclosed. Human discernment of divinely sanctioned law is evidence of God's just and gracious nature; hence, the Jewish law is beautiful. The human heart continues to discern the ways by which God desires for us to live in right relationship to God and in right relationship to one another as we evolve into beings more fully aware of the intricate web that provides for our common, earthly survival and as we travel further from a world where we perceive groups other than our own as an immediate threat.

included especially the ones societies too often cast aside. By closing the chasm that had developed in the relationship between God and human-kind, by the very act of becoming human, Beauty expressed the nature of divine Love. By so doing, God invited humankind to participate in a restored relationship. Incarnate, living among us as the undefiled Word, as more than a model for how we, too, ought to live, Jesus lived the Law mindfully among us. Beauty, in an eternal dance with the Good and with the True, reminded his followers that the greatest commandments were to love God and to serve neighbor.

Jesus, his humanity married in a perfect union with the divine Logos, acknowledged that, in God's imagination, the community comprises all of humanity: Gentiles included alongside Jews; women alongside men; children alongside adults; the poor alongside the rich; the sick alongside the healthy. He demonstrated that a life in right relation to God and to neighbor entails justice—and it looks pretty radical. His was a life that dismissed material gain in preference for the acquisition of wisdom; it was a life that was offensive to many by the company it kept: with "untouchables" such as lepers and paralytics, and "undesirables" such as tax collectors and prostitutes. Widows, orphans, "aliens," and the poor were among the company Jesus kept, as were the "unclean." He embraced us all, demonstrating that God, who is boundless Love, *is* forgiving and merciful by nature.

When Beauty walked among us, he inspired people to desire to live like him. He drew people into his imagination, thus making converts of them, stirring in them the desire to live into the vineyard he described when he spoke of God's kingdom. His Beauty was alluring. Crowds began to amass around him. Troubled by the impact this reality could have on the wider Jewish community still under the oppression of Rome, some in his own community delivered him to the Romans. These leaders, recognizing the wide base of followers he was gathering, and ever-ready to put down a revolutionary threat to their empire, imprisoned him for treason. The Romans desired to aggravate the Jewish leaders, to whose demands they did not wish to appear to acquiesce too readily, lest they appear to be weak. But ultimately, the Roman Empire, in its quest to maintain control over the people, got the spectacle it desired. Roman soldiers crucified Jesus. Jesus was executed for political reasons.[74]

Jesus' death on the cross was the climactic moment of his resistance to the ways of the world, where humans consolidated power to the

74. Raymond Brown, *The Death of the Messiah* (New York: Doubleday, 1994), 1:328–428.

advantage of the few and to the distinct disadvantage of the many. His death was an act of resistance to the demented ways of the powerful who wielded their authority in a manner that secured their own luxuries at the cost of the exploited poor and who legitimized terrifying acts of violence as just. Jesus resisted their ways by refusing to retaliate, for retaliation would have legitimized their lifestyle by making it his own. Jesus resisted such a way of being to his very death. He did not relent to a way of being contrary to his nature, even in the face of torture. In fact, acceptance of humanity included even his torturers, whom he forgave. Then, through the activity of the Holy Spirit, divine Love invited all of humankind to reconciliation.

Jesus' death on the cross shows the lengths to which God will have us go in order *not* to violate another human life. Jesus invites his followers to live likewise: "Then Jesus told his disciples, 'If any want to become my followers, let them deny themselves and take up their cross and follow me. For those who want to save their life will lose it, and those who lose their life for my sake will find it'" (Matt 16:24-25). Those who would save their lives either by acquiescing to Rome or by trying to overthrow it violently would lose their lives because they would either perpetuate exploitation through their acquiescence or wield violence directly in the same manner as the enemy. By so doing, they would betray all hope for the salvation of the community coming into being as a sign of the reconciliation between God and humankind. But, paradoxically, if they would resist political oppression nonviolently and, like Jesus, lose their lives tragically in the process, they would contribute to the salvation of humanity and to the coming of the kingdom by living as Jesus wills for us all to live—without harming human life, so sacred and precious is it. Indeed, followers of Jesus were to be "in" the world but not "of" it (John 17:14-18; Rom 12:1-2). Their resistance would not entail concession to perpetrators of violence, which would enable such abuse to flourish. Rather, the transformation of society that Jesus sought relied on active, nonviolent resistance *en masse*, for the community of followers recognized that the oligarchy of a few could not withstand the solidarity of the many. This relatively insignificant band of people following a carpenter from Galilee threatened Rome precisely for this reason. Rome recognized in them the seeds of rebellion and feared their power. So Rome killed their Galilean leader. But in his act of resistance to the sinful structures of the world, Christ redeemed the world.

It is true that Jesus sacrificed his life. He willingly laid down his life in allegiance to that which is holy. By refusing to harm another, he

holy

continued to express what it is to be perfectly aligned with Goodness, Beauty, and Truth. He did not do so to repay God's honor or to pay the substitutionary penalty. Rather, he laid down his life when every other avenue of resistance to the violent ways of the world were exhausted— and he did so in such a way that he did not capitulate to the ways of the sinful world. He resisted sin perfectly. He didn't become like violent men, even to save his own life.

Once the historical drama had unfolded, Jesus' followers struggled to understand his death. They attempted to give it meaning. They did so using the language and concepts most sacred to them. He was understood as the High Priest, the Suffering Servant, the Paschal Lamb. As centuries passed, and as political memory was lost, it became commonplace to think that this was as God intended it to be— that God designed Jesus' death on the cross as a means to reconcile human beings with their God. Instead of situating it in its political context of resistance to Rome and to the powers of evil, first priests, then monks, and eventually lawyers speculated that God the Father desired Jesus' death. Atonement theories developed to work out the details. Believers understood Christ to be *satisfying* a debt in order to protect God's honor; they saw Christ *substituting* for humankind by taking the punishment in order to appease the Father's justice. But that progression of interpretation skewed the political cause for Jesus' death into a theological rationale that disastrously situated violence and evil in the very heart of God.

NB

If, in any way, the tradition continues to imply that God needed Jesus to be crucified in order for God to redeem the world—whether it is as innocuous a reason as to make a drama so remarkable that it would be remembered, or whether it is as iniquitous a reason as to be the very drama that God had determined necessary from the beginning of time to become the means of redemption—the church will continue to perpetuate the idea that there is evil in the heart of God. I do recognize that if the *sign* of God's ultimate victory over sin, death, and the power of evil is resurrection, this *sign* is reliant on death. Resurrection can, after all, only occur after someone has died.[75] It is possible, however, for Christians

---

75. My critique of Weaver is that Jesus' death becomes necessary because resurrection is tied to death. Speculatively, if the Father required a resurrection and, thus, a death, at the very least we could say that the death need not have been a violent one. The tradition has suggested that because he was sinless, he never should have died. He should have been born, lived his life, then ascended to heaven. In such a frame, Jesus could conceivably have lived to an old age, and when he was falling asleep,

to say that God desired the redemption of the world, that the Beauty of God became incarnate in Christ in order to communicate God's forgiveness to the world and to invite humankind into a reconciliatory process, and that through his perfect resistance to evil and ultimate victory over it, our salvation is achieved "already" and "not yet." In the fullness of time, through covenant for Jews and through incarnation for Gentiles, it is accomplished already. But in chronological time and space, salvation is coming into being through the activity of the Body of Christ, constituted by our participation in resistance to the broken structures of the world and by their transformation. Our salvation is dependent on our cooperation with the divine graces of empowerment, encouragement, and enlightenment. In this is our sanctification. Our collective salvation is dependent on our participation in the ongoing creation of Beauty's vineyard. From the perspective of chronological time, we are participating in its completion, though from the perspective of the fullness of time, it is already fully restored.

NB

We must not say that God desired Jesus' death and certainly not his death by crucifixion. To do so implicates God in Jesus' murder and throws the entire narrative into a tailspin of confusion, where Judas is more obedient to the will of God than are Mary, the Mother of Jesus, Mary Magdalene, and John, all of whom mourn his death. I was aware of this problem as a child, when I asked my Sunday school teacher, "Why does Judas commit suicide if he is only doing what God required him to do?" Now, I refer to this dilemma as the "Judas complex." The confusion of the narrative is only exacerbated if we understand Jesus to offer forgiveness to the very ones who are doing what, in the framework

---

he could have said "into your hands I commend my spirit." His family and friends would have found him dead and would have performed the requisite funerary rituals, thereby making his death widely and publicly known. If, a few days later, he were to have appeared suddenly in the midst of them again, the community would have proclaimed his resurrection. This too would have been incredible. Ultimately, though, we have to work with the historical record of events. The crucifixion is remarkable only because it demonstrates the horrific lengths humans will go in order to frighten and manipulate one another for political ends. Would Christians ever say that God *desired* John Wilkes Booth to shoot Abraham Lincoln? Would they ever imagine that God would *will* James Earl Ray to kill Martin Luther King, Jr.? So likewise must we not say that God willed the crucifixion. I am going yet even further than this to say that God did not desire him to die, and that resurrection is not the *locus* of salvation but its *sign*. It is a faith claim in the trust and hope that God "already" has had victory over sin, death, and evil, and that we are invited to participate in it, albeit only in part, in the here and now.

I am opposing, God requires for them to do.[76] Traditional theories of atonement introduce conflict in the very heart of the Trinity, and this is a problem to which our theologies must attend because our image of God is the image into which we are being transformed. If evil abides there, then we begin to worship what is evil and conduct ourselves accordingly.

Christians ought to conclude that it was possible, even from the beginning of time, for God to see that if the Logos were to become manifest through the incarnation and to live as Beauty would naturally live—perfectly righteously in the face of human sinfulness—a very sinful humanity would retaliate against the holiness they perceived in him. They would attempt to kill him. Conceivably, God could foresee this without willing it, just as a parent might will a child to enroll in the Peace Corps, fully understanding that she might be killed in service to

---

76. I also believe that Catholic theologians need to begin to wrestle with implications of Jesus' full humanity. Would he not have died if someone had snuck up behind him and put a dagger through his heart as a means to assassinate him—not allowing him the time to commend his spirit to God willingly? If theologians answer that he would have known he was about to be killed, then they have accepted some form of Apollinarianism where Jesus has a human body animated by a divine mind. Likewise, if Christians answer that the dagger would not be able to kill him unless he allowed it to have that power over him, then it seems Christians have accepted some form of Arianism, where Jesus is a super species of being not liable to the same laws of physics as those to which other human beings are vulnerable. Jesus would in such a case not be vulnerable to the laws but in control of them. In that case, he would not be fully human. If we ascribe to an evolutionary view of history, which Catholics do, to be human is to be mortal—physically vulnerable to things like gunshots, dagger wounds, and crucifixions. Does Jesus share that state of being with us? In Jesus, the Logos, the Beauty of God, incarnates what it is to be fully human—and his ascension points to the mystical promise that an earthly, bodily life will be enjoyed again in the fullness of time. But on this side of eternity, a side into which the Logos willingly entered, bodies perish, from the effects of gravity if nothing else. If Jesus' body was immune from the effects of gravity, then, again, we have adopted some form of Arianism. Science has shown that death was natural on the planet long before humankind evolved to have self-consciousness and an awareness of sin. Can Catholics begin to say that humans die because we are physical beings, not because we are descendants of a sinful Adam? Could we begin to believe that death is not Christ's enemy—nor is it ours? Injustice and violence, indifference and negligence, ignorance and complacence—these are the enemies of God. Jesus shared the human state of being fully, his human body and soul in full union, too, with divine Goodness, Beauty, and Truth, perfectly resisting injustice and violence—all that destroys life, ultimately even his own. But he refused to engage in those powers. He was killed for striking such a posture in relation to the world. But, for Christians, his very real mortality, signified by his very real death, is not the end of the story. Those powers would not be allowed to have the final say in his life nor, he promised, in the lives of those who followed him.

peace. Even though the parent wills her to go, the parent does not will her to be killed.[77] So likewise with God. If God wanted to express God's forgiveness of humankind through the voice of a human being, and if God wanted to communicate God's desire for reconciliation with humankind—not only with the Jews but with the Gentiles as well—then God might still will for Jesus to come into being in the midst of us despite knowing some human beings would resist his Beauty. God need not be seen as passive in the face of the unfolding drama but actively present as God is always actively present: calling for humans to align with what is Good, Beautiful, and True, calling for them to cooperate with Justice, Compassion, and Wisdom, imploring them to resist what is unjust and evil, negligent and deformed, and ignorant and deceptive.

What God could foresee, too, was their reluctance to align with what is Good, Beautiful, and True. Knowing that some human beings would turn their backs on Jesus and, in essence, on God, divine Love determined that God would nevertheless achieve God's ends without violating the nature of God's power—a power which does not force or compel but allures and attracts. Without violating human free will, when sinful human beings carried through with the evil task of killing the incarnation of Beauty, God the Father would say no. Evil humankind, with their abusive use of power, would not have the final say. Rather, divine Justice would have the final say. God would have victory over evil by bringing life out of death. The people would proclaim Christ's resurrection. And, through the invitation of the Spirit, God would invite the faithful to participate in Christ's resurrection by becoming his hands and feet. They would become his living Body, making him incarnate among us, even still to this day. And in their collective effort to embody him, by living as he would have us live, they would find their salvation, detectible already in the here and now, and ultimately consummated in the eschaton, when the heavenly and the earthly Jerusalem become one.

This restorative understanding of justice offers a different way to understand the cross—a way that does not require Christians to understand violence or evil as operative in the very heart of God. Whereas retributive justice legitimizes violence by saying that God reconciles human debt by calling for a blood sacrifice—even of God's own Being by the willful coming and sacrifice of the Logos in the Person of Jesus Christ[78]—restorative justice, by contrast, opens the way for us to see

---

77. I am grateful to my colleague Gerald Schlabach for this insight.

78. Miroslav Volf, *Free of Charge: Giving and Forgiving in a Culture Stripped of Grace* (Grand Rapids, MI: Zondervan, 2005).

incarnation, not crucifixion, as God's means of forgiveness. God's mercy—God's forgiving nature—prompts Beauty to break into time and space in the person of Jesus of Nazareth. As the incarnation of divine compassion, God "suffers with" humankind in the person of the Son. In his full embrace of human life—an acceptance of life even unto death—Jesus communicates God's forgiveness to humankind. Through the incarnation, God seeks to restore the relationship with all of humankind through conciliatory means. These are the lengths to which Divine Love will go to restore a broken relationship.

According to this restorative model of atonement, God the Son, the Beauty of God, becomes visible. The incarnate one, Emmanuel—God with us—communicates the presence of divine holiness to the world. By bringing holy, *kairos* time, into contact with *chronos* time, Beauty becomes visible through the Word's incarnation and offers divine forgiveness and an invitation to restoration of relationship. If God first required contrition of heart, or a confession, or an apology, God would be transferring the power over redemption to humankind, and just as humans do tragically time and time again, God would be placing the possibility of reconciliation and peace into the hands of those so broken and wounded by the violence that they have endured, that salvation might never come. To be God, however, is to be forgiving—even when the [*Holy*] people do not ask for forgiveness, even when the people do not confess they have done anything that requires forgiveness. By the embodiment of Love, God through Christ unites God's mind, heart, and will with the world, and Jesus teaches his followers how, by grace, they too can live. In this earthly reign, an alternative vision of how to live is experienced. It is more peaceful and just, more gentle and compassionate, more hopeful and wise. The vision he shares is for a right relationship with God made evident through right relationship with one another, in [*holiness*] which humans can only participate through receipt of the divine graces of empowerment, encouragement, and enlightenment.

In this community of the beloved, no one is excluded. For a time, Compassion lived among us, and when the violence of the world exposed its hands by killing the incarnation of Beauty, the people proclaimed his resurrection. In the community's proclamation of the risen Christ, they communicated their faith that God in Christ had achieved victory over sin, death, and the power of evil. Holiness overcame sin; life overcame death; Beauty overpowered evil—nonviolently. And, in the ongoing presence of Truth—our Advocate and Beauty's companion, the Holy Spirit—continues to communicate divine forgiveness and mercy to the world and empowers in us the ability to live likewise, thereby reconciling the world to God and completing the earth's restoration, a reality already achieved in Christ.

The Third Restorative Move: Sending the Spirit

In the third and final move in this restorative model of atonement, God enables humans to live righteously *by sending an Advocate* who, by the power of grace, empowers humans to live like Christ. By the grace that is already in them in the goodness that they retain in their being as creatures of God, and empowered by the source of all that is Good, humans can choose to cooperate with grace and to follow a path to reconciliation that will restore the relationship with God that has been so severely damaged by sin. It is a life of radical love of both God and neighbor. God wills for humans to live as Christ lived. One dimension of our collective salvation consists in the degree to which we live likewise—an ability that we do not possess on our own but that requires God's grace and our cooperation with it. Indeed, the degree to which we cooperate determines the degree to which we will experience this community of the beloved, the Beloved Community, Beauty's vineyard, coming into being within the midst of us, even now.

The heavenly kingdom, the other dimension of our salvation, which God promises will have its consummation in an earthly paradise, is already mystically present in a community where courageous resistance to the "powers that be" is practiced. It is a community organized not by the ways of this world but the ways of God. It is a kin-dom, as Ada Maria Isasi-Diaz has said, rather than a kingdom.[79] This community of peaceful and nonviolent relations is already and not yet. It is already existing and not yet fully restored. Christians live in the hope that, in the fullness of time, the here and now will meet the hereafter in an eternally sustained right relationship. *Kairos* moments are experiences when chronological, linear time intersects with this eternal, holy time. Such moments make worldly authorities shudder, for these moments threaten the status quo. These moments threaten a way that has been created where the few live in a perversity of excess even as the many struggle with a paucity of scarcity. *Kairos* moments challenge the existing structures designed to protect the privileges of those who have the power to create and maintain them.

79. Ada Maria Isasi-Diaz, "Solidarity: Love of Neighbor in the 1980s," in *Lift Every Voice: Constructing Christian Theologies from the Underside*, ed. Susan Brooks Thistlethwaite and Mary Potter Engel (San Francisco: Harper, 1990), 31–40, 303–5.

Churches, small gatherings of followers committed to the way of Jesus, were intended to be the center of this kind of activity in the world. They were to be filled with people who lived alternatively to the ways of the world. By grace, they were empowered to live the ways of Christ, healing the rifts between them. But Gandhi recognized how far the church had fallen from its original vision when he said, "I like your Christ, but not your Christians." Few Christians anymore, including me, seem to bear a striking resemblance to the one they say they follow.

Jesus ignited his first followers with a love for this way. He knew that Beauty's nature is alluring—infectiously so. Converts to his beautiful way of being would, by grace, also desire to live as he lived.[80] Love and embrace were the markers of this new community to which Christ was giving birth. The way of Christ was opposed to the world's hunger for domination and violence. Those living in the way of Christ desired to transform and to embrace all who left greed and imperialism behind, making students of all those who desired to learn how to live this way as well. This was the meaning of the great commission. Followers of Christ were to "go and make disciples of all nations, teaching them everything" Christ had commanded them (Matt 28:19). They were to be fishers of men and women and children—capturing the imaginations of people who wanted to devote their lives to God and this alternative way of being in the world. Jesus had nurtured them in a community of love, of nonviolence, and of concern for the marginalized. The vision was to draw ever more into this way of being in the world.

This, too, may be why he said he came not to unite but to divide (Matt 10:34-39; Luke 12:49-53). He drew a sharp line between the holy and the unholy, the just and the unjust, the greedy and the simple. They would be divided as they were in Matthew 25: those who took care of the hungry, the thirsty, the stranger, the naked, the sick, and the prisoner were separated from those who did not. Those who refused to live compassionately did not participate in reconciliation with the divine, and they did so to the peril of the wider community, though God's extension of grace was and remains generous.

To lose sight of Jesus' teaching about the kingdom of God is to lose the key to the message of the gospels.[81] History confirms time and again how those who live in the way demonstrated by Christ are a threat

---

80. For an extensive history of Christian thinking about the kingdom, see Rita Nakashima Brock and Rebecca Ann Parker, *Saving Paradise: How Christianity Traded Love of This World for Crucifixion and Empire* (Boston: Beacon Press, 2008).

81. Ibid.

to the powers that be, and how they, like Jesus, often meet a violent end.[82] Socrates, Abraham Lincoln, Gandhi, Martin Luther King, Jr., and Romero have gone this way as well. Jesus' posture of peaceful and non-violent resistance, even to the point of death, stands in stark contrast to the brutal and violent stance of his killers. Instead of retaliating, instead of harming another human being, Jesus preferred to die. He sacrificed his life in laying it down. In so doing, Christ revealed not God's embrace of execution but God's preference for nonviolent resistance to crucifixion and torture. If it functions multivalently, the cross should symbolize, among things like transformation and conversion, God's rejection of torture. The cross ought not to symbolize God's collusion in violence. The cross should not symbolize God's atonement by use of capital punishment. Instead of protecting these precious keys and cornerstones of the faith—principles of peace and nonviolence, political resistance, and forgiveness—the community ultimately handed them over to the very powers that killed Jesus. Christianity came to embrace the very forms of power that conspired to take the life of the religion's namesake.

In a restorative construction, God restores the relationship between God and human beings to be whole or "at one" again. This is accomplished through covenant, incarnation, and the ongoing work of the Spirit. The relationship between God and the world is restored not through punitive justice and retributive models of atonement but restorative ones. God does not send Jesus into the world to die. Jesus does not come in order to be killed so that God can reconcile human beings to God's self, as if God were able to forgive humankind only once someone was brutally whipped and tortured to death for the sins of humanity. God sends his Son into the world to share the Good News—that the loving God desires to be in relationship with humankind, God's beloved creation, and that God forgives them. Emmanuel, "God with us," discloses the internal relations of the Trinity and invites all of humankind into a covenant of loving relations. Just as the Father is related to the Son in love, and just as the Father and the Son are related to the Holy Spirit in love, this love overflows into the created order and embraces humankind, drawing God's beloved humanity into divine life. Now incarnate among us, Beauty is present among us, in the flesh, expressing God's inner Being with all of humanity, extending relationship more deeply into the created order, healing the fractures with a forgiving posture, and inviting humankind to reconcile relations with God by

---

82. Walter Wink, *The Powers That Be: Theology for a New Millennium* (New York: Doubleday, 1998).

restoring relations with one another. In word and in action Jesus, who was proclaimed the Christ, discloses God's vision for the beloved and empowers disciples by grace with the promise of the coming of the Spirit to do likewise. Such mercy and compassion are not at odds with God's justice. God's forgiving nature is a complement to God's justice, which desires for the human community to be restored, not punished—drawn, too, into a life of justice, compassion, and wisdom, producing life abundant within communities of loving-kindness.

A restorative imagination resolves issues that have been identified in this chapter with classical theories of atonement. First and foremost, the issue of the conflict within the Trinity has dissipated. Rather than seeing justice and mercy as pitted against each other, such that God the Father cannot forgive until a satisfaction or penalty has been paid, an understanding of restorative justice borrowed from Africa has allowed us to sketch justice working in tandem with forgiveness; forgiveness, distinct from reconciliation, opens the way to restoration. Whereas medieval theories see the Father and the Son at odds with one another in the garden when Jesus asks for the cup of suffering to pass, restorative lenses have enabled us to imagine God as active too in wanting the cup of suffering to pass from Jesus, but not in a way that would require God the Father to abuse power by overcoming the freedom of those involved in the execution. Whereas traditional theories characterize God as violent at worst, actively slaughtering the Son, or passive at best, simply allowing the Son to be slaughtered, this restorative theory characterizes God as engaged and peaceful. God, who is Good and True, was sacramentally present in the situations leading to Jesus' death, as God is present in every situation, calling for justice and wisdom—a justice and wisdom that were abandoned by those soldiers who indicated their allegiance was to Rome, not to God—not to Goodness, Beauty, or Truth. In every moment of the drama, the gospels affirm that Jesus maintained holiness in a posture of peace and nonviolence, ordering his disciples to put their weapons down (Matt 26:52) and offering forgiveness even from the cross (Luke 23:34). Nonetheless, humans used their freedom and chose to kill Christ. They killed Beauty, but three days later, Jesus' followers proclaimed, "He is risen." Life emerged from death in the community that followed in the way of their Christ. They became his risen body, and it walks among us even still in places where the coming into being of Beauty's vineyard is evident.

Whereas traditional theories have a cosmic focus with good battling evil on a spiritual scale, this restorative theory has an earthly focus, understanding the battle between good and evil to be embodied in very real, political situations that continue to visit populations around the globe. Whereas traditional theories are anti-Jewish, insofar as they hold that the teachings of Christ must supersede the previous covenants, this restorative theory honors the Hebraic covenant as efficacious always for those of Jewish descent. Whereas traditional theories suggest that Jesus is obedient to God's desire for his death to acquire redemption, this restorative theory claims that Jesus is obedient to holiness, a holiness that he maintained throughout his life in his refusal to harm another of God's children, and that provoked resistance from leaders whose power was perceived to be threatened by Jesus' integrity. Whereas traditional theories insist that Jesus saves by dying, making the crucifixion the moment of victory, this restorative theory sees his death as tragic. He is another fallen prophet like so many figures before and after him. He nonetheless saves by offering God's forgiveness throughout his incarnation and by living perfectly in resistance to the sinful structures, relationships, and persons of the world. The resurrection is a sign of God's victory over the powers of evil and death that saw to Jesus' execution. And whereas traditional theories contend that his mission was to die to save, thereby confusing Judas's betrayal with obedience to the Father's will for redemption through the cross, this restorative theory maintains that Jesus' mission was to come to live justly and righteously, and that Judas's act was truly an act of betrayal. By grace, Christ empowers others to live as he did through the activity of the Spirit. Those who live righteously and justly act as his hands and feet, contributing thereby to a community of *shalom* and loving-kindness, the kingdom that he describes again and again, the kingdom that I have been referring to as Beauty's vineyard.

The implications of this reimagined theory of atonement invite us to reconsider how Christians might think about Christianity in an age of anguish and anticipation. In situations of domestic violence, like those considered at the opening of this chapter through discussion of the painting by Velarde, a restorative understanding of atonement would never tolerate the kinds of interpretations of Christ that would condition clergy to counsel a woman that God the Father wills her to suffer endlessly at the hands of her violent spouse. It is *not* her religious duty to endure violence. Being beaten is *not* her cross to bear. Violence is *not* a cup of suffering that God the Father wills for her, as it was not God's will for Christ to suffer to redeem us. To accept the beatings is *not* to follow in the steps of Jesus. Rather, her religious duty is to resist evil creatively and nonviolently, just as Jesus did. This may entail moving away from her husband to protect herself and her children. When she does, she ought not to be chastised in church, and she certainly ought to be welcomed to the table. This restorative understanding of atonement affirms that life is valuable, precious, and sacred. Christ came so that his followers may have life, and have it abundantly (John 10:10). Her husband's violence only demonstrates where his loyalties lie—and such loyalties, like those harbored by the ones who mocked, spit on, and whipped Jesus, are certainly not allegiant to a God of Love. As such, this restorative theory is more in keeping with the culture of life embraced by Catholic moral thought and pronounces once and for all a divine "no" on all violence conducted in God's name.

Converts to this way, the way of Goodness, of nonviolence, and of love, will, by the power of the Spirit, follow in the way of Beauty. In community, we all are responsible for the creation of a world in which people flourish, where the needs of those who are struggling are tended to not out of pity or obligation but out of a genuine desire for wholeness—out of a genuine desire for the restoration or "filling up" where there is lack. All of us are implicated in the neglect of those who go without. And the Christian tradition promises that we are forgiven by a God whose nature is to forgive, and whose concern is to inspire in us a will to love as we are loved. So embraced by Love, we are filled by the Spirit of Love with a concern for all to have life and a desire for all to share in the earth's abundance. And by our love and concern for those who share our common humanity, we participate in the development of the beloved community. Baptized into this conversion, we too become incarnations of beauty, and we participate in our restoration—with humanity, with the planet we occupy as gift, and with God. Created for loving-kindness, to live lives of abundance in a world where all are embraced and none are excluded, where all are nurtured and none are abandoned, where all are cradled and none are neglected, we grow in the womb of Love, the source of our being until, one day, we are born. Held and caressed, the beloved at long last will see Love's face, face-to-face.

Hold Fast (2004) by Geoffrey Laurence. Oil on canvas; 78 x 72 inches. Courtesy of the artist.

Chapter 7

Beauty's Lament
On Suffering

According to Greek mythology, King Leucippus's daughters, Phoebe and Hilaeira, were abducted and then forced to marry the sons of Zeus—Castor and Pollux—also known as the Dioscuri. In one depiction, painted by Peter Paul Rubens between 1615 and 1618, the sisters are full-bodied and nude, as women typically are in Rubens's paintings. The scene by Rubens is troubling, for even as the men seize the sisters, their garments flailing, the women apparently submit to and even seem to desire their abductors. One son of Zeus is still on horseback. The other has jumped onto the roadway, catching on his knee the daughter who would otherwise fall to the ground, thereby valorizing him despite the sexual violence overtaking her. The rearing of the horse behind him heightens the aggression of the scene. Facing heavenward, the women appear both to resist and resign themselves to their captors. One daughter reaches out to the heavens while caressing one brother's arm, while the other looks into the eyes of her abductor, his eyes filled with sexual desire, hers not expressing a rejection of him entirely.

Margaret D. Carroll, a scholar of art at Wellesley College, has noted, "Rubens's depiction of the abduction is marked by some striking ambiguities: an equivocation between violence and solicitude in the demeanor of the brothers, and an equivocation between resistance and gratification in the response of the sisters."[1] Carroll goes on to explain how the poet Ovid, in his *Art of Loving*, champions sexual violence by reference to the rape of the sisters: "Perhaps she will struggle at first

---

1. Margaret D. Carroll, "The Erotics of Absolutism: Rubens and the Mystification of Sexual Violence," *Representations* 25 (Winter 1989): 3.

and cry, 'You villain!' Yet she will wish to be beaten in the struggle. . . . You may use force; women like you to use it. . . . Phoebe suffered violence, violence was used against her sister: each ravisher found favor with the one he ravished."[2] Carroll's thesis is that Rubens represents his period's association of princely power with sexual force and dominance in a valorization of violence deemed in his time not only politically expedient but also strategically necessary. Carroll asserts, "Any interpretation of the painting is inadequate that does not attempt to come to terms with it as a celebratory depiction of sexual violence and the forcible subjugation of women by men."[3]

Carroll's interpretation of the Rubens painting is instructive when it is considered in light of Geoffrey Laurence's 2004 painting *Hold Fast*. The modern realist painter has chosen Rubens's depiction of *The Rape of the Daughters of Leucippus* to occupy the ground behind three armed American soldiers, or rather one American soldier depicted at three stages of his psychological evolution. He sits on a bench in the museum where the Rubens hangs, each stage depicted with a different position of the soldier in relation to his rifle. Reading from right to left as in a Hebrew text, the figure on the right is most threatening. New to the military, his gun is cocked in a manner reflective of his personality. His fingers are already on the trigger, and he is eager to shoot. The soldier in the middle holds the barrel of his gun; it is upright and points to the ceiling. He is no longer as eager as he was when he first enlisted. He is bewildered and numb, shaken by what he has seen. The image of the soldier on the far left rests his right hand on the trigger mechanism, his left hand on his knee. He is lost in thought, his eyes looking deep into a helmet on the floor at his feet. Perhaps he is experiencing self-loathing and utter revulsion over what he has done.

By juxtaposing the soldiers in the foreground with the scene by Rubens in the background, Laurence communicates, using a visual vocabulary, that violence begets violence. Laurence has said that he used background imagery initially to achieve an artistic objective: "At first I was using the paintings in the backgrounds to stop deep space from occurring. I go to great lengths to compress the space in my paintings and achieve a tension between flatness and three-dimensionality."[4] In

---

2. Ovid, *Artis Amatoriae* 1.664–80, in *The Art of Love and Other Poems*, trans. J. H. Mozley, rev. ed., Loeb Classical Library (Cambridge, MA: Harvard University Press, 1939), 59; quoted in Carroll, "The Erotics of Absolutism," 4.

3. Carroll, "The Erotics of Absolutism," 3.

4. "American Realist Artist Interview Geoffrey Laurence," http://arifnews24 .wordpress.com/2010/07/07/american-realist-artist-interview-geoffrey-laurence/.

his more recent works, however, he conveys that there is a relationship between the background and the foreground: "I realized that I could play narrative games between the 'painted' space in the paintings in the background and the painted space [in the foreground]."[5] In *Hold Fast*, Laurence critiques the correlation between war and sexual violence, as represented by the Rubens work, and asserts that it continues into the modern day. In private correspondence with me, Laurence wrote,

> I will say that [*Hold Fast*] came about when America invaded and occupied Iraq and that the response to 9-11 (Mission accomplished!) truly and deeply dismayed and depressed me. My belief *is* that violence begets violence. I do *not* believe in an eye for an eye as a solution to hatred.
>
> Two things at that time made deep impressions on me. The museum of Baghdad was looted by criminals, *while the museum was occupied by armed American soldiers who did nothing at all to stop them* and the oldest writings in existence disappeared without trace to this day, [and a] newsreel [showed] American soldiers entering a cafe somewhere in Iraq where men in their 60s and older were innocently and politely drinking tea and discussing whatever. When the Iraqis responded to the sergeant's questions with gestures that they had not understood, as they did not speak English, the sergeant's solution was simply to speak English in a louder voice at them as if they were idiots. I was utterly horrified. . . . America raped Iraq and it was perversely complicit in its being raped.[6]

To comprehend the etymology of violence represented in Laurence's work, one must recall that, in Greek mythology, Pollux himself was conceived when Zeus took the form of a swan and raped the Spartan queen, Leda. W. B. Yeats (1865–1939) imagines Zeus's use of power and Leda's acquiescence to it in this way:

> A sudden blow: the great wings beating still
> Above the staggering girl, her thighs caressed
> By the dark webs, her nape caught in his bill,
> He holds her helpless breast upon his breast.
>
> How can those terrified vague fingers push
> The feathered glory from her loosening thighs?
> And how can body, laid in that white rush,
> But feel the strange heart beating where it lies?

5. Ibid.
6. Geoffrey Laurence, e-mail message to author, August 9, 2015.

A shudder in the loins engenders there
The broken wall, the burning roof and tower
And Agamemnon dead.
    Being so caught up,
So mastered by the brute blood of the air,
Did she put on his knowledge with his power
    Before the indifferent beak could let her drop?[7]

According to Yeats, the "shudder in the loins" that occurred when Zeus raped Leda led to the birth of the primary figures of the Trojan War and eventually to the death of Agamemnon. Laurence's reference to the Rubens painting expresses that the violence of war creates a vicious retributive and vengeful cycle that can lead only to further slaughter and death in spaces both political and domestic. Laurence's perspective is all the more compelling when one learns that he is the son of survivors of the Shoah; Laurence's father was sent to Sachsenhausen and then to Dachau, where Laurence's grandmother, grandfather, and aunt committed suicide; Laurence's mother survived Kristallnacht and escaped to England even as her parents were sent to Terezin.[8]

The consideration, then, of all these things in Laurence's work—rape, war, militarism, genocide—speaks to the existential anguish that accompanies modern life, perhaps even more so for those of us who are trying to hold onto our faith in spite of these realities. Is atheism preferable, as a way to avoid what Elie Wiesel refers to as "the tragedy of the believer"—the torment of faith in the face of pervasive human distress? Is faith in an omnipotent and omnibenevolent God possible in a world filled with "dangerous memories": the destruction of indigenous people on our continent as well as in Africa and Australia, Germany's Holocaust, America's bombing of Hiroshima and Nagasaki, South Africa's apartheid, Argentina's dirty war, Bosnia's genocide, as well as Rwanda's, Cambodia's, and Sudan's?[9] This list represents only a fraction of the atrocities humans have engineered in recent memory. A God entirely Good would not sit idly by, passively watching while we did these things to one another; an omnipotent God would certainly intervene to alleviate suffering in keeping with God's perfect Goodness. And since the atrocities do not cease, so the logic goes, such a God must

7. W. B. Yeats, *Leda and the Swan*, http://www.poets.org/poetsorg/poem/leda-and-swan.

8. "Geoffrey Laurence," http://chgs.umn.edu/museum/responses/laurence/.

9. For a discussion of "dangerous memories," a term coined by Johann Baptist Metz, see chap. 4, "Beauty's Veiling: On Sin."

not exist. David Hume, in *Dialogues Concerning Natural Religion* (1779), poses the issue in this way:

> Epicurus's old questions are yet unanswered:
> Is God willing to prevent evil, but not able?
>   Then, he is impotent.
> Is he able, but not willing?
>   Then, he is malevolent.
> Is he both able and willing?
>   Whence, then is evil?[10]

The word "theodicy," coined by Gottfried Leibniz (d. 1716) from the Greek *theos* ("god") and *dike* ("justice"), refers to the exploration of possible defenses of God given the reality of evil and suffering in the world. In this chapter, despite all the minefields surrounding contemporary discussion of this subject, possible defenses of God's knowledge, goodness, and power in light of the evil and suffering in the world are explored. In broaching these topics, it is essential to address several preliminary issues, namely, that not all suffering is the same, that not all suffering causes transformation of the heart, that the very same suffering that may transform one may destroy another, and that there is a difference between suffering at the hands of nature and at the hands of moral evil.

First, it must be said that not all suffering is the same. Most people of goodwill would agree that there is a suffering that functions like a refiner's fire. As painful as it is to endure at the time, it has a creative effect. It changes someone for the better. It spurs growth into maturity, perhaps, or it enables someone to become more compassionate in response to the suffering of fellow human beings who are enduring the same or a similar kind of struggle. But we must be cautious when we think about pain and suffering as a refiner's fire. It is one thing to say that God can draw good from evil. This I do not dispute. Such transformation is undeniably a good effect of a lamentable anguish. It is quite another thing to say, however, that God designs the suffering as an instrument in order to achieve a certain end or passively allows the suffering to occur in order to accomplish the same. These are insufficient responses to the question of theodicy, because for God to wish this kind of suffering on someone to achieve a higher end, or for God to be passive in the face of suffering, challenges the precept that God is omnibenevolent. Perhaps, one might argue, God desires the good

---

10. David Hume, *Dialogues Concerning Natural Religion* (Charleston, SC: Biblio-Life, 2008).

outcome (maturity, for example) but not the means (suffering)—but then we are back to square one in terms of theodicy, for such a move, in order to protect God's goodness, seems to collapse God's power. Certainly, God's power is such that God could accomplish a development of maturity in humankind without requiring suffering born of moral evil. This is a topic to which we will return in due course.

Second, it must also be said that not all suffering causes a transformation in the heart of one who experiences pain, whether physical, psychological, or spiritual. It is loathsome to suggest that God *allows* the things that cause our anguish—the Holocaust, apartheid in South Africa, or the genocides in Bosnia Herzegovina, Rwanda, Cambodia, Darfur—*in order* to attain a higher end. Some simply do not survive the violence and therefore cannot be transformed, such as the six million Jews who died terrible deaths at the hands of the Nazis, and the countless African men and women who were tortured and killed by members of the South African police services during apartheid. Others, the ones who survive, are often traumatized by what they have seen. What of the children who watched machetes tear their loved ones to pieces in Rwanda? Some suffering simply destroys. So when we dare to speak of these things, we must not suggest that all suffering is constructive. There is a suffering that is nothing but destructive.

Third, suffering that is transformative and that functions creatively for one may simply destroy another. A complex interplay of factors, including previous exposure to violence and the intricacies of one's temperament, including the degree to which the survivor is resilient, collude to enable some to attain greater compassion, while others spiral into a seemingly bottomless abyss. Therefore, we need to be mindful that context matters, and that we cannot speak in broad brushstrokes when referring to the effect of suffering on those who survive. Moreover, we must not further traumatize, victimize, or shame the one who spirals by suggesting she or he is weak. Calls for accountability must be directed squarely and continually to those who have conducted or condoned the atrocities in the first place.

And, finally, while the effects may be similar, ranging from transformative to destructive, there is a difference between suffering at the hands of nature, so to speak, and at the hands of fellow human beings. In other words, there is a difference between natural disaster and moral evil. Moral evil, because it is unnecessary, is uniquely tragic; whatever suffering it causes could, ostensibly, be avoided—which makes its consequences harder to bear. Suffering from nature's events, whether from earthquakes, sandstorms, hurricanes, tornadoes, fires, tsunamis, droughts, disease, and so on, while tragic, are largely unavoidable. Bodies are vulnerable to the forces of nature. Unless the events themselves and their effects have links to human failings and to poor judgment (and with climate change and disease, these are admittedly increasingly in our moral consciousness), there is a degree to which human beings recognize that there is a degree of suffering that will be experienced precisely because we are embodied and mortal creatures, vulnerable to such things as gravity and to the elements of earth, air, fire, and water. Therefore, it is critical to recognize that the focus of this chapter is on the anguish born of moral evil.

For much of my career in theology, even stretching back to my days as an undergraduate student pursuing a bachelor of arts degree in religion and art history, I have been intrigued, perplexed, and sometimes troubled by possible defenses of God in relation to the sufferings of humankind. Twenty years in, I continue to struggle with every dimension of this profound, even most difficult, of riddles—from the hubris of the question itself to the unsatisfying answers it typically elicits. How is it that we can maintain faith in an omnibenevolent and omnipotent God given the intolerable degrees of suffering experienced by human beings? Must we, to make sense of our faith, deny perfect knowledge, goodness, or power as attributes of God in order to account for the depths of pain and sorrow into which existence sometimes carries us? Does God welcome this investigation into the nature of the divine Being, as is suggested in the book of Job, when God commends Job for having spoken well of God after Job has asserted the injustice of his circumstances (Job 42:7)? In order to continue to offer praises to God, must we disengage our capacity to reason? Or does God, in the face of suffering, and as the prophet Jeremiah suggests, invite us to pray using the form of the lament, a type of prayer that requires us to protest in faith to God a suffering disproportionate to our guilt? In this chapter, after differentiating key terms in relation to God's knowledge, we will dare to investigate the nature of the divine Being by visiting each attribute in turn, and I will offer a proposal that simultaneously protects God's omniscience, omnibenevolence, and omnipotence. And then, having proposed an approach to the problem of theodicy, we will turn to the lament, to Beauty's song, as perhaps the most appropriate immediate response to suffering at the hands of moral evil.

On Omniscience

The first attribute of God to defend in constructing a theodicy for an age of anguish and anticipation is divine omniscience, a concept poetically anchored in the Psalmist's words,

Where can I go from your spirit?
> Or where can I flee from your presence?
If I ascend to heaven, you are there;
> if I make my bed in Sheol, you are there.
If I take the wings of the morning
> and settle at the farthest limits of the sea,
even there your hand shall lead me,
> and your right hand shall hold me fast.
If I say, "Surely the darkness shall cover me,
> and the light around me become night,"
even the darkness is not dark to you;
> the night is as bright as the day,
> for darkness is as light to you.

For it was you who formed my inward parts;
> you knit me together in my mother's womb.
I praise you, for I am fearfully and wonderfully made.
> Wonderful are your works;
that I know very well.
> My frame was not hidden from you,
when I was being made in secret,
> intricately woven in the depths of the earth.
Your eyes beheld my unformed substance.
In your book were written
> all the days that were formed for me,
> when none of them as yet existed. (Ps 139:7-16)

Several key terms surface quickly in any conversation about God's omniscience. Often, these terms are used interchangeably, but they need to be differentiated in order to approach more precisely an understanding of God's knowledge, insofar as understanding God's omniscience is possible. These key terms are "providence," "predestination," "predetermination," and "foreknowledge." In this chapter, "providence" will technically refer to God's provision of protective care for the universe God has created and sustains in being. "Foreknowledge" will technically refer to the idea that God can "see" or "know" something in advance, without necessarily willing, planning, designing, or constructing the events that will unfold in time. "Predestination," as distinct from providence and foreknowledge, will technically refer to God's will in regard to human destiny, that is, to one's final end, and which is understood to be God's willing for our eternal happiness in union with God. "Predetermination," by contrast, although sometimes used to indicate one's destiny, will technically refer to God's will in regard to each discrete moment or event in a creature's life. This is typically what people are referring to when they speak of "God's plan"—a faithful trust that all things are unfolding according to God's will for the creation, though here it will be clarified that God's "will" or "plan" never entails sin but rather its sanctification.

Because predestination and predetermination are biblical terms, all Christians wrestle with them. Since both predestination and predetermination tend to collapse human freedom, they are employed more commonly by mainline Protestants who maintain that sin has completely destroyed the human capacity for freedom, making the creature entirely dependent on God and unable to cooperate with God's grace for salvation. While Calvin taught that humans are predestined either to heaven or hell based solely on God's sovereignty, and not at all on the relative merit of the individual, Catholics tend to protect the idea of human freedom by tying predestination to the idea of God's foreknowledge. Catholics tend to suggest that God predestines people on the basis of God's foreknowledge of choices they will freely make throughout their lives. One might also speak of God's plan in the sense that God always wills what is good and is actively engaged in bringing about God's intention, ultimately providing the best for creation. This approach tries to protect human freedom in relation to an understanding of God's providential care.

In terms of theodicy, God's knowledge is the easiest to protect among the trio of knowledge, goodness, and power. Protecting the attribute of God's knowledge in light of evil and suffering can be accomplished by defining omniscience in terms of foreknowledge and distinguishing it from predestination, on the one hand, and predetermination, on the other. If omniscience means that God knows everything that is going to occur because God has predetermined each moment, and indeed everything is unfolding according to God's divine plan, then God's goodness is collapsed by definition. God is implicated in the evil and violence of the world by *determining* it. Indeed, God is, in such a view, evil's author, which protects divine knowledge at the expense of divine goodness. The idea of God's foreknowledge, however, protects the character of God as both omniscient and good if explained by reference to how God can see something in advance without necessarily willing in advance whatever is going to occur. In such an imagination, God could *see* in advance, for example, that the Holocaust was going to occur without *willing* it to occur.

In such a view, God is certainly not evil's author. But our theodicy is as yet incomplete, and Hume's articulation of theodicy stands: If, on the one hand, God can see that something as horrible as the Holocaust is going to occur but does nothing to prevent it (and thereby *allows* it to occur), God is complicit at best, morally obtuse at worst, and we have collapsed God's goodness. If, on the other hand, God wants to prevent the Holocaust from occurring but cannot, we have collapsed God's power. Nonetheless, at this stage, my point is simply to recognize that foreknowledge, as distinct from some conceptualizations of predestination and predetermination, protects the idea of human freedom and suggests that some things (i.e., sinful things) not only *can* occur but also *do* occur, outside the will of God.

Philosophers have long debated the question of whether anything can happen outside the will of God. In "On the Will of God," Thomas Aquinas responds to the question "Whether the Will of God Is Always Fulfilled" in the affirmative: "The will of God must needs always be fulfilled."[11] Thomas speaks about cause and effect and that all things will conform to the universal cause eventually: "An effect cannot possibly escape the order of the universal cause."[12] Also, "Hence that which seems to depart from the divine will in one order, returns to it in another order; as does the sinner, who by sin falls away from the divine will as much as lies in him, yet falls back into the order of that will, when by its justice he is punished."[13] In answering this question, Thomas stresses that sinful actions are in no way willed by God. "He in no way wills the evil of sin, which is the privation of right order towards the divine good."[14]

In the second paragraph of the reply to objection one, Thomas draws a distinction, too, between the antecedent will of God, and the consequent will of God, emphasizing, however, from the start, that God wills only what is good.

> To understand this we must consider that *everything, in so far as it is good, is willed by God*. A thing taken in its primary sense, and absolutely considered, may be good or evil, and yet when some additional circumstances are taken into account, by a consequent consideration may be changed into the contrary. Thus that a man should live is good; and that a man should be killed is evil, absolutely considered. But if in a particular case we add that a man is a murderer or dangerous to society, to kill him is a good; that he live is an evil. Hence it may be said of a just judge, that *antecedently* he wills all men to live; but *consequently* wills the murderer to be hanged. In the same way God *antecedently*

11. Aquinas, ST, I., q. 19, a. 6.
12. Ibid.
13. Ibid.
14. Ibid., I., q. 19, a. 9; I., q. 79, a. 1-2.

wills all men to be saved, but *consequently* wills some to be damned, as his justice exacts. . . . Thus it is clear that whatever God simply wills takes place; *although what He wills antecedently may not take place.*[15]

This distinction between the antecedent and consequent will of God is an idea to which I will return when I consider divine omnibenevolence in the next section. For now, there are several important points to keep in mind in relation to God's knowledge. First, according to Thomas, God wills only that which is good. Second, God does not will the evil of sin. Third, the evil of sin occurs even though it is not willed by God. Thus, Thomas answers the question before us, "whether anything can happen outside the will of God" in the affirmative. Sin happens outside the will of God. Evil happens outside the will of God. God is not the author of sin. Fourth, and finally, Thomas provides a word of hope. The good that God desires for the creation will be achieved ultimately. In other words, according to Thomas, the antecedent will of God, which wills for a good creation to have union in the Goodness of divine life, will take place ultimately, though not all human beings may experience such an end despite God's desire for them to enjoy it. Such beings will cease to be. Indeed, for God in *kairos* time, the good already has been achieved, and perfectly so. From our vantage point, by contrast, in *chronos* time, we continue to await the consummation. In *Beauty's Vineyard*, I have been suggesting we play a key role in bringing the kingdom into being.

On Omnibenevolence

The second attribute of God that requires a defense in constructing a theodicy for an age of anguish and anticipation is divine omnibenevolence, a concept that, like omniscience, is also poetically anchored in the psalms: "O give thanks to the Lord, for he is good, for his steadfast love endures forever" (Ps 136:1). Challenges to an ability to maintain omnibenevolence as an attribute of God when considering the questions posed by theodicy, however, are typically twofold. First, theologians must answer how evil, with its attendant suffering, coexists in a world created by a God said to be entirely good. Second, theologians must address how a God said to be entirely good *allows* or *tolerates* this evil and suffering to persist in the creation God cherishes as beloved. If we can comprehend the existence and nature of evil in a world created by an all-good God, and if we can protect the good character of God in face

---

15. Ibid., I., q. 19, a. 6, ad. 1; emphases mine.

of the evils we experience, we will be closer to an adequate theodicy for an age of anguish and anticipation.

Earlier, in the chapter on "Beauty's Companions: On the Good and the True," I spoke to the first of these challenges by reference to Augustine's solution to the problem of evil. I discussed how Augustine, drawing on the thought of Socrates as relayed by Plato, understood there to be something of a continuum between Absolute Goodness and nothingness—or between Absolute Being and absolute nonbeing. Augustine understood the human experience of evil to be located somewhere along that continuum. He thought that experiences of things we call evil are not experiences of something *per se* but rather are experiences of privation, of corruption, of the lacking of goodness to varying degrees. I explained how, according to Augustine, a goodness that is entirely corrupted, or that which is absolutely evil, has absolutely no Goodness, or Being, in it. Thus, absolute evil has no essence. Absolute evil is nothingness. As such, Augustine understood absolute evil not to exist. What humans experience and name "evil" is, properly understood, according to Augustine, an experience of corrupted Goodness, or of a lacking of Goodness to a high degree.

As controversial as it is to call absolute evil "nothingness," this concept is helpful for an aesthetic theology such as the one I am constructing. If we conceive of the universe sacramentally, as participating, as we suggested earlier, in the Being of God and nestled deeply within God's womb, so to speak, and if we conceptualize evil as having its own substance or essence, then we have entered the existence of evil, a substantial *thing*, into the Being of God. This is deeply problematic. A retrieval of Augustine's Neoplatonic idea, then, gives us the ability to think of evil, instead, as a lacking of substance, as a privation of the good, in humans who are coming to being within the Being of God. As created beings, we are lacking the fullness of God's Love, Goodness, Beauty, and Truth; but God is infusing divine Love, Goodness, Beauty, and Truth into the creation first through creation, and then through processes of sanctification. We are in gestation, in a very real sense. God is developing divinity—holiness—within us and is filling us up where we lack.

But our theodicy is yet again incomplete. Hume's articulation of theodicy continues to stand. The idea of privation, or corrupted goodness, provides a satisfactory philosophical explanation for how evil or, if you will, a lack of being, coexists with an omnibenevolent God. But if, given our understanding of foreknowledge, God can foresee that humans are going to actualize a privation of goodness that leads eventually to holocausts, atomic bombs, genocides, and so on, and if God does nothing to prevent these things (and thereby *allows* them to occur), God remains, as I said before, complicit at best, morally obtuse at worst, and we continue to collapse a perfection of God. If, on the other hand, God wants to prevent these moral atrocities from occurring, but cannot, we have again collapsed God's power. Nonetheless, at this stage, we must recognize that privation, divorced from any accounting of evil as an essence independently occurring in the universe, protects the idea of God's omnibenevolence.

The second issue—how a God said to be entirely Good abides these experiences of evil and suffering and *allows* them to persist even in the creation that God cherishes as God's beloved—requires further examination. Indeed, most proposals that try to resolve this problem of theodicy (and there have been many) tend in some way to collapse God's goodness. The shortcomings of most of these theodicies can be quickly grasped by holding each proposal against a parenting analogy.

One possible solution, for example, is that God allows or uses suffering to test our faith. But if a father tested the faithfulness of his child by either setting one's own house alight or by allowing an arsonist to set it aflame as a means to test whether the child would call out to him for assistance, he would most likely be arrested for child endangerment. If a child were then admonished for failure to worship such a father, the abusive nature of the father would be even more apparent. Yet Christians often embrace this view of a God who allows us to suffer as a means by which to test our faith, and who, despite such an interaction, mandates our worship.

A second possible solution is that God allows or uses suffering as an occasion to deliver a message. Maybe, some preachers said in the 1980s, God allows the HIV/AIDS pandemic to persist in order to deliver a message about the sinfulness of sexual promiscuity. But if a father, disquieted by his child's sexual promiscuity, permitted the development of a biological weapon and allowed it to be unleashed on all of humankind in order to use the outbreak as an occasion to deliver a message to his son, he would most likely be arrested for crimes against humanity. Yet Christians often embrace this view of a God who allows us to suffer as a means to deliver a message and again who, despite such an interaction, mandates our worship.

A third common possible solution is that God *uses* or *allows* suffering as a catalyst to bring about a change of heart. But if a father was displeased with his unrepentant children who were disobeying his rules, and he *invited* or *allowed* bullies from the neighborhood to come rough them up and even kill a few of them in order to teach them a lesson, he would most likely be arrested for child abuse, if not murder. Yet Christians often embrace this view of a God who *uses* suffering or *allows* us to suffer in order to bring about a change of heart. Again, despite this interaction, we are expected to worship God.

Indeed, these are arguments that have been given currency again by Eleonore Stump, the Robert J. Henle Professor of Philosophy at St. Louis University, in her book *Wandering in Darkness: Narrative and the Problem of Suffering*.[16] In a nutshell, in her 668-page book, Stump attempts to defend Thomas Aquinas's theodicy, maintaining that it is as relevant now as it was in the thirteenth and fourteenth centuries. According to Stump, Thomas understood God to allow humans to suffer for two morally justifiable reasons: suffering enables the person to avert the worst possible end (i.e., hell—self-willed isolation from God), or this suffering enables the person to attain the best possible end (i.e., heaven—union with God).[17] In either case, the suffering enables a change of heart: either conversion to God or a deepening in the relationship with God. Referring to the latter, Stump writes, "The experience of suffering enables them to open in a deeper way to the love of God."[18] She refers to the distinction that I discussed in the previous section, between the antecedent will of God and the consequent will of God, to say that antecedently God does not will human beings to suffer but, due to the actualization of sin, the consequent will of God wills us to suffer in order to effect the changes of heart mentioned above. Conversion to God is effected through suffering. According to Stump, suffering is willed by God in the consequent will because it is the best possible means by which God shepherds us, either to relinquish freely our resistance to God or to enable cooperatively our living union with God.[19] In my mind, however, it is certainly possible to conceptualize a God still more perfect yet who would never sit idly by while permitting God's precious creation to suffer so miserably, often at the hands of people who have embraced moral evil. Even if God draws the good of conversion from moral evil without intending the evil, we can do better theologically.

In order to see the absurdity in the argument before us, let us consider the case of moral evil executed on September 11, 2001. On the terrible night after those planes hit the towers, a palpable sense of com-

---

16. Eleonore Stump, *Wandering in Darkness: Narrative and the Problem of Suffering* (Oxford: Oxford University Press, 2010).

17. Ibid., 387, 390, 452.

18. Ibid., 399.

19. Ibid., 166, 456.

munity formed among New Yorkers, who flocked to the streets and lit candles, some crying for the deceased, wounded, and missing, and still others praying for peace and the return of the sense of safety and security that had been lost. On that night, and the days following, I heard many Christians express their piety by saying things like, "God is testing us—will we continue to believe in the face of this violence?" or "God allowed it to happen to remind us how life is precious," or "God allowed it to happen to draw us to Him again." Now, I realize these are expressions of faith in the face of absolute horror, and that such sentences function as recitations of faith in the midst of sheer terror. But these responses too are concerning as should, by now, be evident. The God-image operating behind them is ghastly; they depict God as a monster who allows thousands to be killed in order to test or generate faith ("will we continue to believe?"); to deliver a message ("to remind us how life is precious"); or to effect a change of heart ("to draw us to Him again"). They are recitations of the arguments I have already dismissed as theologically problematic. Does God truly *idly* sit by as these horrors unfold?

To be clear, for God to wish New Yorkers to live in peace affirms God's Goodness. But for God to accomplish peace among New Yorkers by permitting members of al Qaeda to take down the World Trade Towers, an act that God is said to have permitted in the recitations of faith above, for a greater end—whether for the demonstration of faith, the communication of a message, or the transformation of heart—collapses both God's goodness and God's power. It depicts God as negligent at best, impotent at worst. If God foresees the violence but allows it to occur in order to bring good from it, God is implicated in the violence itself and the attribute of goodness is collapsed. If God foresees the violence and cannot do anything to stop it, God is impotent in the face of violence and the attribute of power is collapsed. By characterizing God as passive in the face of violence when God could have prevented the deaths of 2,977 people but chose not to in preference for testing faith among the faithful, delivering a message about the preciousness of life or, conversely, effecting a change of heart, this theodicy, this defense of God, fails miserably. It is easy to conceive of a God greater than this, who is not impassive in the face of atrocity. In such constructs as these, those who died simply became God's pawns in bringing out goodness in survivors. The ones who died seem to be expendable in order to achieve God's higher aims. This is a reprehensible image of God.

Perhaps the instinct at this point is to suggest that God does miraculously intervene at times, and thus does not idly sit by as evil is unleashed. Some Jewish lives were spared during the Holocaust; the South African resistance led to the liberation of the country; miraculous stories of survival circulate from Bosnia Herzegovina, Cambodia, Rwanda, and so on. If *this* is our resolution, however, a new conundrum is introduced. If we insist that God does miraculously intervene, the obvious dilemma arises: why does God only intervene sometimes, for some people—but not always, for all people? Does God intervene only for the faithful? Does it become a contest then over who can rally more "prayer warriors" to prove the strength of faith and to see who God favors?

I, for one, hope not. The way through this conundrum is not to look for miracles (though I believe miracles are occurring all the time) but to look not only at the attribute of God's goodness (and of absolute evil as nonbeing) but also at the attribute of God's power and, considered together with an understanding of God's foreknowledge, to construct a plausible theodicy for the twenty-first century, a defense of God informed by theological aesthetics and by an understanding of Christ as divine Beauty.

On Omnipotence

The third and final attribute of God that requires a defense in constructing a theodicy for an age of anguish and anticipation is divine omnipotence, a concept that, like omniscience and omnibenevolence, is also poetically anchored in the Psalmist's assurance of divine protection:

> You who live in the shelter of the Most High,
>   who abide in the shadow of the Almighty,
> Will say to the LORD, "My refuge and my fortress;
>   my God, in whom I trust." (Ps 91:1-2)

That God is powerful is without dispute; however, the nature of that power is an issue of enormous consequence. If humans are created in the image of God, and if we imagine God to be a deity who exerts divine power by overcoming, overwhelming, prevailing over, subduing, suppressing, subjugating, repressing, conquering, defeating, having triumph over, trouncing—indeed, by *over*powering—then it is no wonder that Christians have justified overcoming, overwhelming, subjugating, repressing, and conquering as their birthright, for this is precisely the God-image into which they believe they are being transformed. But is power understood as coercive force an adequate definition of perfect power when applied to God's omnipotence? Or are there better accountings yet?

Arthur McGill, when he was the Bussey Professor of Theology at Harvard Divinity School, in a book first published in 1982 and called *Suffering: A Test of Theological Method*, takes up the question of the nature of God and God's power. In his chapter on the Trinity, he asks, "*What is God within himself, in his inner nature and fundamental character?*"[20] By revisiting the debate between Athanasius and Arius, McGill searches for the decisive mark of divinity in God the Father and finds it not in the Father's absoluteness or eternal nature (as it was for Arius) but in the Father's love and self-communication.

> Between the Father and the Son there exists a relationship of *total and mutual self-giving*. The Father and the Son are not just entities who contain within themselves a divine level of reality, and who tenaciously hold onto what they have, in the fashion of Arius' God. The Father and the Son have divine reality in a *state of action*, in the action of total self-communication. In fact, Athanasius' point is that this state of action, this act of self-giving is the *essential mark of God's divinity*. . . . Because the Father holds nothing back but gives all his glory to the Son, and because the Son holds nothing back but offers all that he has to glorify the Father, God within himself is supreme in the order of love.[21]

God's exercise of power, then, is in keeping with the internal being of God as Love, as self-giving, and as self-communication. McGill stresses the idea that "God exercises his power in Jesus Christ in the mode of service, and not in the mode of domination."[22]

> God exercises his power in relation to men through self-giving love and service. There is no possibility that by some fluke God should suddenly decide to suspend this kind of powerfulness and become a Gentile lord who dominates his creatures with violent power. God has a specific character, a specific kind of powerfulness within himself. He can no more dissociate himself from that mode of power than he can dissociate himself from his own inner reality.[23]

Jesus, as the Son of God who expresses the inner nature of God through the incarnation, reveals too the perfect expression of God's power, an expression in keeping with the nature of God the Father.

20. Arthur McGill, *Suffering: A Test of Theological Method* (Eugene, OR: Wipf and Stock, 2006), 64.
21. Ibid., 76.
22. Ibid., 79.
23. Ibid.

"When Jesus stands opposed to all acts of violence and to all violent powers, and when he acts to free men [*sic*] from those forces which oppress and torment them, he does so as the revealer of God's own essential life."[24] McGill concludes with the assertion, "Force is no attribute of God."[25]

> God's divinity does not consist in his ability to push things around, to make and break, to impose his will from the security of some heavenly remoteness, and to sit in grandeur while all the world does his bidding. Far from staying above the world, he sends his own glory into it. Far from imposing, he invites and persuades. Far from demanding service from men in order to enhance himself, he gives his life in service to men for their enhancement. But God acts toward the world in this way because within himself he is a life of self-giving.[26]

If we take seriously, then, the challenge to rethink our understanding of the nature of perfect power not as the ability to coerce, but as the ability to attract, as theological aestheticians are wont to do, or as an ability to draw a will that is free, even if damaged, to desire what is Holy, what is Good, Beautiful, and True, then the divine image into which we understand ourselves to be artistically shaped by God has an entirely different cast. We too, as images of God, should be less apt to exert our power in terms of overwhelming, subjugating, and conquering than in terms of attracting, persuading, and alluring. Even when we think of God's "mighty" act of creation, we might, in keeping with the science of our day but read in a faithful light, see the act of creation not as a coercive act to overpower but as a gentle action of attraction between two potential charges, one positive and one negative—a potential that God actualizes by creating them, their nature attracting them to one another, such that they fall out of balance and explode in a silent "bang" which produces materiality and which, over billions and billions of years, expands to produce what we know as the universe. My point is that, in this telling, God creates not through a coercive, forceful act but by means of a persuasive act, an act in keeping with the nature I am describing.

The consequences of this reassessment of the nature of God's power are far-reaching, particularly when applied to the sources of our anguish in the modern world. These consequences are thoughtfully explored in an episode of *On Being* when host Krista Tippett sat down with South

24. Ibid.
25. Ibid., 82.
26. Ibid.

African Quaker cosmologist George Ellis on the occasion of his reception of the 2004 Templeton Prize for research at the intersection of science and religion. They discussed "Science and Hope."[27] During the interview, Ellis shared with the audience his belief that ethics, like the laws of physics, are deeply embedded in the nature of the universe, waiting to be discovered. He referred to the ethical nature of the universe by drawing on the Greek word *kenosis*, which means to empty oneself, to let go, to give up, to forgive, or even to sacrifice oneself completely for the sake of the other.[28] "Kenotic ethics," he noted, are central in the thought of the apostle Paul, who wrote in his letter to the Philippians:

> If then there is any encouragement in Christ, any consolation from love, any sharing in the Spirit, any compassion and sympathy, make my joy complete: be of the same mind, having the same love, being in full accord and of one mind. Do nothing from selfish ambition or conceit, but in humility regard others as better than yourselves. Let each of you look not to your own interests, but to the interests of others. Let the same mind be in you that was in Christ Jesus,
>
>> who, though he was in the form of God,
>>> did not regard equality with God
>>> as something to be exploited,
>> but emptied himself,
>>> taking the form of a slave,
>>> being born in human likeness.
>> And being found in human form,
>>> he humbled himself
>>> and became obedient to the point of death—
>>> even death on a cross.
>> Therefore God also highly exalted him
>>> and gave him the name
>>> that is above every name,
>> so that at the name of Jesus
>>> every knee should bend,
>>> in heaven and on earth and under the earth,
>> and every tongue should confess
>>> that Jesus Christ is Lord,
>>> to the glory of God the Father. (Phil 2:1-11)

27. "Transcript for George F. R. Ellis—Science and Hope" (May 2007), http://www.onbeing.org/program/science-and-hope/transcript/1158.
28. Ibid.

Ellis's treatment of *kenosis* is not a trite one but is informed by his resistance to apartheid and by his study of such figures as Gandhi, Martin Luther King, Jr., and Nelson Mandela. He says of *kenosis* that "it is counterintuitive" and "incredibly unnatural."[29] "To be beaten up and not to retaliate. It requires incredible courage, devotion, dedication in that extreme kind or form. The life of Christ, of course, is the ultimate kind of example."[30] He explains that

> [Gandhi] trained his followers to accept suffering, [and] not to retaliate. And by doing so, he reached into the heart of the British oppressors. But after a while, the pain is incredible at that deep level. . . . The training is incredible. Gandhi spent about fifteen years studying and thinking before he did it. So did Martin Luther King.[31]

Ellis, with Tippett, discusses the spectrum that kenotic ethics runs, from small everyday acts of forgiveness to the far end of self-sacrifice. But Ellis turns, in time, to the case of the United States and its war with Iraq. He pulls out a letter that he received "from a man called David Christie" and points to a practical application of *kenosis* that demonstrates well the kind of perfect power that is proper to God but that is paradoxically exemplified through the expression of a kind of powerlessness. The letter reads:

> In 1967 I was a young officer in a Scottish battalion engaged in peace-keeping duties in Aden town in what is now Yemen. The situation was similar to Iraq, with people being killed every day. As always, those who suffered the most were the innocent local people. Not only were we tough, but we had the power to pretty well destroy the whole town had we wished.
>
> But we had a commanding officer who understood how to make peace, and he led us to do something very unusual, not to react when we were attacked. Only if we were 100 percent certain that a particular person had thrown a grenade or fired a shot at us were we allowed to fire. During our tour of duty we had 102 grenades thrown at us, and in response the battalion fired the grand total of two shots, killing one grenade-thrower. The cost to us was over 100 of our own men wounded, and surely by the grace of God only one killed. When they threw rocks at us, we stood fast. When they threw grenades, we hit the deck and after the explosions we got to our feet and stood fast. We did

29. Ibid.
30. Ibid.
31. Ibid.

not react in anger or indiscriminately. This was not the anticipated reaction. Slowly, very slowly, the local people began to trust us and made it clear to the local terrorists that they were not welcome in their area.

At one stage neighboring battalions were having a torrid time with attacks. We were playing soccer with the locals. We had, in fact, brought peace to the area at the cost of our own blood. How had this been achieved? Principally because we were led by a man whom every soldier in the battalion knew would die for him if required. Each soldier in turn came to be prepared to sacrifice himself for such a man. Many people may sneer that we were merely obeying orders, but this was not the case. Our commanding officer was more highly regarded by his soldiers than the general, one must almost say loved. So gradually the heart of the peacemaker began to grow in the man and determination to succeed whatever the cost. Probably most of the soldiers, like myself, only realized years afterward what had been achieved.[32]

This, Ellis concludes, is "*kenosis* in action."[33] Its expression of power achieves transformation rather than destruction. And he believes this kind of power is rooted in the very being of God and is therefore embedded in the creation the Creator gives as gift to the beloved.

Given the kind of kenotic power about which Ellis speaks, and about which McGill writes, is our theodicy still incomplete? This definition of power, in tandem with God's foreknowledge and God's benevolence, does not "allow" suffering to occur, doing nothing to prevent it. God is always active, not passively or idly standing by in the face of suffering, but self-giving and self-communicating in the ways that I have been arguing throughout this book: by expressing God's self through goodness made evident in justice, through beauty made evident in compassion, through truth made evident in wisdom. God does not allow people to suffer; God actively resists moral evil by attracting wills to cooperate with divine grace and by alluring wills to convert willingly to the ways of holiness—but never by overcoming the human will, which by overwhelming another's freedom would constitute an abuse of God's power. While it is true that God's power in relation to nature is such that it can speak existence into being and even to create out of nothing, such acts of creation did not violate the human will, a dimension of the creation that, as sacred, must not be coerced.

Such a construction suggests that, given God's perfect knowledge, God can see that humans will enter into moral evil without willing them

32. Ibid.
33. Ibid.

to fall into sin. When they do, God is not complicit or passive. God's perfect goodness wills a better world for human beings to experience. And God's perfect power, because it is not coercive but subversive in that word's most positive sense, does not overwhelm human freedom but attracts it to cooperate with what is good. So we can explain how things called "evil" and that lack perfect goodness to varying degrees exist in a world created by an all-Knowing, Good, and Powerful God. God creates because it is better for the world to exist than not to exist. When humans exercise their freedom and actualize what is sinful (which was only a potential in a creation that was essentially good), God is actively present to the creation, attracting wills that are free to cooperate with graces of empowerment, encouragement, and enlightenment. Through this activity, God is active in creation, infusing greater and greater degrees of justice, compassion, and wisdom in the world—restoring it to a state of union with the Goodness, Beauty, and Truth that are its source.

If we return to consideration of the moral evils of our day, our theodicy maintains that God can see horrible events that are going to occur, but God resists them by sacramentally imploring the wills of human beings to stand down and to embrace God's will. God's presence empowers, encourages, and enlightens right action, but not every will chooses to cooperate. Even so, God exercises power in a way appropriate to God, which never overpowers human freedom but constantly works within the proper parameters so as not to collapse the constraints that love places on power.

Such a view might even be applied to the night Jesus was betrayed. God the Father and God the Spirit were present to God the Son, desiring what they always desire: cooperation with Goodness, Beauty, and Truth by expressions of justice, compassion, and wisdom. These options were available to Jesus, who demonstrated perfect obedience to them by not returning violence with violence, by healing one harmed by the sword, and by forgiving those who killed him. These options were available, too, to the soldiers when they arrested Jesus, but in their freedom they resisted what was right. These options were available to the priests and judges who conspired to have him killed. These options were available to the Romans, who in their freedom chose to beat and torture Jesus rather than to cooperate with their consciences which must, at some level, have been telling them that what they were doing was wrong. And these options were available again to the soldiers who crucified him, who nevertheless overrode their consciences and pounded nails into his living flesh. In every moment, God the Father and God the

Spirit were present to God the Son. They were not idle, as God is never idle—but always actively present and engaged, calling us, persuading us, and working in us through grace to cooperate with Goodness, Beauty, and Truth and, by our dance with grace, incorporating us into the Body of God, the Body of Christ, actively creating what I have been calling Beauty's vineyard.

One can only wonder if Geoffrey Laurence's image of the American soldiers sitting before Rubens's painting of *The Rape of the Daughters of Leucippus*—a painting that he titles *Hold Fast* and that was painted in the same year that Ellis won the Templeton Prize—is also a reference to the ethic of *kenosis* that Ellis says is deeply embedded in nature, waiting to be discovered, and described so well by David Christie's letter. What if America, after the collapse of the Twin Towers, had held fast and had refused to act in the way that al Qaeda expected? What if America had not acted out of an instinct for revenge, retaliation, or vengeance, responses that can only escalate the cycle of violence? What if, instead, America had responded in a way of keeping with an ethic of *kenosis*? What if America had "held fast"? Would peace and security have been hastened?

In his interview with Krista Tippett, Ellis said, "Often, the true nature of things is paradoxical. And the Christian paradox is that the true nature of power is in weakness and suffering. That is the true nature of power. And it is transformative." He went on to say that the true nature of security "is very simple. You are secure if you have no enemies. So how do you change enemies into friends is the true question which underlies security." Maybe Geoffrey Laurence paints the soldiers holding fast in order to demonstrate a power quite unlike the kind valorized by Rubens and represented in the Dioscuri's rape of the daughters of Leucippus. Perhaps Laurence is advocating in his work for the paradoxical power of *kenosis*.

Beauty's Song: On Lament

Despite the most advanced theodicies we can imagine, the human condition is mysterious, its riddles never ending. Any journey of faith is a venture from the heights of joy to the depths of sorrow and back again. These are rhythms that ought to find their deepest expression in our prayer and in our worship. Instead, it seems that we are too often encouraged to suppress our doubts, anxieties, and disappointments and to sing only praises to God. We may go hungry, witness war, terror, and violence, suffer illness, and lose loved ones, but we are to give thanks to

God. This conflicted existence, however, where what is genuine is kept from God in preference for a confused reverence, prevents the formation of an authentic relationship with God. Instead, expressing our inner spirit in all its complexity is intrinsic to us as human persons. We share the state of our being with our closest friends. Those with whom we are in most intimate relationships, our spouses, our life partners, our dearest friends, see us at our best and our worst. Yet, in the presence of God, we often feel best advised to keep such things as our doubt and even our anger hidden. Because they are genuine, however, these aspects of human existence—varying degrees of faithlessness, confusion, and hopelessness—ought to find reflection in the liturgy of the church and in the prayers we utter. Otherwise, our praises can ring hollow. Indeed, they often are.

The biblical witness, especially Hebrew Scripture, does not model, nor does it even encourage, an issuance of praise without a serious appraisal of the depths into which our human experience can take us. Scholars point out that the biblical form of the lament follows one common pattern of the movement of faith that finds frequent use in the Bible: people cry out, issuing a complaint about their present circumstances; they ask God for assistance; they wait expectantly for God's divine response to their cry for help; and, regardless of the receipt or nature of the response, people offer praise to God. Issued in the form of a lament, it is a praise that is not empty, however, for it is written within the context of great sorrow.

The first element of a true lament is the utterance of a complaint. Denise Dombkowski Hopkins writes in her book, *Journey through the Psalms: A Path to Wholeness*, that the language used in the complaint is "meant to be provocative and evocative, to draw us into sympathy and outrage."[34] In addition to writing about one's own suffering, the complaint models the naming of the enemy. Hopkins's argument is prophetic, given the grave situations afflicting us in the modern world:

> The theme of enemies and evildoers in the laments can help us to name social enemies, and thus relates to crucial social issues of our times. We must, in our impersonal world, be able to ask who is responsible for societal suffering and identify those who are guilty of destruction and dehumanization in our communities. We must show solidarity with the poor against existing power structures. The enemies in the . . . laments thus can become for us, as they were for ancient Israel, the

---

34. Denise Dombkowski Hopkins, *Journey through the Psalms: A Path to Wholeness* (New York: United Church Press, 1990), 63–64.

structural enemies in our own society; supra-individual representatives of the chaos opposing God's good order for the world.[35]

Sometimes, the enemy so named is God. Although Christian faithful are often reluctant to engage in such direct confrontation with God, Hopkins argues, "[lament-enemy language] urges us to work with God now to transform and make new" by "pushing us to face the world and its pain now."[36] As an indictment against God, the lament's complaint can accuse the Holy One of "negligence or hostility."[37] In a state of disorientation, the lament understands "God . . . in the disorientation, absent or acting unjustly."[38] Hopkins recognizes that "when enemy language and accusation of God are found within the same [biblical lament], it is clear that the enemies are not the cause of the [lamenter's] distress; God is."[39] Hopkins appreciates how bold such an accusation is, especially where the tradition of the lament has been all but lost. She argues, however, "to be angry with God is not impious but an acknowledgment that God matters to us. . . . The angry response is part of being truly human."[40]

The form of the lament provides people of faith with assurance that, being in relationship with God, we can express our frustration in the midst of profound, unrelenting, and unwarranted human suffering. Indeed, it is even more than that. God *invites* us into such a relationship, where sincerity, honesty, and truth are valued. Because expression of pain and anger is a phenomenon so basic to human experience, the form of the lament enables us to cross boundaries in the search for meaning from within the wisdom of our diverse and often quite distinct traditions. In the context of the sources of anguish we have been discussing, from violence against women to genocide and still more, the form of the lament provides us the means to articulate our anger at the very existence of these acts of moral evil that leave us vulnerable. The implication is not that we believe God sent these sources of suffering to test us or to deliver a divine message or to elicit a change of heart; rather, the point is that we are in relationship with a God to whom we can take such anguish, even when we are angry, and know we are accepted—and we can trust that God is working always in us and with us and by us to generate a good, holy, and beneficent final outcome.

35. Ibid., 64.
36. Ibid., 70.
37. Ibid., 74.
38. Ibid.
39. Ibid.
40. Ibid., 76.

The very form of the lament requires the faithful to complain in faith to God. It requires the faithful to request God's help and to anticipate a call to become involved in resisting the things that cause our anguish. The lament encourages us to listen acutely for what role we might play in a divine response, for just as Christ demonstrated radical love in his ministry to the poor, the prostitute, the leper, and the orphan, so are we, in an age of anguish, called to respond to the world with the same kind of radical love we witness in our teacher.

Finally, the lament leads us to praise. We sing not only when our suffering has ended; we sing even in the midst of our sorrow. We sing because despite our doubts, our fears, and our frustrations, we are a community of faithful ones. We are a community of hope. We sing praises because we trust in the compassion of a God who will hear our cry and who will deliver us. We sing because we are confident that God is delivering us now, even before our cry reaches to the heavens. We sing because we believe God is working among us already, leading us to be the change we wish to see in the world. We sing because we hope.

Chapter 8

Beauty's Imagination
On Hope

When a military dictatorship seized rule of Argentina in 1976, Jacobo Timerman was editor of the Buenos Aires newspaper *La Opinión*. In that role, he published critiques of the government for its policies of cruelty and repression against the Argentine people, and he condemned the violent methods used by the rebels opposing the regime.[1] Allegedly, for distribution of such "subversive propaganda," as well as for being of Jewish descent, Timerman was arrested without any official charges filed against him, taken to a clandestine prison, and tortured from April 1977 until his release in the fall of 1979. The next year, he published his memoir, *Prisoner without a Name, Cell without a Number*. About the experience of torture, he wrote:

> In the long months of confinement, I often thought of how to transmit the pain that a tortured person undergoes. And always I concluded that it was impossible.
>
> It is a pain without points of reference, revelatory symbols, or clues to serve as indicators.

1. A previous version of this chapter was published by in Kimberly Vrudny, "Deforming and Reforming Beauty: Disappearance and Presence in the Theo-Political Imagination of Ricardo Cinalli," in *Visual Theology: Forming and Reforming the Community through the Arts*, ed. Robin M. Jensen and Kimberly Vrudny (Collegeville, MN: Liturgical Press, 2009), 67–92.

Encuentros V (1993–1994) by Ricardo Cinalli. Pastel on tissue paper layers; 2.84 x 1.95 meters. Private collection.

A man is shunted so quickly from one world to another that he's unable to tap a reserve of energy so as to confront this unbridled violence. That is the first phase of torture: to take a man by surprise, without allowing him any reflex defense, even psychological. A man's hands are shackled behind him, his eyes blindfolded. No one says a word. Blows are showered upon a man. He's placed on the ground and someone counts to ten, but he's not killed. A man is then led to what may be a canvas bed, or a table, stripped, doused with water, tied to the ends of the bed or table, hands and legs outstretched. And the application of electric shocks begins. The amount of electricity transmitted by the electrodes—or whatever they're called—is regulated so that it merely hurts, or burns, or destroys. It's impossible to shout—you howl. At the onset of this long human howl, someone with soft hands supervises your heart, someone sticks his hand into your mouth and pulls your tongue out of it in order to prevent this man from choking. Someone places a piece of rubber in the man's mouth to prevent him from biting his tongue or destroying his lips. A brief pause. And then it starts all over again. With insults this time. A brief pause. And then questions. A brief pause. And then words of hope. A brief pause. And then insults. A brief pause. And then questions. . . .

When electric shocks are applied, all that a man feels is that they're ripping apart his flesh. And he howls. Afterwards, he doesn't feel the blows. Nor does he feel them the next day, when there's no electricity but only blows. The man spends days confined in a cell without windows, without light, either seated or lying down. He also spends days tied to the foot of a ladder so that he's unable to stand up and can only kneel, sit, or stretch out. The man spends a month not being allowed to wash himself, transported on the floor of an automobile to various places for interrogation, fed badly, smelling bad. The man is left enclosed in a small cell for forty-eight hours, his eyes blindfolded, his hands tied behind him, hearing no voice, seeing no sign of life, having to perform his bodily functions upon himself.

And there is not much more. Objectively, nothing more.[2]

Even as Timerman was undergoing interrogation at the hands of the regime, Argentine-born and European-trained artist, Ricardo Cinalli (b. 1948) was coming to maturity as an artist. South American and European influences coincide in his work in intriguing ways, particularly in images from his "blue box" series. In some, grotesque figures share space with crucifixions in the confines of a small box; in still others, ladders or grotesques occupy spaces otherwise empty. What is Cinalli

2. Jacobo Timerman, *Prisoner without a Name, Cell without a Number*, trans. Toby Talbot (New York: Alfred A. Knopf, 1980), 32–34.

expressing through these images, categorized as surreal by critics? Is he saying, as the British intellectual Edward Lucie-Smith interprets, that Christ is impotent to improve human conditions—particularly in situations where poverty and political strife coalesce to create militarized regimes opposed by armed resistance? Lucie-Smith considers the "flood of new arrivals" to Argentina between 1905 and 1910 and then writes of Cinalli's *Encuentros V*:

> Here are specifically European fragments tumbled together in an alien and alienating setting. The Corpus Christi, back deliberately turned, is a reminder of the strong influence of Catholicism; it also speaks of the fact that religion has nonetheless failed to heal the divisions in Argentine society. Christ looks down in pity at the mangled limbs heaped below, but is powerless to offer help. He Himself, the image tells us, is brutally divided.[3]

Cinalli's artistic imagination as depicted in his "blue box" series, read through lenses informed by a theopolitical reading of torture, the prophetic, the grotesque, and real presence, offers a counterpoint to Lucie-Smith's interpretation. In pastel on tissue paper, Cinalli explores issues like those Timerman once contemplated in ink on newsprint and then later on the pages of his memoir. By depicting a detainment cell, Cinalli bears witness to Christ's navigation of time, testifying to his compassionate presence among the tortured during Argentina's "Dirty War," even while promising his presence, too, in an afterlife for those

3. Edward Lucie-Smith, "Ricardo Cinalli," in *New Art from Latin America: Expanding the Continent* (London: Academy Group, 1994), 85–86. If the brutal division of which Lucie-Smith speaks is the denominational divide within Christianity, it should be noted that, according to the statistics compiled by the Archdiocese of Buenos Aires, 90 percent of the total population of Argentina was Catholic in 1976, so the impotence of the larger church to unite in opposition to the government seems misapplied here. See www.catholic-hierarchy.org/diocese/dbuea.html#details. In the unlikely event that the brutal division of which Lucie-Smith refers is the one about which Cavanaugh writes, referring to the church's divided ecclesiology, then Lucie-Smith has a valid point. Because of its ecclesiological imagination, Cavanaugh argues, the Corpus Christi was ill-prepared to oppose the regime, for it had abrogated its authority over the body to the state, and retained only its authority over the soul and things spiritual. This is the thesis of his book. See William T. Cavanaugh, *Torture and Eucharist* (Oxford: Blackwell Publishers, 1998). Two monographs have been published about Cinalli's career. Edward Lucie-Smith and Giorgio Cortenova, *Ricardo Cinalli: Accade? Il flusso disordinato degli esseri, nel vortice discontinuo dell'essere cose?* (Milan: Mazzotta, 2004), and Raul Santana, *Cinalli: Dreams, Flesh, Shadow, Memory* (Buenos Aires: Centro Cultural Recoleta, 1998).

who have been killed. By facing a pile of grotesques on the floor of the cell, Cinalli's Christ confronts the demonic—the abuse of power and violence that is all too familiar in the earthly realm and represented by the Argentine state. He extends a prophetic invitation for the Christian community to band together as the Body of Christ and, like Christ, to resist the oppression of the state.

By affirming the essential goodness of creation, Cinalli's Christ informs his disciples how to live with hope in an age of anguish and anticipation. He suggests that collective incorporation into the Body of Christ through the Eucharist can empower a movement to resist the moral evil of regimes like the one that seized control in Argentina. His work expresses Cinalli's courageous indictment against those who deform Beauty by the exercise of torture. And his image provides reason to hope too that those who resist idolatrous power will enliven Beauty again by re-membering the Body of Christ in a community that nonviolently resists political oppression. Beauty's vineyard is precisely this—the realization of an entire community working together as the Body of Christ to repair the world—so it is fitting to conclude with an extended reflection on hope in conversation with Cinalli's drawing.

Torture

A small cell is the site of a crucifixion in Ricardo Cinalli's *Encuentros V* (1993–1994). Within the cell, there is an exchange between a crucified man and the grotesqueries at his feet. In terms of composition, two inverted triangles form the shape of an invisible hourglass, suggesting that time is among the topics of this image, moving the viewer's imagination from the linear or *chronos* time of earthly life to *kairos* or fullness of time—time from God's vantage point. Unlike the cell that Timerman describes, this one has an "escape hatch," an eye at the top through which an illuminating light streams into the space. The light makes visible the brilliant blue walls of the "box," not the dingy gray one that one might expect to find when one encounters the cement walls of a cell intended for purposes of solitary confinement or torture.[4] Given

---

4. Many of the testimonies of torture include references to color. For example, Alicia Partnoy in *The Little School: Tales of Disappearance and Survival in Argentina* (Pittsburgh, PA: Cleis Press, 1986) takes note of color through the hole in her blindfold, or its effect when the blindfold has been removed. See also Kate Millett's analysis in "The Little School: Argentina and Brazil," in *The Politics of Cruelty: An Essay on the Literature of Political Imprisonment* (New York: W. W. Norton, 1994), 232–33: "For those who have disappeared into the Little School and the darkness inside its

the artist's Italian ancestry and fascination with all things Roman, the hole is likely a visual reference to the *oculus* of the Pantheon in Rome, the sole source of light filtering into that space from the realm of the gods, suggesting that God can see what occurs without willing or allowing what is transpiring in this cell. Looking upward through it, one sees that the peaceful night sky, sprinkled with stars, is disturbed only by smoke as if from a furnace next door.[5]

The dominantly Catholic Argentina of Cinalli's birth and formative years shaped his theopolitical consciousness. After riding the ebbs and flows of the Great Depression and the Second World War, Argentina's growing urban working class began to seek political voice, competing for power with a military junta on the one hand and Marxist rebels on the other. The uneasy coexistence of these movements and their competition for power dominated the political landscape of Cinalli's youth. In 1973, when Cinalli was in his mid-twenties, Juan Perón's government, now returned from exile, was democratically elected. It promised to elevate the concerns of the working classes and to advocate for free trade, but peace was not to accompany the administration's ascendancy. An oil shortage contributed to Argentina's economic troubles even as rival groups continued to use violent means to acquire political ends.[6]

---

blindfolds, the world has disappeared as well. Perhaps because of this, Partnoy is poignantly aware of color. At the very moment of her arrest, she had looked up: 'The sky was so blue that it hurt.' On her first morning in the Little School, she wakes to find that 'someone had retied her blindfold during the night' and now 'the peep hole was smaller but still big enough to see the floor; blood on the tiles next to a spot of sky blue.' She is being led from one wing of the Little School to another: 'While they opened the iron grate into the corridor, she thought for a minute of the sky blue spot. She could have sworn that it was a very familiar color, like the sky blue color of her husband's pants; it *was* him, lying on the hall floor, wounded.'"

5. The literature on torture from Argentina is clear that Nazism influenced the tactics of the regime. Because of the anti-Semitism of the junta, Jews suffered severely for their ethnicity in the torture chambers. By showing the smoke outside the cell, Cinalli is acknowledging the relationship between Germany and Argentina. See, for example, Timerman, *Prisoner without a Name*, esp. 130–45.

6. Leonardo and Clodovis Boff emphasize the complexities of the political maneuverings of populist governments and their impact. "The populist governments of the 1950s and 1960s—especially those of Perón in Argentina, Vargas in Brazil, and Cárdenas in Mexico—inspired nationalistic consciousness and significant industrial development in the shape of import substitution. This benefited the middle classes and urban proletariat but threw huge sectors of the peasantry into deeper rural marginalization or sprawling urban shantytowns. Development proceeded along the lines of dependent capitalism, subsidiary to that of the rich nations and excluding the great majorities of national populations. This process led to the creation of strong

Perón died in 1974; his third wife María Estela Isabel Martínez de Perón (Isabel Perón) took the reins as leader of the government, but she was speedily overthrown by a military coup in 1976.

The coup inaugurated the period of Argentina's "Dirty War." A series of military dictatorships controlled Argentina between 1976 and 1983. The junta implemented a policy of arresting anyone suspected of opposing its control. Human rights groups estimate that, in those seven years, the regime was responsible for the disappearance of over thirty thousand people. Because those considered subversive were arrested secretly and often executed without trial, few dared to protest. The famous exception is the Mothers of the Plaza de Mayo, a group of mothers of the dead and disappeared who demanded information from the army about the whereabouts of the abducted through peaceful vigils and marches they conducted weekly between the years of 1977 and 2006.[7]

Ricardo Cinalli was studying art in London for much of the period of the dictatorships. His drawings demonstrate, however, that his attention was never far from the political situation in his homeland. In his "blue box" series, he explores the cells of the clandestine prisons where "the disappeared" were taken. He studies the sites where their invisibility was verified in isolation from a community of family, friends, and even memory. He bears witness to the rooms that testified nonetheless to the truth that some of the disappeared were still, in fact, alive—that they were indeed still visible. Cinalli examines where the prisoners were confirmed, by their own confession, to be enemies of the state—admissions often coerced by electrical shock through prods attached to sexual organs. But Cinalli's investigation proves to be not only of the physical space of the torture cell but also of the moral meaning of what transpired in that very real, physical space, even if, in many cases, all evidence of cells of this kind was destroyed.

In his seminal book *Torture and Eucharist: Theology, Politics, and the Body of Christ*, political theologian William Cavanaugh studies the Chil-

---

popular movements seeking profound changes in the socio-economic structure of their countries. These movements in turn provoked the rise of military dictatorships, which sought to safeguard or promote the interests of capital, associated with a high level of 'national security' achieved through political repression and police control of all public demonstrations." Leonardo Boff and Clodovis Boff, *Introducing Liberation Theology* (Maryknoll, NY: Orbis Books, 2006), 66–67.

7. Perceiving that the current government is not hostile or indifferent to recovery of the disappeared, members had their final march around the plaza in January 2006. Weekly marches have continued, however, to raise awareness of other social issues confronting Latin America.

ean regime under Pinochet to untangle the typical justification for torture—that pain is inflicted in order to get truthful information from the
one being interrogated—from its underlying motivation. Rather than
seeking information, the torturers enact what Cavanaugh refers to as
a "perverse liturgy": they participate in a drama that reifies the façade
of their power and authority by degrading the prisoner to the point
of humiliation. Despite the brutality, and because all else is withheld
from the prisoner, the captive becomes dependent on the state, thereby
reinforcing the illusion that the state possesses an all-encompassing
power. Cavanaugh writes,

> The victims are made to speak the words of the regime, to replace their
> own reality with that of the state, to double the voice of the state. The
> state omnipotence becomes manifest in the horrifying production of
> power, what Scarry calls a "grotesque piece of compensatory drama."
> Torture may be considered a kind of perverse *liturgy*, for in torture the
> body of the victim is the ritual site where the state's power is mani-
> fested in its most awesome form. Torture is liturgy—or, perhaps better
> said, "anti-liturgy"—because it involves bodies and bodily movements
> in an enacted drama which both makes real the power of the state and
> constitutes an act of worship of that mysterious power.[8]

The torturers achieve their objective by inflicting blows until the
tortured one appeases them by producing, Cavanaugh skillfully documents, "the reality in which [the state's] pretensions to omnipotence
consist."[9] It is not the production of information that is desired. Rather,
the goal is a confession of putrescence. Since such filth is not human,
torture is legitimized in the mind of members of the regime: "Torturers
humiliate the victim, exploit his human weakness through the mechanism of pain, until he does take on the role of filth, confessing his lowli-
ness and betraying cause, comrades, family, and friends."[10] Thus, even

8. See Cavanaugh, *Torture and Eucharist*, 30. His reference is to Elaine Scarry,
The Body in Pain: The Making and Unmaking of the World (New York: Oxford Univer-
sity Press, 1985), 28. While Cavanaugh's book pertains to the particular context of
Pinochet's Chile, he allows for a transference of context. He writes, "Although it is
beyond the scope of this book to explore the atomizing pathologies of all the different
types of modern states, I will not discourage the reader from drawing analogies from
Pinochet's Chile to other contexts where such analogies are warranted" (*Torture and
Eucharist*, 15). Indeed, he also uses illustrations from Argentina and Uruguay, "given
the close collaboration between the security apparatuses of these countries during
their military dictatorships and the similarities of the methods used" (ibid., 23n4).

9. Ibid., 31.

10. Ibid.

as "the regime's world swell[s] to enormous proportions . . . the world of the victim dissolves into nothing."[11]

Acquiescence to the imagination of the torturers assumes an important role in the mythos of the regime, Cavanaugh goes on to analyze, given the larger project of the state to disintegrate and "disappear" resistance. In the public square, as word of disappearance and torture spreads, even as it is denied by the state, fewer and fewer are willing to take risks by speaking out against the atrocities and violations they know to be happening. Cavanaugh explains the strategy of denying the practice of torture while simultaneously distributing information about its existence:

> For this type of strategy to be effective, the state's power cannot simply remain hidden. Disappearance and torture is rather a dance of visibility and invisibility, a macabre striptease of power in which the regime both conceals its security apparatus and at the same time assures that its presence is widely known. The sheer terror of torture must be invisible to public scrutiny, but its power must nevertheless be manifested for the state to achieve its goals of social control. Disappearance and torture is a game of the shadows, always lurking just out of sight, behind the curtain of the temple. The omnipotence of the state must be made present, but it is most powerful precisely when it is invisible, internalized in the anxieties of the people. The liturgy of torture realizes the state's terrible might, but it remains out of grasp yet palpable, felt like a nausea in the viscera of society.[12]

And so in secret locations throughout the countryside, the "perverse liturgy" of torture erases the lives of the disappeared as members of a wider community, diminishing them as human beings, cutting them off from all normal and functional relationships, exchanges, and even from memory, dulling all sensations except for pain. Memory of the past and hope for the future are made remote by the immediacy of pain, a pain that "shrinks the world down to the contours of the body itself; the enormity of the agony is the sufferer's only reality."[13] Often, the isolated individual disintegrates: "The feeling and reality of powerlessness in torture is so extreme that the subject is no longer subject, but mere object. The ego is dissolved because it cannot sustain the processes necessary for self-preservation. In fact, death, the very negation of ego, becomes

---

11. Ibid., 36.
12. Ibid., 53–54.
13. Ibid., 37.

desirable."[14] It is more than individuals, then, who disappear. "Torture is consonant with the military regime's strategy to fragment the society, to disarticulate all . . . parties, unions, professional organizations—which would challenge the regime's desire to have all depend only on it."[15] In sum, "the net effect of this strategy was the disappearance of social bodies which would rival the state."[16]

Kate Millet, in her book *The Politics of Cruelty*, aptly deconstructs the rhetoric of the state relating to disappearance:

> The ability to "disappear" a human being is such an awesome power that the verb itself, grammatically intransitive, becomes transitive and now takes an object. A new passive is also created: one does not disappear, one is disappeared. The word is further detached from its nearly abstract connotations of perception or impression and transformed into a specific act: "to disappear" someone is to erase a presence, perhaps even an existence, through capture.[17]

Such power again serves to inflate the idolatrous confidence of the state's omnipotence. "Government now causes its citizens to exist or cease to exist. These magical feats of appearance and disappearance, the condition of being seen or being invisible, present or not present, border on conjuring. The state's very efficacy in abducting its targets," Millett goes on, "not only has the effect of making them cease to be but perhaps also to have never been. Since the fact of their detention is not recognized or recorded officially anywhere, the 'disappeared' can be killed with the same ease as they can be detained until broken through torture."[18]

Key to breaking open the meaning of *Encuentros V*, then, is proper identification of the "blue box" as a torture cell which situates the image in Argentina's experience of torture. Though prompted by Argentina's

---

14. Ibid., 40.
15. Ibid., 38.
16. Ibid., 47.
17. Millett, "The Little School," 228.
18. Ibid. I cannot help but comment that, even as I write, there is news of Ingrid Betancourt's rescue from a Colombian jungle, where she was held for nearly seven years. Betancourt was a presidential candidate in Columbia, until the Revolutionary Armed Forces of Colombia (FARC) kidnapped her at a checkpoint approaching a demilitarized zone that had been overrun by FARC guerilla fighters. Though her family periodically received recordings of Betancourt during the years of her captivity, they sometimes went months on end without knowing whether she had been killed by her captors. It is a timely case in point that disappearance and non-existence are not synonymous.

recent past, the cell in Cinalli's image represents all chambers—even Golgotha—where torture has been exercised as a means of advancing or maintaining totalitarian power. Cinalli's image is not another memoir of torture; his is not merely a narrative about Argentina's violent past. Instead, the cell provides Cinalli with the stage on which time itself is dramatically navigated.

A marvelous light streaming through a hole in the ceiling illuminates the cell. No longer gray and dreary, the cell opens to a world beyond itself. Without denying the physical reality of what has transpired within its walls, the image expresses that there is more, not only physically—with a world beyond the confines of the cell visible through the hole allowing light to filter into the space—but also metaphysically. The *oculus* suggests the omniscient nature of God who sees all—even the obscene tactics of those trained in techniques of torture.[19] From the realm of *kairos* time, the transcendent Christ flickers into *chronos* time and space, reminding the viewer of God's presence. Taking the posture of the cross, he courageously confronts the grotesqueries at his feet with the "dangerous memories" of his own torture, suffering, and death, thereby sharing in the suffering of the afflicted one in the cell, reduced to grotesqueries at the foot of the cross by the torturer's blows.[20]

In *Encuentros V*, Cinalli expresses that the prisoner is never alone—that another Being is *really present*. Another Being, also intimately familiar with the horrors of torture, is compassionately present to *suffer with* the battered

---

19. Intentional or not, the hole in the cell imagined by Cinalli has a double meaning for, in testimonies of torture, a cell with a hole often was much preferred by prisoners to one without. Timerman, for example, writes: "I miss my former cell—where was that?—because it had a hole in the ground into which to urinate and defecate. In my present one I must call the guard to take me to the bathroom. It's a complicated procedure, and they're not always in the mood. [Sometimes they] don't respond to my call. I do it on myself. Which is why I miss the cell with the hole in it." Timerman, *Prisoner without a Name*, 4.

20. "Dangerous memory" is a theological concept developed by Johann Baptist Metz. According to him, dangerous memories are "memories which make demands on us. There are memories in which earlier experiences break through to the centre point of our lives and reveal new and dangerous insights for the present. They illuminate for a few moments and with a harsh and steady light the questionable nature of things we have apparently come to terms with, and show up the banality of our supposed 'realism.' They break through the canon of the prevailing structures of plausibility and have certain subversive features. Such memories are like dangerous and incalculable visitations from the past. They are memories that we have to take into account, memories, as it were, with a future content." Johann Baptist Metz, *Faith in History and Society* (New York: Seabury Press, 1980), 110.

one, even in solitary confinement. God's own presence there bears witness to the atrocities committed within those fetid walls. This Christ displays a vulnerability to be *present with* rather than to have *power over*. But, by alluding to metaphysical time and space in the image, Cinalli appeals not only to Christ's very human compassion for the tortured but also to God's divine objectivity and perfect judgment on what has transpired in the cell. This Christ, making incarnate the mind of God, challenges worldly authorities who abuse their stations by the manner in which they wield their power. Christ's wounded body condemns the act of torture performed in that space. And he demonstrates a way of life that calls for discipleship. Only by re-membering him, by becoming his body, by becoming his hands and his feet, Cinalli suggests, will the mystical Body of Christ be able to resist oppressive regimes to establish a new world order based on the inviolable dignity of every human person. Christ sees such dignity in the grotesque figure bloodied by torture *and* in the torturer, whose will, though twisted, is veiling an image still bearing too God's own. In all of these ways, Cinalli's image possesses prophetic power.

The Prophetic

The image of Christ, stationed in the cell, strikes a prophetic posture. In our contemporary world, the word "prophet" seems to be employed most often in fictional stories and fanciful tales with imaginary settings where there is a character toting a magical gift—an ability to read palms, crystal balls, or tea leaves, perhaps, in order to utter grim omens about one's destiny already fully determined. A prophet, therefore, in the popular imagination, has come to signify someone who can predict the future. But such an understanding fails to capture the meaning of the biblical figures. When readers face the biblical texts and encounter prophets, it is vital to recognize that, in ancient Israel, a prophet was someone who had a rare gift to be sure, but it was not foremost an ability to read the future. It was a God-given ability to interpret the "signs of the times" so accurately that the Truth they uttered was in resonance with God's own. They were messengers of God who were sensitive to subterranean tremors—societal patterns entirely predictable but easily forgotten by the masses, for they are inconvenient truths. Israel understood the prophets to be mouthpieces for God, commonly uttering oracles of doom because of the people's unrepentant posture but also sometimes oracles of hope because of the promise that, when God's people turn from their wicked ways, the disaster they were inviting by their opposition to God's good and holy will for them might yet be prevented. They could continue in their unrepentant posture and face war and certain death or turn to justice and righteousness and avert disaster.

As one who could communicate God's word to humankind and enunciate it in human language, the prophet was, in the Hebraic sense, the one who called the people to account when they had deviated from the just, compassionate, and wise course that God intended for all of humanity. The prophet was compelled to remind the people of the covenant into which they had entered and of their responsibilities within such a sacred relationship—responsibilities especially to live in right relationship with God which overflowed into just and right relationships with other human beings.

Amos, for example, saw disaster looming for Israel. The Assyrian army was threatening its borders. But Amos believed that if only the folks in the Northern Kingdom could be convinced to change their ways, they could prevent the disaster awaiting them. If only they would demonstrate justice in their courts, he pleaded with them, a justice that would be made evident by a genuine concern for the poor, war could be avoided. Because they believed that they worshiped faithfully, however, and because they offered their ritual sacrifices according to the schedule they had determined to be pleasing to God, they dismissed Amos. They believed they were righteous before God. They believed their material possessions were a sign of God's favor. But Amos knew they were deceiving themselves. Prophets understood that the suffering of the poor was a violation of the covenant. They knew that the injustice that perpetuates poverty and its attending endemic social problems violated God's will for human community and for human thriving. Amos issued a warning in God's own voice. He proclaimed God's dismay with the people. On behalf of God, Amos uttered God's displeasure, especially because of the people's mistreatment of the poor:

> Ah, you that turn justice to wormwood,
>   and bring righteousness to the ground! . . .
> Because you trample on the poor
>   and take from them levies of grain,
> you have built houses of hewn stone,
>   but you shall not live in them;
> *you have planted pleasant vineyards,*
>   *but you shall not drink their wine.*
> For I know how many are your transgressions,
>   and how great are your sins—
> you who afflict the righteous, who take a bribe,
>   and push aside the needy in the gate. . . .

Seek good and not evil
    that you may live;
and so the LORD, the God of hosts, will be with you,
    just as you have said.
Hate evil and love good,
    and establish justice in the gate;
it may be that the LORD, the God of hosts,
    will be gracious to the remnant of Joseph. . . .
In all the vineyards there shall be wailing,
    for I will pass through the midst of you,
        says the LORD. . . .
I hate, I despise your festivals,
    and I take no delight in your solemn assemblies.
Even though you offer me your burnt offerings and grain offerings,
    I will not accept them;
and the offerings of well-being of your fatted animals
    I will not look upon.
Take away from me the noise of your songs;
    I will not listen to the melody of your harps.
But let justice roll down like waters,
    and righteousness like an ever-flowing stream. (Amos 5:7, 11-12,
    14-15, 17, 21-24; emphases mine)

Because they were attuned more closely to the Good, Beautiful, and
True Being of God and perceived God's just, compassionate, and wise
desire for God's beloved—all of creation—the prophets discerned that
the conflicts that erupted too often among human beings resulted most
often from people of privilege wielding power over the social order in
such a way that neglected the material needs of the masses—of those
oppressed, exploited, and marginalized by the manner in which power
was exercised for the privilege of the few and to the distinct disadvantage of the many. The prophets recognized that the sufferings of the
poor and marginalized were related to injustices inflicted on them by
the powerful, those who would feel threatened or harassed or incon-
venienced at the mere mention that some—even just a few—sacrifices
would have to be made in order to extend the same privileges more
widely. More profoundly still, the prophets interpreted that social unrest inevitably came as a result of senseless inequality. Prophets were
clear that God willed otherwise. God willed for repentance and for just
relations to be established in the human community. But the people
chose otherwise. It was the obstinate and unrepentant human heart
that selected the way of discord and disorder rather than concord and
harmony. By their exercise of injustice, humans invited clashes within

and without the borders of their nations. Humans created the conditions of needless suffering and paid the price.

If we read the prophets neither as beings whose gifts were so rare that they have become extinct nor as historical chroniclers of God's involvement in human affairs but as wise beings who had a heightened sensitivity to the suffering of the poor and marginalized and who understood the suffering of these precious ones to be a violation of God's Good, Beautiful, and True intention for human flourishing, these texts sing with relevance once again. The prophets come alive, imbued as they are with contemporary significance as we face the injustices in our world that are creating situations where people living in poverty continue to struggle for survival even while some, the privileged few, live in luxurious comfort—luxuries acquired often in ways intricately related to the suffering of the poor. This truth is becoming ever more painfully evident in our increasingly complex, interdependent global world, where corporate CEOs respond to shock waves from a movement demanding fair trade and where people living in poverty are buried under the collapse of the first world's stock portfolio. We live in a world where it is no longer possible to deny that our own humanity is bound up in one another's.

Prophetic messages are a burden to carry; rarely do people want to hear what prophets have to say. Their messages are easily dismissed. Just as the residents of the Northern Kingdom in ancient Israel brushed Amos aside as a nuisance, an annoying pest, so too in our own day, in an age of anguish and anticipation, it is inconvenient to listen to the prophets. And there are false prophets among us, as there were in ancient Israel, who proclaim things that are easier to bear. They teach that if individuals would make better choices—if only they would be more responsible, if only they would work harder, if only they would take advantage of their public education and engage in less promiscuity, if only they would take fewer drugs, if only they would find legitimate work rather than prostituting themselves—then the problems of the world would disappear. Individual behaviors like these certainly have a role to play in the problems of our world, but some prophets among us condemn another set of behaviors, behaviors that permit, even glorify, the acquisition of perverse amounts of wealth even when children go hungry on the streets beneath the corporate towers, penthouses, and gated communities that hide the powerful from view. Choices made in the upper echelons of society, from the White House to Wall Street, create cultures where women, denied access to education, employment, or independence, are constrained to such a point that they trade sex for money. The abuse of power in the White House and on Wall Street create situations in which men of color, disempowered politically and economically, too often exercise dominance in the domestic and sexual spheres, raping women and abusing children, sometimes turning to drugs and alcohol to escape the inertia of their lives. In such conditions, where predictable realities produce desperate circumstances, disease proliferates. And behind them all are choices, both individual *and* structural. While the political climate in the United States fosters the sense that it is either/or, it is both/and—and it is going to take the cooperation of both sides to repair what is broken.

True prophets are present among us still. Understanding that people cannot build what they cannot imagine, prophets help populations to see as they see. They are able to imagine how societies could look differently than they do and they draw people into another imagination of how to structure themselves and their lives together in the public square. They are present to remind us that, if we are to live in a world without war, without poverty, without preventable disease, we must first imagine a world without injustice, a world without inequality, a world without misery. They will remind us that war is a consequence of inequality. Conflicts break out between people who fight for land and its precious resources thought to be scarce. When there is too wide a gap between those who live luxuriously and those who live in want, an energy born of resentment, seething with righteous indignation, will inevitably boil over—often in destructive and intolerable ways. History is filled with examples. God continues to stand in opposition to the conditions of poverty and injustice out of which wars emerge. Cinalli, whom I am calling a modern-day prophet, imagines a different world—a world that confronts the demonic and creates something new.

The Grotesque

The physical space within the cell is empty—its former inhabitants dead, transported, or released. The room is occupied now only by the haunted memories of what has unutterably transpired there, Christ's prophetic stance blinking in and out. The figures at the base of the crucifixion, certainly a visual reference to *Three Studies for Figures at the Base of a Crucifixion* by Francis Bacon, are grotesques. Whereas the viewer knows Bacon's grotesques are at the base of a crucifixion only because of the title given to the triptych by the artist, Cinalli presents the viewer with a visual crucifixion. Littering the entire bottom half of the scene, amputated body parts—with a broken torso, a beheaded skull with elongated neck, reverent limbs with hands as if still folded and legs as if still kneeling in prayer only now detached and twisted—pile on top of one another. The head that rises from the mound at the base of the cross refers visually to the right panel of Bacon's *Three Studies*. The scream of Bacon's figure is metamorphosed here into a scream of another kind—not the existential scream rising from the depths of Bacon's despair, but the moan of one being tortured, his deformed body representing the distorted project of his torturers.[21] Colored a dirtied white, these body parts recall images of classical sculptures with proportions like those of the *Doryphoros*, but they also convey the pallid tones of death. Like Christ, the victim in a heap at the foot of the cross has been tortured to the point of death. He is killed by the injustice and violence of those who pound the nails into his flesh, even as he is killed by those complicit through their indifference and negligence, by their willful ignorance and complacence. The scale of these body parts threatens to overcome Christ, who risks disappearance in their presence.

Cinalli's invocation of the grotesque is far from unique in the history of art. Wilson Yates, in his book *The Grotesque in Art and Literature: Theological Reflections*, traces the form of the grotesque back to caves in ancient Roman times, documenting it as well in the art of the Middle Ages and Renaissance. In each period, he explains, the grotesque is based on forms in this world—or just enough so that viewers are able to recognize that which they distort: "They are part of our 'familiar world'—though transformed in images difficult to decipher, images that are foreign."[22] Trying to account further for the category of the grotesque, Yates goes on to identify the grotesque as that which humankind recognizes in itself, yet wishes to suppress:

> The grotesque refers to aspects of human experience that we have denied validity to, that we have rejected, excoriated, attempted to eliminate and image as a distorted aspect of reality. Because this reality belongs to our world, it cannot be destroyed. But it can be relegated to the underground. It can be literally and metaphorically hidden

21. As Timerman wrote, "It's impossible to shout—you howl" (Timerman, *Prisoner without a Name*, 33). "Those in great pain are reduced to inarticulate screams and moans, or words which convey little of the actual experience of pain ('throbbing,' 'stabbing,' 'burning'). Pain does not merely resist language but actively destroys it, in extreme cases reducing the sufferer to the sounds he used before he learned to speak" (Cavanaugh, *Torture and Eucharist*, 34).

22. Wilson Yates, "An Introduction to the Grotesque: Theoretical and Theological Considerations," in *The Grotesque in Art and Literature: Theological Reflections*, ed. James Luther Adams and Wilson Yates (Grand Rapids, MI: Eerdmans, 1997), 40.

in the subterranean, in the cavernous world of our experience. . . .
It confronts us with questions about the nature and character of the
world and the center that has exiled it.[23]

Yet, Yates argues, the concept of the grotesque grows more complex
still, for in the grotesque, the center and the boundary ultimately confront one another: "The grotesque takes us to the boundary of the world
as we have created it, for the center we have created we have deemed
righteous and the face of evil we have hidden. But in entering this world,
the unmasking begins."[24] The grotesque is frightening not because of
its unfamiliarity, Yates argues, but because of its intimacy: "For as we
dwell with the grotesque . . . we see the hidden face of human evil
emerge. We see that the face of the grotesque is not so bizarre, so alien
to our experience as we had thought in our first encounter, for the face
of the grotesque is about the way we are."[25] Frightened by the evil
lurking just beneath the surface, humans hasten to cover it with a shiny
veneer to hide it, to fool others into believing that goodness will prevail
when, in truth, at least according to some theories of the grotesque,
death conquers all.

Grotesqueries, then, are expressions of anthropological assumptions
about the innate capacities of the human person. Indeed, if it is true
that Cinalli was influenced by the grotesques of Francis Bacon, their
very *raison d'etre* in *Encuentros V* is to invite a dialogue with Bacon on
the truth about the human condition. Both Bacon and Cinalli share a
desire to press at that which is deeper, to get at that which is beyond the
surface of things. Unlike that of Bacon, however, who rejected the idea
of a reality beyond the natural,[26] Cinalli's sense of what is deeper was
shaped by the dominance of the Catholic intellectual tradition in the
country of his birth and its sense that a divine Being, perfect in nature,
is the cause of all that exists. This key difference in their presuppositions
about reality leads to two differing conclusions about human nature.

For Bacon, the grotesques at the base of the crucifixion drive to
despair because the philosophy underlying his work emphasizes the

23. Ibid., 40–41.
24. Ibid., 56–57.
25. Ibid., 57.
26. Yates notes that "Bacon is nonreligious in any traditional sense, a nonbeliever
in any theistic sense. God is not, or if God is, God is not accessible to us: there is
no tradition or archetypal myth that can endow our life with ultimate purpose or
meaning" (Wilson Yates, "Francis Bacon: The Iconography of Crucifixion, Grotesque
Imagery, and Religious Meaning," in Adams and Yates, *The Grotesque in Art and
Literature*, 154).

idea that there is a superficial façade over the human being, who is composed of a substantial evil. The human being is essentially evil, ugly, and deceptive. According to Yates, "When we both listen to [Bacon's] words and study his work, it is not difficult to see that he provides us images of human existence that are coherent and consistent in their articulation and, taken together, suggest a rather well-defined view of the human condition. The view," assesses Yates, "is a dark one. We are creatures with a unique propensity for violence and inhumanity who are anxious and despairing, isolated and alienated, who live in the shadow of death and the awareness of the ultimate futility of life itself."[27] Yates goes on to say that, for Bacon, "we are, finally, creatures . . . who do not realize the nobility, the love, the goodness that we imagine ourselves embodying."[28] Instead, humankind embodies the monstrous: "Bacon's own radical existentialism brings us into the land of despair, for it is a vision that sees the truth of us all finally located in our libidinal needs, our savage impulses, our survival instincts . . . our propensity for evil."[29]

Despite this unrelenting and desperate view of the human condition, Yates insists, "It is important not to flatten Bacon's thought into a one-dimensional understanding of cynicism or nihilism. His understanding is much richer than that."[30] In order to provide support for his case, Yates points to the ambiguities within Bacon's works and to the poems and stories that often influenced them: "He gives us powerfully and directly the facts of our mortality, our caughtness, our passion as unequivocal parts of our lives, but at the same time he pulls us into a recognition that we know and do not know what they finally mean."[31] Yates collects evidence from interviews with the artist to suggest that, for Bacon, "The artwork . . . becomes a means to insight and purgation, to some sense of release and freedom."[32] Such a catharsis might bring healing by breaking the cycle of violence, at least temporarily. Nonetheless, Yates observes that the "real presence" of evil in Bacon's work symbolizes the essence of what it is to be human:

> The panels, void of all sensibility of any emotion that suggests human grief, or compassion or guilt, portray in their rawness the face of the

27. Ibid.
28. Ibid., 157.
29. Ibid., 190.
30. Ibid.
31. Ibid., 158.
32. Ibid., 161.

demonic in the guise of what Russell has called "a needless voracity, an automatic unregulated gluttony, a ravening undifferentiated capacity for hatred." . . . It is the real presence of evil that Bacon gives us in *Three Studies*.[33]

The figures at the base of Cinalli's crucifixion offer an alternative anthropology. For Cinalli, exposure to the transcendent philosophy pervasive in Catholic thought provides him the sense that, because the power of God pertains only to what is possible, God could not create a perfect world. An entirely perfect being is, by definition, uncreated—not contingent on another. So God could only create that which is lesser than God.[34] That which is lesser than God has the potential for sin, for evil, for immorality, a potential actualized in our primordial past and into which each of us enters and to which each of us will eventually and inevitably capitulate. Cinalli's tradition attempts to account for why, in a world said to be created by a good and loving God, it is possible that cells of the kind depicted in Cinalli's drawings exist for the express purpose of torture in the first place. They are created by sinful beings, people whose vision is so distorted by veils of sin that they cannot see the Good, Beautiful, and True wish of God for them. The "perverse liturgies" they enact in the cells, to recall Cavanaugh's phrase, are interactions with evil, deformity, and deception, with a rejection of God—though God is mystically present, always giving them the possibility to choose by grace a still more excellent way.

By positioning the viewer behind Christ yet on the same level as the mound of grotesques at his feet, Cinalli invites the viewer into his debate with Bacon about the meaning of the human condition. Do the grotesques represent a primal evil in the human person, or do they point to a veiling of an essentially good nature? Do they express something of the nature of the perpetrator, or do they represent a distortion of who the perpetrator is meant to be? In Yates's analysis of the grotesque, he writes, "Certainly, when we consider the grotesque dimension of [Bacon's] work, we are dealing with a distortion taken to such an extreme that we are forced to

33. Ibid., 176, 178.
34. According to Thomas, God's power pertains only to that which is possible— ST I., q. 25, a. 3. To create another entirely perfect Being is a contradiction of terms, for to do so would be to create a second "all-powerful," a second "all-good," and a second "all-knowing" being, and there cannot be two beings who have power over all things, who are the essence of all goodness, or who are the very composite of all knowledge. To share power, goodness, or knowledge with another would create a lacking in the first, thus collapsing perfection.

deal with the violence both to the image and to that to which the image points."[35] The double entendre of the image is witnessed in the ugliness of the mouth, with its broken teeth, cracked lip, and foul odor (one imagines) reeking in the space. Its scream releases the "howl" that Timerman describes in his memoir, remembering torture; but it also epitomizes the vile arrogance of those commanding and conducting it. Yates's analysis of Bacon's scream also applies to Cinalli's: "It is the essence of horror, ambiguously encountering the viewer as an anguished cry of unleashed pain or fear or hatred that shrieks of destruction; grotesque in form, violent in image, it confronts one violently."[36] The amputated lower legs of the subject are twisted—they are positioned as if kneeling in prayer, even as they strike the last position commanded by the torturers. The violated body that is mangled at Christ's feet in Cinalli's *Encuentros V* point both to the tortured one and to the torturer. Violence has been committed to the body, mind, and spirit of the one violated in this space, in this cell. But the violence of the image points, in effective ways, to the evil of the torturer. In reference to the grotesques at the base of Bacon's cross, Yates recalls poet Stephen Spender's response, "These appalling dehumanized faces, which epitomize cruelty and mockery are of the crucifiers. . . . If they are not always the people who actually hammer in the nails, they are those among the crowd which shares in the guilt of cruelty."[37]

Cinalli does not avoid the horrific distortion of Beauty that evil makes manifest in this world by polishing over it with platitudes of faith and hope; rather, he confronts human savagery by looking squarely at the brutality of torture. Cinalli's grotesques function to bear witness to the extremes of the human condition, the "sinfulness" of human nature (for lack of a stronger word) that puts the boundary and the center together in a single cell. Yet unlike Bacon, he does not leave the viewer there; he does not permit the state to terrorize with its rhetoric of control in its bid to dominate the private sphere and the public square. Instead, he invokes a "theology of the cross" to confront atrocious ugliness with a radical invitation for incorporation into the Body of Christ.[38] Beauty

---

35. Yates, "Francis Bacon," 150.

36. Ibid., 176.

37. Ibid., 174, quoting Stephen Spender, quoted in James Thrall Soby, "A Trail of Human Presence: On Some Early Paintings of Francis Bacon," MoMA, *Members Quarterly* 2, no. 4 (Spring 1990): 10.

38. This theme of an unveiled veiling, of a present absence, of a revealed hiddenness, was conceived of and coined by Martin Luther to describe the enigmatic spiritual discovery that God is often most profoundly experienced when least expected—even in conditions of apparent abandonment and rejection. Known as

extends an invitation for the people of God to enliven the Body of Christ and to abandon the project before them that allows the Body of Christ, the real presence of Beauty, to disappear entirely.

Real Presence

In Cinalli's pastel, the rectilinear light and diminishing point meet at the "neck" of the hourglass composition, guiding the viewer's eyes to the exchange between Christ and the oversized, faceless head moaning at his feet. The vantage point of the viewer makes it such that the exchange between them is both visible and hidden from view. In this, the focal point of Cinalli's image, violence threatens again to proclaim victory. Christ's body is "disappearing"—his elbows, abdomen, thighs, and lower calves are already transparent, "amputated" at the same points as the tortured body beneath him, enabling the viewer to see more of the cell and the grotesque imagery through those parts of his body that have become invisible. Cinalli asserts in his drawing, however, that Christ is not defeated. As the embodiment of the Beauty of God, Christ confronts the grotesque presumptions of the torturer. With Latin American features, one imagines, since his face is turned from the viewer, he appears as a compassionate presence to the disappeared of Argentina.[39] Christ's body is present to the grotesques at his feet in all their complexity. In solidarity with those who were tortured, Christ remembers the position he was forced to take by his own torturers. He strikes the pose again, hovering over the grotesques in the cell now threatening to overtake him. The cross, however, is absent. The torturers, Cinalli seems to say, will not have the final word. No longer among the tortured, for he is resurrected from the dead, Christ has had victory over the evil among them. He is really present. In Christ's presence and transcendence, Cinalli makes a visual play on the meaning of "appear-

---

the *theologia crucis*, or the theology of the cross, this idea of God's paradoxical revealed hiddenness, or hidden revealed-ness, was born in Luther's estimation that "the inexpressible majesty of God" would crush humankind upon seeing it. Such a belief contributed to his understanding that, in the disclosure of God's presence to humankind, there is simultaneously a withholding; in the presence, there is simultaneously an absence of God. The hiddenness protects us from a glory too great for us to comprehend. Having access only to the "back side of God" is a concept with a long tradition in the Lutheran tradition of *theologia crucis*. For an insightful analysis of the tradition from a feminist and liberative perspective, see Deanna A. Thompson, *Crossing the Divide: Luther, Feminism, and the Cross* (Minneapolis, MN: Fortress Press, 2004).

39. Cf. *Encuentros V*, where the features of the crucified one are more distinct.

ance" and "disappearance," calling to memory the history of Argentina's painful past even while expressing the heart of his theopolitical imagination. Disappearance is not the story of *Encuentros V*, only its backdrop. Appearance, through the "real presence" of God, compassionately present in solidarity with the captured—this is the message of Cinalli's encounter.

In Roman Catholic theology, "real presence" is the term that is used to describe the belief that, in the Eucharist, Christ is really present, body and blood, humanity and divinity, in what formerly was bread and wine. Opponents of this position have balked at the scholastic philosophy necessary to understand how the "forms" of bread and wine could be changed into, or how they could be "transubstantiated," into a new "substance." Luther, for example, argued that the body and blood of Christ were understood to be "truly and substantially present in, with, and under the forms" of the consecrated bread and wine, though later regretted acquiescing to the language of Aristotelian philosophy in order to make his point, finally supporting language of a "sacramental union."[40] In his mind, the communicants at the table ate and drank the eucharistic bread and wine in the presence of the true body and the true blood of Christ himself. Other Protestants advocated for the Eucharist as a "Holy Mystery,"[41] or a "spiritual presence,"[42] while still other denominations were, and even today still are, sometimes chided by these as advocating for a "real absence," understanding communion to be a memorial of the Last Supper, at which Christ is symbolically present.[43]

There is more at stake in the question than the whirl of semantics here suggests. If the bread and wine are understood to transubstantiate and become the body and blood, then the recipients of such gifts can likewise be understood to be physically transformed. By receipt of the consecrated bread and wine, they are thought to become that which they receive, just as Ezekiel became that which he received when eating the scroll on which were inscribed the laws of God (Ezekiel 3). They are mystically incorporated into the Body of Christ. If, however, communion is celebrated as a remembrance, then the table fellowship calls Christ's life and death to mind in the believer without necessarily being understood

---

40. Cf. *Augsburg Confession*, Article 10.

41. See *This Holy Mystery: A United Methodist Understanding of Holy Communion* (Nashville, TN: The General Board of Discipleship of the United Methodist Church, 2003).

42. *Westminster Confession of Faith*, chap. 29.

43. Zwingli, for example, promulgated this view. See Ulrich Gäbler, *Huldrych Zwingli: His Life and Work*, trans. Ruth C. L. Gritsch (London: T & T Clark, 1986, 1999).

to work a fundamental change in the recipient. With transubstantiation, recipients are understood to be more and more deeply transformed into the Body of Christ, constituting the real presence of Beauty in the world by mystically becoming Christ's hands and Christ's feet.

When Lucie-Smith interpreted Cinalli's image, he concluded that Cinalli depicts the failure of Christianity, so broken is it within itself that it is unable to heal a broken society. Either the Corpus Christi in Cinalli's pastel represents the power of God, and as such possesses the power to confront the terrors unleashed by Argentina's violent regime with the capacity to bring them to their knees and thereby transform the society, Lucie-Smith suggests, or the Body of Christ is like any other, vulnerable to the tortures humans inflict on one another and, as such, impotent to respond. Since horrors of torture continue to our own day, Lucie-Smith creates the impression that we must conclude with him that God/Christ/the church are impotent and, therefore, that Cinalli's pastel is nihilistic, finally about nothing more than hopelessness and the requisite despair one must have when confronted with violence of the kind in Argentina.

This, however, is not our only interpretive option. Given the Catholic eucharistic imagination, with its understanding of the transformation of the recipient as an "ingrafted" member of the glorified Body of Christ, we can hear Cinalli sounding an imperative through his images. Will the church be absent by "disappearing"—by going into hiding, as the state desires, so that the state's agenda in the cell can succeed? Or will members of the Body of Christ be present by appearing before the regimes of the captors to resist oppression? In the words of Cavanaugh, will the church enter cowardly into "the imagination of the state" or courageously into "the imagination of God"?[44]

Such an imperative has implications for how the Christian, as a member of the Body of Christ, is to live in such a way as to bring the kingdom of God into fuller being in our time and space. According to the *Catechism of the Catholic Church*, the church's destiny, as the people of God, *is to become* "the Kingdom of God which has been begun by God himself on earth and which must be further extended until it has

---

44. For a stark contrast between these two imaginations, see William Cavanaugh, "Making Enemies: The Imagination of Torture in Chile and the United States," *Theology Today* 63, no. 3 (October 2006): 307–23. He is clear that his "appeal is by no means limited to the church. We should cooperate across religious boundaries to foster alternative imaginations and alternative bodies. If we tell the truth, we will resist the politics of fear that makes torture thinkable" (see ibid., 323).

been brought to perfection by him at the end of time."[45] Through its history, the church has struggled to maintain a proper balance between the earthly and eschatological dimensions of the kingdom of God. The church has struggled to imagine how the community might anticipate being again in the immediate presence of God in the hereafter while simultaneously recognizing the beginning of that experience already on earth in the here and now. In short, it has struggled to live into the imagination of the "already" and the "not yet."

This imbalance has led some within Christianity to believe that the kingdom of God will be experienced *only* in the next world, with the cross merely opening the gates to the kingdom, so to speak, in the hereafter. Such an approach tends to denigrate the here and now, thereby accepting and even at times legitimating suffering by looking *only* to the promise for the coming day when "mourning and crying and pain will be no more" (Rev 21:4). In the twentieth century, when technological advances introduced new heights of obscenity into the "science" of human torture, some have been accused of the opposite tendency. Some have been accused of suppressing the importance of the soul's eternal fate to elevate the significance of the needs of the physical body and its protection in the here and now.

Especially in the Latin American world, theologians, pastors, and Christian base communities, responding to the unique political situations in their own countries, situations such as those depicted by Cinalli, have been accused of this second tendency. Without necessarily denying Christ as Redeemer, they have developed a method of doing theology that emphasizes political action in this world by promoting an idea of Christ as liberator of the oppressed. Such an approach understands God to hold a "preferential option for the poor."[46] Leonardo and Clodovis Boff, Brazilian theologians providing an account of liberation theology, write:

> In liberation, the oppressed come together, come to understand their situation through the process of conscientization, discover the causes of their oppression, organize themselves into movements, and act in

45. *Catechism of the Catholic Church* (Vatican City: Libreria Editrice Vaticana, 2000), 782; cf. *Lumen Gentium* 9.2, http://catalog.hathitrust.org/api/volumes /oclc/44788139.html.

46. Of this preferential option for the poor, the Boffs write: "God is especially close to those who are oppressed; God hears their cry and resolves to set them free (Exod. 3:7-8). God is father of all, but most particularly father and defender of those who are oppressed and treated unjustly. Out of love for them, God takes sides, takes their side against the repressive measures of all the pharaohs" (Boff and Boff, *Introducing Liberation Theology*, 50–51).

a coordinated fashion. First, they claim everything that the existing system can give: better wages, working conditions, health care, education, housing, and so forth; then they work toward the transformation of present society in the direction of a new society characterized by widespread participation, a better and more just balance among social classes and more worthy ways of life.[47]

Reading Scripture with eyes attentive to the sufferings of the poor, theologians of liberation advocate for political activism as an authentic expression of Christian piety. Sometimes they have been criticized for neglecting a more contemplative, prayerful piety.[48] In its best articulations, however, liberation thought comprehends the strength of unity in plurality and emphasizes activism in this life without denying the promises of the hereafter and the importance of a contemplative life in attaining it. Liberation theologians have legitimately tried to retrieve from history the situation of Jesus' death by crucifixion. Their investigation suggests that Jesus was a threat to Rome because of the revolutionary potential of his leadership. People were amassing around him, attesting to healings and other miraculous signs even as they were listening to him preach about their inherent dignity as persons created and loved by God. Such a message opposed a religious authority that cooperated with an oppressive regime, as well as a governing body that preferred to view the masses merely as a mechanism to the comfort and security of the elite. Jesus' message was therefore threatening to the echelons of power, with Rome suspecting him of insurgency and with Jerusalem fearful that his ministry could destroy them all. Thus, liberation thought concludes, Jesus was put to death for political reasons.

By retrieving the fuller historical context of Jesus' life within the political climate of the Roman Empire, liberation thought forces the issue. If followers of Jesus are to live like him, they too will recognize the inherent dignity of the poor. They will advocate for systems of justice that recognize the rights of the underprivileged. And when this brings them into conflict with worldly rule, as it inevitably will, martyrdom may result, just as it did for Jesus of Nazareth, and just as it has for

47. Ibid., 5.

48. The Boffs admit there is a temptation within liberation thought to disregard mystical roots of faith "from which all true commitment to liberation springs" in an overemphasis on political action. They write, "It is in prayer and contemplation, and intimate and communitarian contact with God, that the motivations for a faith-inspired commitment to the oppressed and all humankind spring and are renewed" (ibid., 64).

people who have followed "the way": Martin Luther King, Jr., Oscar Romero, and so on. Latin American liturgies are filled with the names of "subversives" who, by opposing governments controlled by military militias, drug traffickers, and corrupted leaders, advocated for the ones who suffer the most under these regimes.[49] Many of them were the disappeared of Argentina. And it is they who, finally, are the subject of Cinalli's drawing.

Cinalli's compassion for the disappeared is evident in the depiction of Christ's disappearing body. Cinalli presents viewers with a Christ who "suffers with" by disappearing alongside those who have been tortured by Argentina's military junta, recognizing that they are the ones who, as members of the Body of Christ, picked up their crosses to follow him (Mark 8:34) by daring to resist the idolatry of the state. Cinalli implies that there is an eternal future for those "disappeared" by the state, and that the invisibility wrought by death is, likewise, permeated by the "real presence" of Christ whose body is simultaneously "really present" to them in heaven.

Quite unlike Lucie-Smith's reading of Christ's invisibility as impotency, Cinalli is making a theological assertion about power. There is a "power over" that can manipulate captives to the interests of the captors, but this is not God's way. Rather, expresses Cinalli, God's way is a power that is demonstrated paradoxically through vulnerability. It is a power that generates community around such innate desires as wishing to ensure that every mouth is fed, that every body is clothed and sheltered, and that every thirst is quenched. It is a power that exposes the idolatrous aspirations of the state. The state's power is not ultimate power. Perceptions of reality are easily manipulated. But the truth, according to Cinalli, is that there is a transcendence to the universe. Visibility does not cohere with existence, nor invisibility with nonexistence. Though Christ disappears from view, he exists, and he is in solidarity not with the perversions of the empowered but with the afflictions of the tortured ones; he is really present among the disappeared—both dead and alive—through the compassionate presence of those who long for

---

49. Again, consider the perspective of the Boffs: "Liberative hermeneutics will stress (but not to the exclusion of other aspects) the social context of oppression in which Jesus lived and the markedly political context of his death on the cross. Obviously, when it is approached in this way, the biblical text takes on particular relevance in the context of the oppression now being experienced in the Third World, where liberating evangelization has immediate and serious political implications— as the growing list of martyrs in Latin America proves" (ibid., 35).

their return, and through those who resist their oppression by refusing to be silenced by fear. Implicit within such seeing is a revolutionary power residing in a community refusing to despair, refusing to give up in the face of violence, refusing to believe that torturers will have the final say. There is, in other words, in this Christ, revolutionary potential.

Rather than presenting viewers with an impotent Christ, Cinalli confronts viewers with the radical presence of God born out of a distinctly South American experience of disappearance and torture inflicted on those resisting oppression under a military junta. Cinalli's encounter with God is through One who endured torture on the cross; he depicts God in solidarity with the "prisoner without a name," sharing the sufferings of those souls tortured in the "cell without a number."

The image functions sacramentally, inviting a *metanoia*, or a conversion, of the viewer's heart. Will the viewer serve the state? Or will the viewer choose to oppose the powers identified with this world and to stand, like Christ, in solidarity with justice and with love—to stand nonviolently on the side of those who oppose injustice, regardless of the personal cost that such a stance requires—even if the cost is life itself? Only in this conversion, his image conveys, does one become more than a "convert" or a "believer" but a disciple of Christ in the truest sense of the term. Only in this conversion is the Body of Christ able to realize its potency to stand over and against the injustices and perversions represented by the grotesques tearing at Christ's flesh, attempting to deform Beauty. Only in this conversion is the Body of Christ given flesh to give form, again, to Beauty—to "re-member" Beauty in the development of a community committed to the establishment of just relations and compassionate concern for the ones neglected by the imperfect systems the world engineers, tolerates, and perpetuates. Such a reclamation of Beauty puts flesh, again, on the Body of Christ, creating a community strong enough to withstand the perversities of the state and its attempt to silence and "disappear" any kind of resistance.

Such reclamation of Beauty promises to unite that which is divided. Converts to this way of being are empowered, encouraged, and enlightened by God's own breath to restore the earthly creation by just, compassionate, and wise engagement in the world. Beauty saves by absorbing recipients deeper into the source of Love, simultaneously creating a capacity for deeper love within them. And Love's effects are experienced, even if imperfectly, even if intermittently, even if incrementally, in this world. They are experiences of resistance to injustice. They are experiences of compassionate accompaniment through suffering. They are experiences of hope for reconciliation with neighbor and with

God. Even in situations of disappearance, they provide evidence of the real presence of God. And they offer hope for the coming into being of Beauty's vineyard among us, which is God's imagination for creation. If it sounds naïve, let us be mindful of Jesus' words, "Truly I tell you, whoever does not receive the kingdom of God as a little child will never enter it" (Luke 18:17). Our hope resides in Beauty's prophetic imagination, activated among us by the Holy Spirit to live into the imagination of Beauty's vineyard.

Beauty's Anticipation
On Workers

The Gospel of Matthew preserves another parable set in a vineyard that Jesus is said to have told his disciples. The parable comes in the gospel after a man approached Jesus, asking him what humans needed to do in order to inherit eternal life. After Jesus told him to keep the commandments, the person persisted. Jesus responded, " 'If you wish to be perfect, go, sell your possessions, and give the money to the poor, and you will have treasure in heaven; then come, follow me' " (Matt 19:21). The questioner walks away grieving, because he owned many things. Turning to his disciples, Jesus laments, "Truly I tell you, it will be hard for a rich person to enter the kingdom of heaven" (Matt 19:23).

In order to explicate further his principle that in the kingdom of God the "first will be last, and the last will be first" (Matt 19:30; 20:16), Jesus next tells them a parable about laborers who are called to work in a vineyard (Matt 20:1-16). The parable reflects the conventional practice of bringing extra laborers into the vineyards at harvest time. In Jesus' day, as in our own, landowners were known to exploit labor in order to yield a greater profit. Trusting that his audience would not miss the allusion to the vineyard as a site of great injustice for those living in poverty, Jesus reimagines the vineyard and its landowner anew and attempts to draw his audience into a new imagination, the possibility of a heavenly vineyard firmly planted on earth, a vineyard of justice and mercy rather than of injustice and exploitation.

Jesus recounts how an owner of a vineyard contracted with workers early in the morning to work all day for an agreed upon wage.[1]

---

1. The landowner offers one denarius for a day's work. This would be the equivalent of about twenty dollars for a day's hard labor. First-century hearers would

At nine o'clock, seeing the amount of work that remained, the owner found others in the marketplace and brought them into the vineyard to work as well, promising to pay them what was right. He did the same at noon, and again in midafternoon. In the early evening, he admitted still more laborers into the vineyard. At sunset, a manager emerged in order to give each worker what he was owed—granting the men who arrived at day's end, as well as at noon, the same payment as that given to those who arrived early in the morning. The manager paid them the same wage regardless of how many hours each one contributed, to the exasperation of those who had come early to pluck the vines. Those who had come early, and who had worked the longest, cried foul, insisting it was not fair that those who came late in the day, and who had not even broken a sweat, should receive the same payment as they who had toiled all day under the heat of the scorching sun. The owner of the vineyard emerged, insisting that no harm had been done to them, for they had agreed to work for the wage. It was his prerogative, he insisted, to be generous—giving the same amount to those who arrived at noon as well as to those who arrived later in the day.

It is easy to imagine listeners to Jesus' parable being aghast when they heard this story. How unfair for those who had worked so little to be paid the same as those who labored all day! Theirs is a reasonable reaction. Is Jesus likening God to the owner of a plantation, of sorts? Was the landowner intending to create tension between the laborers, inspiring envy among them? Was he inattentive to best practices in management? Wasn't the landowner unfair—giving those very much who by contrast had produced very little? If it is a parable about the afterlife, is Jesus revealing that even those who have performed very few good works can inherit eternal life—the same reward as those who have labored for God every minute of their lives? Clearly, Jesus reveals that the kingdom of God is not about righteousness based on a rigid ledger of hours worked or units produced. How could the owner of

---

have recognized that one denarius is not a living wage, but they too would have understood that people desperate for money would work for a day's wage, however inadequate. See Luise Schottroff, *The Parables of Jesus* (Minneapolis, MN: Fortress Press, 2006), 209–17. This is a context that workers in the vineyards of South Africa as well as the United States and elsewhere would surely recognize today as well. In addition to wine lands, we might extrapolate meaning for migrant labor and exploited farm workers who pick tomatoes, oranges, and cucumbers, etc., for thankless wages. See Deborah Barndet, *Tangled Routes: Women, Work, and Globalization on the Tomato Trail* (Lanham, MD: Rowman and Littlefield Publishers, 2002).

the vineyard be so cavalier, so reckless, so foolhardy, to distribute grace with such abandon?

Readers of the parable commonly interpret the vineyard to be the kingdom of heaven in the sense of a paradise received in a heavenly afterlife, and the payment to the laborers the grace from God necessary to enter it—a grace that Jesus claims that God the Father distributes generously. Many sermons throughout the ages have suggested that the meaning of the parable is that those who are baptized as infants, and who remain faithful for their entire lives, receive the same gracious entry to the heavenly afterlife as those who enter the vineyard, or the church, later, even in the dusk of their lives, even on their deathbeds. Some understand Jesus to suggest that God receives those "deathbed converts" who confess faith just before they die, often after a lifetime of self-indulgence, in the same way as God receives those who had lived uprightly and faithfully for their entire lives.

While this interpretation constructs a beautiful image of a God who is generous and hospitable, even in ways that would seem to border on reckless, Luise Schottroff, whose interpretations guided us in the chapter on "Beauty's Story," is critical of this line of interpretation. She writes, "The generosity of this landowner offers only a weak hint at what God's generosity means."[2] And she emphasizes that the wage offered even for a day's labor was not enough to support a family. In other words, the landowner did not offer a living wage. Therefore, "a landowner who on one occasion pays unemployed people a denarius is a counter-image" to the God she desires to worship.[3] She goes on to say that those who listened to Jesus in situations of oppression would "not recognize God in the landowner. On the contrary, the parable, with its sharp analysis, illuminates economic misery and its causes at the time of the Gospel of Matthew."[4]

But I believe there is a more profound interpretation still. What if the kingdom of God about which Jesus speaks is not restricted to the afterlife? What if there are implications to Jesus' teachings about the kingdom of heaven for the here and now? After all, Jesus tells the parable after lamenting how difficult it is for those who are rich to enter heaven. The relationship between how life is lived in this world and its implications for the next is a theme Matthew emphasizes from Jesus' teaching more than once. Judgment Day entails separation of the sheep

2. Schottroff, *The Parables of Jesus*, 216.
3. Ibid.
4. Ibid.

from the goats, according to the Gospel of Matthew, on the basis of care for the hungry, the thirsty, the sick, and the prisoner (Matt 25:31-46). Within this larger context of Matthew's understanding of the interrelationship between heaven and earth, the parable of the workers in the vineyard takes on deeper meaning. Jesus teaches about the kingdom of God present here and now, an interpretation consistent with how Jesus instructed his disciples to pray earlier in the same gospel, that God's will be done "on earth as it is in heaven" (Matt 6:10).

Indeed, the parable provides only a shadow of what is vivid in Jesus' imagination, its characters and figures only dim and imperfect examples of what the kingdom of God can be. For the vineyard is the focus of the parable, not the landowner. The owner searches for laborers to work in the vineyard, promising to pay them out of the vineyard's yield. If Jesus intends the kingdom of heaven to represent not only the realm of the hereafter but also a peaceful society overflowing with generosity in the here and now, then Jesus' teaching has to do with the role of the faithful in contributing to such a community of loving-kindness. The workers in the vineyard play a role that stands in stark contrast to the ways of the world.[5] The fence around the vineyard becomes the demarcation of the community's parameters. Set apart from the rest of the world, but within it, the vineyard functions quite differently from the insatiable ways of the world exhibited outside its fences. The members of the community mark the boundary of this vineyard, those who enter in to maintain justice and righteousness in a realm of *shalom* and loving-kindness and whose inhabitants live off the fruits of the community's collective labor. They may squabble with one another as the vineyard is incrementally perfected to have its culmination with a heavenly Jerusalem that is squabble free, but their squabbles are right-minded. Their disagreements with one another seek greater justice for one another.

Within such a vineyard, the laborers, those who toil for the owner, might be those who do the will of God not only with an eye to the hereafter "in heaven" but also with a heart for the here and now "on earth." The workers in the vineyard might be those who experience a conversion, to be sure—but not a conversion from one religion to another or from unbelief to faith—but a conversion of heart, to the way of Jesus, to the way of loving-kindness, to the way of justice and compassion. Their faith in "the way" will guide them to live attentively to the poor, the widow, the

---

5. Ada Maria Isasi-Diaz, "Solidarity: Love of Neighbor in the 1980s," in *Lift Every Voice: Constructing Christian Theologies from the Underside*, ed. Susan Brooks Thistlethwaite and Mary Potter Engel (San Francisco: Harper, 1990), 31–40, 303–5.

orphan, the immigrant, the prostitute, the leper. They might be the ones who, like Christ and the prophets before him, resist injustice, recognizing the inherent preciousness and inviolable dignity of all human life. They might be the ones who, like an ideal landowner, give generously out of the harvest, sharing riches with abandon and without condition, endowing everything they own to the service of the community. Like the perfect land-owner, they put everything they earn back into the vineyard, so that the community thrives, dependent as it is on the well-being of the collective.

This interpretation understands the payment, the grace, the fruit, to be the yield from the vineyard itself. The vineyard is the source of the abundance from which the ideal landowner—the true God, the just God—draws to give the workers what is right. The "first fruit" of this labor is the emergence of the kingdom itself—the vineyard coming into being with lush vines, plump fruit, juicy grapes. It is the genera-tion of a more just dwelling place, paradise regained yet still awaiting completion, coming into being within the midst of those whose justice, compassion, and wisdom contributes to its creation.[6] Such a community requires the investment of the collective—even of those who can give it only a little. The harvest of such a community is living in safety and security, where neighbors attend to one another's needs, where there is no tension between the haves and the have-nots because everyone has more than what is adequate for survival. The owner extends the pay-ment, after all, from the vineyard's yield. Payment is equitable precisely because all of the workers are collectively the recipients of the vineyard's harvest; the workers are collectively recipients, for they reap what they sow. They receive the gift of the peaceable kingdom emerging in their midst. If they receive only a denarius now, just think what they could be paid when the vineyard truly flourishes.

Whether they come to the vineyard early in the morning, as it were, and toil for such a vision of generosity and justice every hour of their lives; whether they convert to a commitment to justice "at noon" but embody it not as fully as those who labor in the vineyard from the early morning; whether they can give only a little because they recognized the beauty of such a way in the twilight of their lives or because there were obstacles that prevented them from embodying it as fully as the first, the reward will be the same. The enjoyment of the kingdom is theirs to appreciate. God is already, indeed, present among them.

---

6. For more about this vision of paradise, see Rita Nakashima Brock and Rebecca Ann Parker, *Saving Paradise: How Christianity Traded Love of This World for Crucifixion and Empire* (Boston: Beacon Press, 2008).

Pressing the parable forward through the ages, echoes of Jesus' words can be understood in our own day to be an invitation to enter into the vineyard, to labor in it each day, in order to bring about a community of peace and loving-kindness *on earth* as it is in heaven. We can read in the pages of this text sacred to Christians an invitation to participate in the creation of such a sacred unity of heaven and earth in the here and now, a beautiful community that recognizes that where one is diminished, all are diminished, and that where one is nourished, all are nourished. The parable's lesson for an age of anguish and anticipation is profound. If we recognize the intricate degree to which humans are interrelated and interdependent on one another not only for our own survival but also for true human thriving in the most holistic sense, we will want to ensure that no one is left outside the vineyard's fences. Imagining with hope the world as it can be, as Jesus does by setting the parable in a reimagined vineyard, the message of the parable is that every contribution in bringing about such a community is valued by God. Do something, Jesus implores us—even just a little something—to alleviate and to prevent human sorrow and suffering, to prevent human anguish. Because like the prophet Jeremiah, he recognizes that in seeking the well-being of the city, we will find our own (Jer 29:7). He promises that, in God's imagination, all works of mercy, compassion, and justice are valued. Such a conversion of heart will be its own reward, as a first fruit of a new world coming into being. Only in this way, as the incarnation of his hands and his feet, can the promises of Beauty's vineyard be realized.

Index of Biblical Citations

Index of Subjects and Names